The JUBAK PICKS

50 Stocks That Will Rebuild Your Wealth and Safeguard Your Future

JIM JUBAK

CROWN
BUSINESS
NEW YORK

CROWN BUSINESS is a trademark and CROWN and the Rising Sun colophon are
registered trademarks of Random House, Inc.

Library of Congress Cataloging-in-Publication Data

Jubak, Jim.
The Jubak picks / Jim Jubak.—1st ed.
p.   cm.
1. Stocks. 2. Investments. 3. Investment analysis. I. Title.
HG4661.J83 2008
332.63'22—dc22   2008027685

ISBN 978-0-307-40781-8

Printed in the United States of America

Design by Lauren Dong

10 9 8 7 6 5 4 3 2 1

First Edition

For Marie always, for Finn once more,

and for Luna for the first time

Contents

PART I

How You Can Put This Winning Strategy to Work for You

How I Made 14.9 Percent a Year—

and How You Can Rebuild

Your Wealth

THE PURPOSE OF THIS BOOK IS VERY SIMPLE: TO MAKE YOU MORE money in the stock market. By outperforming the stock market as a whole in the good times. By keeping your money as safe as possible in the bad times. And by rebuilding your wealth as quickly as possible when the bad times are over.

In good times, the Jubak Picks strategy I explain in the pages that follow will beat the market. I know because I've used this strategy to run an online portfolio that has returned 360 percent in its first eleven years. In that same period, the Standard & Poor's 500 stock index was up 68 percent.

Not all of those eleven years have been good times, of course. In the bad times, my long-term track record shows my strategy doesn't always make money. But it loses less than the stock market as a whole. No investor, not you and not me, can make money all the time, especially when the entire market plunges in a grinding bear market. At those times, you want a strategy that plays good defense. In the first year of the bear market, nine months of the bear market that began in October 2007, my Jubak's Picks strategy actually managed to make money. The Jubak Picks were up 5.8 percent while the Dow Jones

Industrial Average lost 18 percent. As the bear's claw dug deeper into the market, my Jubak's Picks portfolio swung to a loss. For the first full year of the bear market, my strategy lost 15.1 percent. That's still painful, but it is significantly less painful than the 21.9 percent loss for the Dow Industrials or the 23.7 percent loss for the S&P 500.

When the bear market ends, my strategy will help you rebuild your portfolio. And rebuild it much faster than the stock market as a whole. How do I know? Because that's exactly what the Jubak's Picks did after the 2000 bear market finally came to an end in October 2002. For the twelve months from September 30, 2002, to September 30, 2003, the Jubak Picks returned 37.7 percent. The Dow Industrials and the S&P 500 each returned 22 percent. For the twenty-four months ending on September 30, 2004, my strategy returned 80.2 percent. The Dow Industrials returned just 33 percent and the S&P 500 37 percent.

Great offense. Decent defense. Great recovery after a bad market. The Jubak's Picks delivers all three. So how does this strategy work?

Most stock picking starts from the bottom up.

One method begins with some kind of formula for picking the best stocks by looking at the *fundamentals* of a company's business: how fast the company is growing profits, its profit margin, the size of its debts, or its cash flow. The system then gives you a way to judge whether a stock with this or that fundamental character is cheap or expensive. A buy or a sell, in other words.

Another relies on charts and other indicators of a stock's price momentum or some other technical measure of past performance that predicts future performance. This kind of *technical analysis* tells you how to use things called moving averages, Bollinger Bands, relative strength indexes, cups and handles, and Japanese candlesticks to find stocks that are trending up or down.

The two approaches seem as different as night and day. But they do have this in common: both start with individual stocks, and *both are wrong.*

Picking individual stocks that beat the market consistently, using either method, turns out to be hard work. Research shows that most professional money managers can't do it. And most individual investors can't either. Most investors who try to run their portfolios this way wind up trailing the stock market indexes such as the Dow Jones Industrial Average or the Standard & Poor's 500. They'd be better off simply buying a fund that tracks a market index.

I think the reasons for that are pretty simple. Identifying the past characteristics of an individual stock, using any system fundamental or technical, that will make a stock go up in price in the future is pretty much like looking for a needle in a haystack. An added challenge is that those "winning" characteristics change over time as the economy and market change, and that other investors are poking through the haystack too, bidding up the price of any easy-to-find needles.

I think this whole approach to stock picking is upside down.

Why? Well, because financial research has shown that *a majority of the money you'll make (or lose) in the financial markets comes from being in the right class of asset at the right time.* If you get that big call right—the decision to have your money in oil stocks or drug stocks or technology stocks—then making money by picking the right individual stock or bond gets a whole lot easier. You've got the tide flowing with you, the wind at your back, the downhill ahead—pick whatever image you like. By picking the right asset class, you increase the odds that whatever individual stock, fund, or index you pick will be a winner that beats the market averages.

In this book I'm going to teach you how to beat the stock market averages, how to keep your money safe, and how to rebuild your portfolio after a bear market by using exactly that kind of odds-altering strategy.

And I know that what I teach you will work.

How do I know?

Because I've used exactly this strategy to run a public portfolio on the Internet for the last eleven years and counting. In the portfolio's first ten years—the ten years cited on the cover—this strategy returned 339 percent. In the first eleven years that I've run this portfolio, called Jubak's Picks, on the MSN Money Web site, this strategy has returned 360 percent. That's an average of 14.9 percent a year since I started this portfolio on May 7, 1997.

That looks pretty good compared to the returns for the three major stock market indexes during the same period. The Dow Jones Industrial average in that eleven-year time span was up 6.1 percent annually on average. The Standard & Poor's 500 Stock Index was up 5.8 percent. And the NASDAQ Composite Index was up 7 percent.

You can trust this performance number. The record isn't the result of going back in time and reconstructing trades to make the numbers look good or turning vague buys into real buys when it suits me and ignoring them when it doesn't. Every single buy and sell I've made in those eleven years has been clearly published as a buy or sell at the end of a column— marked out with the clever title of "Buy" or "Sell" and then tracked while I held the shares and for about a year after I sold them on the page that lists the complete Jubak's Picks portfolio at the current time. Every quarter for those eleven years I've reported in my column how the portfolio has done in that quarter, for the year to date, and for longer periods. Some reports, such as those during the bear market of 2000–2, were downright painful to write. It wasn't exactly fun to write those reports during the bear market that started in the fall of 2007 either. Up through the second quarter of 2008, my strategy was in the black even as the market tanked. But in the third quarter of that year, the bear clawed me for a painful loss. The black ink for the bear market turned to red. And it isn't much consolation to me that the loss from the Jubak's Picks strategy for the first year of the bear was just 15 percent against 22 percent for the Dow Industrials. It's important to lose less money in a bad market, but a loss is still a loss. My record is my record, warts and all. And it's always been available to anyone who cared to click.

Let me give you a real-life example—one from my online portfolio—that shows how my system works.

Start with a Top-Down Approach by Finding an Odds-Shifting Trend

Start with a macro trend in the United States or, better yet, the global economy. The bigger the better. You're trying to put as big a wind at your back as you can in an effort to shift the stock market odds in your favor.

You don't have to be an economist or anything with a fancy title to come up with these trends. You can uncover them with careful observation of everyday life and from reading the daily newspaper or whatever online source of news has taken its place for you.

But I've done the heavy lifting for you. In Part II (chapters 3–12) I'll give you ten such odds-shifting macro trends and name the best individual stocks, mutual funds, and exchange-traded funds you can use to profit from the ten trends.

What are those ten big trends? Let me list them very quickly. In the book you'll find a chapter devoted to each.

- *Go where the growth is*—and that means putting some money in the developing economies of China, India, Brazil, and the rest of the gang.
- *The rise of the global blue chips.* These companies are emerging from the world's developing economies to challenge Coke, IBM, and Wal-Mart on the global stage.
- *The world is getting wealthier and older at the same time.* So who's going to manage all that retirement money?
- *Inflation, the beginning of a new era.* After twenty years of low inflation, the world is headed for a decade of constantly rising prices.
- *The world may not be running out of oil—then again, it might be—but it sure has run out of cheap oil.* How to make back in the stock market what you pay at the pump and more.
- *The commodities crunch.* The developing economies are demanding more iron, more copper, more nickel, more coal—and that's set off a boom for mining companies and the companies that equip them.
- *Food, the new oil.* It's turning out to be as hard to increase food supplies as it is to find new oil. We're looking at a decade of higher food prices driven by competition with biofuels and the fact that people in the developing world will eat more pigs, chickens, and other sources of protein as their incomes rise.
- We've delayed and dragged our feet, but *environmental problems*

have become so pressing that it's time to save the world—and make a buck doing it.

- The technology sector doesn't look anything like it used to, but fortunately the same rules still apply to what I call *"hidden tech" stocks.*

- It used to be that stocks and bonds from the United States got a premium in the financial markets just for showing up. Investors were willing to pay more because the U.S. markets were so stable. Even after the 2007–8 financial crisis, they're still among the world's best, but now they've got *company from Canada, Australia, and, of all places, Brazil.*

One of these—a trend that you've undoubtedly noticed yourself every time you fill up your gas tank or pay the electricity bill—is the rising cost of energy. And that, with a little elaboration, qualifies as a macro trend. I'd phrase it like this: oil and natural gas prices are headed up in the long term. Even the drop in prices in 2008 hasn't changed the long-term trend.

I then break that macro trend down into its parts. In this example, the trend really is made up of three parts:

- Global demand for oil and gas is headed up because of the fast-growing economies of China, India, and other developing countries.
- Global supplies of easy-to-discover and easy-to-produce oil are headed down because the easily exploited reserves in easy-to-explore places have largely been discovered.
- Global energy supplies are increasingly subject to disruption by everything from governments intent on nationalizing their oil to terrorists to outright war.

I've made important progress even by this step. I've identified an asset class, a group of stocks that move together, that's likely to be moving up. If you can figure out which stock groups are moving together and which aren't, and then move between them in time to catch some of the ups and avoid some of the downs in those groups, then you should be able to beat the returns you'd get either from investing in a stock market index or from trying to pick the best stock.

By moving into strong stock groups, you pick up on the momentum effect. Common sense and any experience you may have as an investor say that stocks that have been going up tend to keep going up. Academic research says this effect lasts for anywhere from six to eighteen months and gradually gets weaker. Common sense says that a company delivering good news will continue to deliver good news for a while. A company with a product that clicks will see sales rise for more than just the quarter when the product was introduced. A company that discovers new efficiencies and reduces costs will reap the benefit for quarter after quarter. Academic research supports this: a company that reports surprisingly strong earnings results in one quarter stands a good chance of reporting better-than-expected earnings for the next two quarters.

By moving into strong stock groups, you pick up on the expectation's lag effect. Common sense and experience tell us that we don't change our minds easily. Reality often has to hit us over the head repeatedly before we revise our opinions. Investors and Wall Street analysts aren't any different. In the great bull market for oil stocks, for example, analysts had to see month after month of oil prices at $40 a barrel before they decided to use $25-a-barrel oil in their calculations instead of $15 or $18. Wall Street analysts aren't unusual. It takes most investors months or quarters to catch on to a trend. The good news here is that you and I don't have to buy into a trend on day 1 to make money. We can be reasonably late and still make reasonable profits.

By moving out of stock groups as trends start to fade, you avoid being the last buyer. We've all been there and done this: we buy into a stock that's been a rocket just at the point where the rocket starts to run out of gas and fall back to earth. By constantly staying alert on the news on each trend—focusing on the potential turning points I identify in the "Ripped from the Headlines" section at the end of each chapter—you've got a good chance of not buying in when a trend and a stock are about to fade and of getting out when a trend and a stock have exhausted their momentum.

And since you're constantly on the lookout for new trends and groups of stocks that will make you money, I think you're less likely to buy into overpriced manias for "must-own" stocks. One great way to avoid feeling that you must own this stock or that one, no matter what the price, is to have lots of other great alternative investments always in front of your eyes. If you've got three or four stocks competing for your limited pool of investment cash (hey, every investor, even Warren Buffett, has some limit), you've got to be more critical of each of them in order to decide among them. That lets you take the kind of deep breath investors often need in order to avoid doing something stupid.

My strategy has done all that for my portfolio already—and notice that I haven't even bought a single stock yet.

Next step: I then look at the macro trends that I've identified to see what features in a company or stock the stock market is likely to value over time. This is a critical stage in tilting the odds in your favor. The macro trends that I've identified put the wind at my back; now I have to find the right sail—buy the right specific stock or stocks—to catch it. In this example by taking apart the macro trend I come up with this definition of the kind of energy stock that I want to buy. Looking at the results of breaking down the macro trend into its parts, I come up with this list of features:

- Since global demand for oil and gas is rising, according to my breakdown of the trend, I want to find an oil or gas company with growing reserves.
- Since the global supply of easily discovered and produced oil is falling, according to my breakdown of the trend, I want to find an oil or gas company with unconventional supplies that until recently couldn't be recovered using current technology.
- Since global energy supplies are increasingly subject to disruption by political unrest, according to my breakdown of the trend, I want to find an oil or gas company that operates in a politically and militarily stable area.

FROM TOP-DOWN TO BOTTOM-UP

After I do my top-down assessment of macro trends and choose asset classes, I then shift to a bottom-up approach by using fundamental screening and technical charting tools to put together a list of candidates (see Part III). For example, I used these tools to look for oil companies that were close to or above the industry average in profitability and that showed faster-than-average revenue growth over the last year. I then looked at the characteristics of the top ten companies that turned up on that list to see where their oil and gas reserves were located and how much of these reserves came from unconventional sources. And then finally I looked at the charts of each of these ten stocks to see the likely near-term trend in price. Were any showing signs of exhaustion? Getting ready for a breakout? On a steady climb? Or headed down like a falling knife?

Ideally, the top-down and bottom-up approaches meet up at the perfect single stock (or, even better, a short list of a few perfect stocks). In each chapter in this book I'll give you a list of five or so stocks that fit each trend.

In this case, after going through these steps, I picked Devon Energy, a relatively small oil and natural gas producer with a big presence in the oil shales of Texas. Until new technology came along in the 1980s, extracting the natural gas trapped in these rock formations was seen as either impossible or too expensive. Now, however, thanks to new drilling and extraction techniques, Devon is producing increasing volumes of oil and gas from these formations—in good ol' safe Texas—at a time when production in the United States from conventional sources is falling. Devon Energy is also extraordinarily profitable, with a gross operating margin of 81 percent when the industry margin is 66 percent. Net income is growing by 130 percent a year (over the last five years) when the industry average is 44 percent.

I added shares of Devon Energy to my online Jubak's Picks portfolio on July 18, 2006, at $59.53. As of July 7, 2008, the shares had climbed 98.9 percent in price.

What I like about that gain—proof that picking the right large-scale trend and then using the best stock-picking tools to choose a specific stock can increase your gains in the stock market—is that shares of Devon Energy outperformed the stock market as a whole and the average oil and gas producer's stock during that period. While shares of

Devon Energy were gaining 98.9 percent, the Standard & Poor's 500 was up 12 percent and the energy sector as a whole was up 52 percent.

Devon Energy really did have the wind at its back—and my strategy had shifted the odds in my (and my readers') favor.

I think you can find winning stocks like Devon Energy at home by doing what I do in my office at your own computer. I don't have a gaggle of employees. I don't have a staff of hundreds, dozens, or even one. I've written every word in every column over those eleven years and researched every buy and sell myself. I don't have access to sophisticated trading systems or hugely expensive Wall Street databases. (Want to see my office? Check out the disorganized mess behind me in any of my MSN Money videos.) Over the years I've deliberately tried to use only tools that were available for free to individual investors on the Internet—on our site, MSN Money, and on other free investing sites—or that cost at most a few hundred dollars. I do subscribe to a few newsletters or e-mail alerts (total annual cost less than $1,000) to help me out in areas that aren't my strong suit, such as market timing and technical analysis. (I'll give you a list of some of these in Chapter 2.) But there's nothing here most investors with $50,000 socked away in an IRA or 401(k) can't find or afford.

In the ten chapters that form the heart of this book, I'll give you ten macro trends that can help you find stocks as profitable as Devon Energy. In each chapter I'll explain the trend and why I think it will be around for at least five to ten years. I'll provide you with lots of examples and enough detail so you can decide for yourself whether or not this is a trend that you'd like to invest in. (I don't want anyone following me blindly. From the beginning, the goal of my online column, "Jubak's Journal," has been to create educated investors, not guru-following robots.) At the end of that explanation I'll give you a bulleted list of news to watch for so you can judge when this trend is getting stronger or weaker, or even ending. And after that I'll give you a list of specific stocks (and mutual funds and exchange-traded funds, for investors who don't or can't invest in individual stocks) that fit this trend. In each chapter I'll give you at least five stocks with detailed explanations of why I like each stock for this trend. In addition, each chapter includes a list of "brief mention" stocks that you can use either as alternatives to main picks or as additional choices to overweight a specific trend in your personal portfolio.

After these "top-down" trend chapters, I've included "bottom-up" chapters on fundamental and technical analysis that will introduce you to the basic tools I use to find the perfect stock in an asset group and how to decide if it's a good time to buy. Even great stocks show swings in price that make them cheap at one moment (buy them now) and too expensive at another moment (buy them later). You don't have to be a big believer in the possibility of timing the market to try as hard as you can to buy stocks when they're cheap and sell them when they're expensive. I've also included a chapter that explains how my strategy automatically helps you play defense in a down market.

At the very end, in the very last chapter, I've combined all those stocks listed in individual chapters into one master list of the fifty specific stocks I recommend. I've summarized the reason that I believe each stock belongs on the list and noted the macro trend that makes each stock a buy. This master list is a kind of quick reference guide to every stock in the book.

So that this master list of fifty stocks won't go out of date, I've used it to create an online portfolio on "Jubak's Journal" on MSN Money.com. Once a month I'll update that online page with commentary on what has changed for the trends in this book and the stocks on this list. I'll flag stocks from this list that are selling at particularly attractive prices and indicate those that are starting to look like candidates for a sell because the price has run away from the fundamentals. If anything changes so much at a specific company that it no longer makes a good vehicle for riding a trend, I'll drop it from this online list and replace it with another stock so that the Jubak Picks stocks in this book remain as up-to-date as possible. And I'll track the performance of each of these fifty stocks and the list as a whole over time as well. Anyone clicking on the page will be able to see how this strategy has fared and how my individual stock picks have performed.

2

GETTING YOUR HEAD ON STRAIGHT

If It's So Easy, Why Is It So Hard?

My STOCK-PICKING STRATEGY—IDENTIFY A BIG TREND, FIND A stock that embodies it, and then keep that wind at your back for long-term gains—seems like common sense, doesn't it?

It *seems* easy, so therefore the world should be awash in investors who beat the indexes by 200 percent or more in the long run. But we know that's not the case, no matter what you hear people saying during the neighborhood cookout.

The reason it's hard is simple: our emotions keep getting in the way. Think back—not so far back at that—to how you felt when the financial markets were coming apart in the fall of 2008. Many days lots of us thought: invest now? You've got to be kidding, right?

When the stock market could drop 785 points in a day? And when government bank takeovers wiped out the owners of both stocks and bonds? About when financial mainstays like Lehman Brothers, Wachovia, WB, and Bear Stearns were disappearing overnight.

Yet at the same time, through our fear, we remembered that advice of Warren Buffett to buy fear and sell greed. And perhaps we even remembered the way investors phrased it in blunter centuries: buy when the blood runs in the streets.

Think it's easy to invest at a time like that? What you need is a stock-picking strategy that recognizes every investor is overwhelmed by conflicting emotions from time to time, and gives you a way to work through those emotions and buy low and sell high more times than not.

The Jubak Picks strategy is designed to do exactly that. I've paid some painful emotional dues in the stock market over the years, but out of that I've come up with a strategy that includes the emotions that all investors feel. Let me tell you a personally painful story that illustrates exactly what I mean. This isn't ancient history either. The lessons in this story apply perfectly to the bear market of 2007–8.

The worst year I ever had as an investor was 1999. Like many other investors, I had packed my portfolio with technology stocks at the end of 1998 because that was the group with the trends at its back. New products were tumbling out the door and immediately turning into revenue. Consumers were genuinely excited about the next big thing. Capacity couldn't keep up with demand, and technologies were moving so fast that before a low-cost manufacturer could get a cheaper knockoff to market, the next hot product would have left the knockoff in the dust. As a result, the technology-heavy NASDAQ Composite Index climbed by 86 percent in 1999. But even with this outsized gain, my online portfolio on MSN Money, Jubak's Picks, still beat it, with a return that year of 102 percent.

What a disaster. Because after a year like that you get an exaggerated view of your own abilities. You think you can do no wrong. Every pick is going to be brilliant and extremely profitable. There's no challenge you can't meet. In other words, you get very full of yourself. That was a bad state to be in entering 2000, the year that the technology market crashed and the NASDAQ Composite fell by 39 percent.

And me? Well, my brilliance continued to astound me. I actually called the March market break, when the technology sector started to crater. I remember reading John Rothchild's *The Bear Book* that spring to learn more about bear markets in stocks and then writing in April that we had entered a bear market and that bear markets aren't just corrections. They last much longer than a few months and can stretch on for two years or more. Following Rothchild's conclusion that history showed that the best thing to do in a bear market is to sell early, I started to sell some positions.

Since I have a record of every buy, sell, dividend, and split for the eleven years of Jubak's Picks, I can tell you exactly what I sold. Out went Broadcom on January 21, 2000, with a 794 percent return since my buy on June 29, 1998. Out went Metromedia Fiber, a stock no longer with us, on March 7, 2000, with a 149 percent gain since my buy on June 25, 1999.

When the bottom fell out, with the NASDAQ Composite falling from its all-time high of 5,049 on March 10, 2000, to 3,221 on April 14, I kept on selling. Out went National Semiconductor on April 28—my 47 percent gain since December 14, 1999, wasn't as good as the 101 percent I was showing at the high, but hey, it seemed pretty good amid the carnage. Same with Vitesse Semiconductor: I sold on May 3, 2000, with a 33 percent gain—down from a 110 percent gain—since my October 29, 1999, buy.

If only I'd kept on selling or at least kept the cash I'd raised so far on the sidelines.

But I didn't. In fact, I started to buy technology stocks again in June, just three months after they had crashed in March. On June 16, for example, I bought Atmel and BroadVision.

I didn't think the bear market was over when I bought these stocks. I just thought I was so smart that I could buy shares smashed in the initial sell-off, profit in the inevitable bear market rally, and then sell my positions before the bear reasserted itself and stocks started falling again. With my amazing investing skills, why shouldn't I be able to pull this off?

After all, I'd managed to buy Broadvision at $27.83 on November 5, 1999, and then sell it on March 10—near what turned out to be the top for technology stocks—at $89.46. That was a 221 percent gain in four months. Why couldn't I do something like that again?

By June 16, moreover, Broadvision was trading at just $49.81—a 44 percent drop from my March 10 selling price. The stock had rallied from its absolute bottom on May 25 and looked like it had the momentum to go higher. I figured it had room to run up another $20 a share and still be significantly below its March high. And then I'd sell with another great short-term profit.

But look at what the "success" of 1999 had done to my thinking. Instead of thinking like a long-term investor, I was thinking like a short-term trader. That put a whole lot of the burden for making a profit on my skills as a market timer. But I was so full of myself after 1999 that I neglected to remember that I'm just a mediocre market timer and that I don't exactly excel at calling changes in direction in the overall market or in individual stocks. In my general overconfidence I was betting that one of my weakest sets of investing skills would be more than enough to navigate one of the most treacherous stock market environments.

You can guess how this particular trade turned out. Instead of having weeks to run higher, Broadvision peaked on June 21, just days after my buy. By the end of the year shares of Broadvision would be down almost 80 percent from their June high. And I'd still be holding my position.

Why? Because once you've headed down the road toward investment folly, it's very hard to reverse your own bad thinking. Indeed, each bad decision increases the odds that your next decision will be a bad one too. So once I had a big loss in a stock I decided that I just had to hang on until I broke even. Because I had outsmarted (or outlucked) everyone in 1999, I must be smarter than them in 2000, and the stock market was simply wrong. It would see reason (my version) soon and prices would rebound to where I knew they should be.

Thinking like that took my Jubak's Picks portfolio down to a 17.2 percent loss in 2000, a year in which the NASDAQ Composite Index fell 39 percent and the Standard & Poor's 500 Stock Index 10 percent, and then another 23 percent in 2001, when the NASDAQ dropped another 21 percent and the S&P 500 13 percent.

But these losses, as big as they were, weren't the worst effects of my bad thinking. By 2001 I had gotten so caught up in trying to reverse my stock market losses in technology stocks that I pretty much completely forgot that there were other groups of stocks to invest in.

While I was battling myself to stay with Broadvision and the other technology stocks that I bought even later in this debacle, I was missing out on the beginnings of big moves in other groups.

For example, 2001 was the beginning of the boom in commodity stocks that's still running. Copper miner Freeport McMoRan Copper & Gold was up 56.4 percent in 2001 and would climb another 25.3 percent in 2002. Iron ore miner BHP Billiton was up 8 percent in 2001 and 34.4 percent in 2002.

In those years you could have also seen the beginnings of what would become a huge rally in railroad stocks. Shares of Burlington Northern Santa Fe edged up 2.5 percent in 2001, fell 7.2 percent in 2002, and then took off in 2003, climbing 26.7 percent. Similarly, these were the years for catching the beginnings of the farm boom. Shares of farm equipment maker Deere & Co. fell 2.8 percent in 2001 but climbed 7.1 percent in 2002.

Investing in any of these would have been better than riding Broadvision down to my final September 4, 2001, sell at $2.35 a share.

It wasn't until I finally gave up, sold, and took my losses in technology that I could start to see the rest of the stock market again. In 2003, my vision restored, Jubak's Picks would climb 45.1 percent, a year when the NASDAQ Composite finally rebounded 50 percent and the S&P 500 climbed 9 percent. The next year Jubak's Picks returned 29.5 percent to the 8.6 percent return on the NASDAQ and the 9 percent return on the S&P 500.

The point of this story for investors looking to recover from the bear market of 2007–8 is that the Jubak Picks strategy is designed to keep you from getting bogged down in your past losses and to help you rebuild your wealth as quickly as possible.

There's a whole school of investing research, behavioral finance, that studies the kinds of mistakes that I made in 2000, 2001, and 2002. Behavioral finance is the study of how our psychology gets in the way of smart investment decisions. It's even got a name for what I did in 2000–2—actually, several names, since my behavior was built on more than one mistake.

First, there's the *endowment effect*. That's the tendency investors have to place a higher value on a stock that they own than others would. The classic endowment effect experiment, described by James Montier in his exhaustive book *Behavioral Investing: A Practioner's Guide*, starts with the distribution of some good—often university-logo mugs—to a random 50 percent of a class of college students. A few minutes later the students who have the mugs are allowed to sell them to the students who don't. The average asking price among the students holding the mugs in one experiment turned out to be $5.25. (The mugs sold at the university store for $6.) But the average bid for the mugs was just $2.50. Even though they'd held the mugs for only a few minutes, the owners of the mugs valued them at more than twice what students who didn't own mugs were willing to pay.

Owners of mugs (or stocks, more to the point for us) are reluctant to part with what they own, and they tend to assign a higher price to what they own simply because they own it. One reason for this, behavioral finance posits, is that once we own something it biases our information gathering and decision making. We don't listen to management's conference call with an objective ear but instead tend to hear the information that reinforces our decision to own what we own.

The endowment effect gets reinforced by what's called the *status quo bias*. Faced with a decision to buy or sell, the majority of investors do neither. They'll hold because change in any direction is more frightening than simply standing pat. After all, making any decision leaves you open to the scary possibility that what you decide will be wrong. Standing pat, which in reality is a decision, seems to minimize the chance that we'll make a mistake by buying or selling.

At first a decision to stand pat rather than buy or sell seems puzzling, especially if the stock you're thinking about is deeply underwater. Why not sell and put that turkey behind you?

Behavioral finance points out that investors are loss-averse. We don't weigh potential gains and losses equally. In fact, we tend to dislike potential losses two to two and a half times as much as we like gains.

This all leads to the behavior illustrated by the story of my portfolio in 2000–2. I held on to what I owned because it was more valuable to me than to potential buyers. I didn't sell because whenever I listened to information about what I owned, I heard more of the "facts" supporting my decision to hold and fewer of the "facts" supporting a decision to sell. Given a choice to sell, and the potential to make another mistake, I chose instead to hold. And finally, I put off selling as long as I could because until I sold I really didn't have a loss. The stock could always come back if I just held on, reasoned the loss-averse part of my brain.

Even after experiencing this behavior myself, I still find it shocking how strong these psychological biases can be and how destructive they are to investors' portfolios. Well into 2005, whenever I spoke at a conference I could count on investors asking me when I thought their shares of Lucent Technologies (now Alcatel Lucent) or Nortel Networks would come back. I certainly understood the anxiety behind the question. Before the technology crash Nortel had traded at a high of $83.88 a share. It fell first to a range of $25 to $35 a share in 2005, and then it kept tumbling. On April 23, 2008, Nortel traded for about 77 cents a share once you adjust for the stock's 2006 reverse split.

There's another, equally destructive side to this behavior. It's called *revulsion*. In investing workshops I gave after the technology bear market of 2000–2 was finally over, I frequently saw this psychology at work. I expect to see revulsion again in full force after we've finally worked our way through the bear market that started in 2007.

Revulsion works like this. Take a big enough beating in the stock market—or in other sphere of life—and you will do everything you can to avoid that arena of activity completely in the future. For example, I'm three years older than my brother. When I was fourteen, I loved to play strategy games. A fourteen-year-old should be able to regularly trounce an eleven-year-old at those kinds of games, and I did. And after a while my brother simply refused to play. (Well, actually he came up with a very smart wrinkle. He would play one of my favorite strategy games with me if I played a more luck-based game that evened the odds with him. And because he so hated the strategy games and I so loved them, he demanded a premium. He'd play one strategy game with me if I played three or five or seven luck-based games with him.)

Not playing board games with your brother, however, doesn't do any damage to your portfolio or to your ability to reach your financial goals. Avoiding the stock market in revulsion after a bear market or other losses does. Reaching your financial goals gets a lot harder if you can't bring yourself to tap in to the 10 percent annual returns that stocks deliver in the long run.

Saying, as a lot of investors did after 2000–2 and as a lot of investors will after 2007–8, that you won't buy stocks (or, in the case of 2007–8, stocks and real estate) just dooms you to the worst of all possible investing returns. I guarantee that your revulsion will fade over time and leave you thinking about getting back into stocks or whatever asset you've been avoiding at just about the time prices are getting set to peak. If you buy then, you'll be setting yourself up for another period of big losses and then subsequent revulsion that will keep you from earning profits from the early stages of the next rally that would make up for some or all of the losses you took earlier.

Buy high and sell low—it's tough to make a buck investing like that. Warren Buffett put it this way: "Most people get interested in stocks when everyone else is. The time to get interested is when no one else is. You can't buy what is popular and do well."

Research shows, however, that most people don't do well. The actual returns of mutual fund investors lag the returns of the funds they've invested in because investors tend to pull money out of the funds near bottoms and put money back in near tops. The actual returns of the great bulk of investors lag the returns earned by the stock market indexes for the same reason.

Buying an index fund, putting the same dollar amount into the fund at regular intervals (dollar cost averaging), and sticking with it for the long term is one way around the pitfalls described by behavioral finance. You won't fall prey to the vast majority of psychological traps that kill the returns earned by most investors because that strategy simply has no place for them. Because you hold for the long term and don't sell, you can't sell in a panic. Because you add money at regular intervals, no matter what the market is doing, you can't suffer from crippling revulsion. You've found a strategy that successfully works around the tendency of your own psychology to cost you money.

Sticking to that strategy isn't easy. You have to continue to put new money into your portfolio on a regular basis even when the markets are really scary, and you have to avoid the temptation to put more money in when the markets are rallying and look especially tempting. You have to refuse to give yourself a pass under "extraordinary" circumstances. No saying, "Well, this is a bad market, so I'd better sell and resume my indexing strategy when things look safer." No deciding to switch from your buy-and-hold index into something more exciting when some parts of the stock market leave you behind in the dust.

Most of all, you must have the discipline to be willing to accept the returns that the stock market gives you. Those returns aren't bad at better than 10 percent a year over the long term—before inflation, of course. In fact, they're pretty spectacular when you compare them to the returns from other strategies, such as putting your money in a savings account or in U.S. Treasury bills. But it's only normal to lust after higher returns in whatever is the hot idea of the moment. To be a successful buy-and-hold index investor, you have to successfully resist the temptation to chase performance.

To be a successful investor of any kind, you do have to figure out a strategy that minimizes the damage done by your own psychology. Buy-and-hold indexing does that. But I think it's an awfully difficult discipline for most of us to follow. To follow it, you have to give up the very normal human desire for bragging rights. Let's be honest—we all like to brag. We like to casually drop a mention of the stock that went from $10 to $120 in weeks. (Of course, we never brag about the stocks that went from $120 to $10, do we?) We like the feeling of being an insider that comes from knowing about the hot next play on hybrid car batteries or what South American oil company has just struck it rich under miles of water and salt in the South Atlantic. (It's Petrobras, by the way. Now, be honest. If you knew that, wouldn't you feel really pleased with yourself?)

Buy-and-hold indexing with dollar cost averaging doesn't give us anything like bragging rights with the neighbors. That can be a big problem in a culture such as ours, which seems saturated in stock picks, financial gurus, and the latest numbers from the soaring Mumbai or Shanghai stock markets. It's tough enough to resist buying a Wii, a Prius, or a pair of Jimmy Choos just because everyone else has one or because Carrie wears them on the big or little screen. It takes an even tougher cookie to be able to resist the siren call of the current money culture.

The Jubak Picks strategy is designed to help you avoid the worst performance killers and to earn you just enough bragging rights in the money culture so that you won't be tempted to break discipline and go on a damaging search for stock-market status.

By monitoring macro trends, for example, and trying to move into rising trends and out of falling trends, you can avoid getting locked into paralyzing status quo and endowment effect traps. By focusing on long-term trends, the strategy enables you to avoid the kind of short-term scattershot trading that can kill performance. By keeping in mind that the goal is always to find the best trend to back, you can avoid getting locked in on a single group of stocks or being so revolted that you abandon the entire market.

I understand the value of investing in what you know. When what you know happens to be the hot sector of the moment, the returns from that kind of focus can be phenomenal.

But there's even more to be said for spreading your attention over a manageable number of different sectors. For one thing, it keeps you from overvaluing stocks simply because they're the stocks that you know best. For another, it forces you to constantly make comparisons between stocks on the basis of valuation, business performance, and momentum.

And, of course, it gives you plenty of opportunity to dazzle your friends by turning to them and saying, "I just heard about this little Australian iron ore company that the Chinese want to buy." Everybody wants to be the center of attention from time to time.

Last of all, investing in a variety of trends keeps the game fresh and interesting. One of the pleasures of investing that enables me to keep doing it year in and year out with the kind of attention required to have any shot at beating the market indexes is all I learn about stuff that I never thought I'd know anything about. Twenty years ago I had to learn about computer chip technologies. Today it's the structure of the Chilean utility industry and ore grades in South Africa's gold mines. Tomorrow it will be something different.

The need to constantly learn about what are initially strange and alien parts of the global economy also helps keep you humble. It's a constant reminder of what you don't know and what you need to learn. And it's not a bad thing if that humility leads you to an accurate assessment of when you need to ask for help or even pay for it. I know, for example, that I'm not a great technical analyst, maybe not even average. So I pay money to subscribe to the newsletters and online alerts of people like Dan Sullivan of *The Chartist* or Phil Erlanger of *Erlanger Squeeze Play* or John Murphy on StockCharts.com, who are really good at technical analysis and market timing. The cost—about $300 or so for any one of these services—is money well spent to compensate for my weakness.

No one can know everything and no one can be good at everything. No one can be coldly analytical at all times and in all markets. That's why I've tried to design an investing system that deals with investors as we are and not as we might hope to be. The Jubak Picks strategy is designed to keep you in the market during short-term market upheavals since the trends that you're following in your portfolio will outlast and overpower any short-term correction. And it's designed to keep you buying when everything seems bleak and stocks are cheap since you have faith in the long-term power of the trends that you're following in your portfolio.

And now you're ready to hear about my ten macro trends—and the fifty stocks—that will help you beat the market and rebuild your wealth over the next ten years, and maybe more.

PART II

Ten Trends to Safely Rebuild Your Portfolio

3

GO WHERE THE GROWTH IS

The Rise of China, India, and the Rest of the Gang

WELCOME TO THE NEW GLOBAL ECONOMY, WHERE THE DEVELoping economies of the world—China, India, Brazil, Russia, Vietnam, Indonesia, and Saudi Arabia—are driving global demand for everything from raw materials such as oil to finished goods such as wireless phones and services such as air travel.

Want some examples?

• Global wireless phone sales grew by 12.5 percent in 2007. Not bad growth. But in China the market grew by 14 percent after growing by 18 percent in 2006. And wireless growth in India makes China look like it's standing still: growth of 48 percent in 2007 on top of 100 percent growth in 2006.

• Domestic air travel is growing at an annual rate of 8.1 percent in China. In Brazil it climbed 19 percent in 2005 and 12 percent in 2006. The Indian market has been growing at better than 14 percent a year over the last three years. In the United States, domestic air traffic grew by about 2 percent in 2007.

• Between 2000 and 2006, when global demand for oil grew by 8 million barrels a day, China alone accounted for 32 percent of that growth. The economies of the Organization of Petroleum Exporting Countries (OPEC)—developing nations such as Saudi Arabia—accounted for 22 percent of global demand growth. The United States, in contrast, accounted for *just* 12.5 percent.

- In the United States the Federal Reserve worries if economic growth gets much above 2.5 percent a year. Anything above the speed limit might be too fast for a mature U.S. economy and lead to inflation. The European Central Bank sets its speed limit even lower, at somewhere around 2 percent. And in Japan, well, the country is still trying to generate enough economic growth to make inflation a worry. In the developing world, though, growth just won't slow down. In China, 11 percent economic growth in 2007 reduced the country's economic plans to a shambles. In India, 8 percent growth now seems like the slow lane as the country accelerates to close the growth gap with China. For the twelve months ended in March 2007 the Indian economy grew by 9.4 percent, the second highest growth rate since 1950. In Vietnam, it was 8.3 percent in the first nine months of 2007; in Russia, 7 percent. Even Brazil, the laggard among the big economies of the developing world, is seeing growth finally accelerate from 2.5 percent toward 5 percent.

That growth set off a boom in the stock—no matter what stock market it trades on—of any company with a piece of the pie. Five years ago the total market capitalization of Asia's stock markets was just $1 trillion. At the end of September 2007, they showed a value of $6 trillion. The Chinese oil company PetroChina, which trades on the New York Stock Exchange, was, as of July 2008, the second most valuable company (measured by stock market value) in the world, behind only ExxonMobil. The Shanghai stock market climbed 130 percent in 2006 and another 116 percent in 2007. A correction in the first half of 2008 lopped 25 percent off the index, but Shanghai stocks were still up 271 percent since the beginning of 2006.

I expect this kind of runaway outperformance to resume after the crisis of 2007–8 ends in 2009–10.

The single most important trend today for investors is the rise of the developing economies of the world. I can't emphasize that enough.

And if you want to make money in the stock market in the next decade, you've got to be invested in this trend, even when it looks like the news from the global economy turns extremely negative, as it did in the summer and fall of 2008. Stressed by the global financial crisis that started in the U.S. subprime mortgage sector, stock markets in Russia and Brazil went into free fall, and both had to be closed on the worst days in order to limit the chaos. There were runs on banks in Hong Kong and India. Economists began predicting that economic growth in China would fall by 20 percent.

But these were all simply speed bumps in the progress of the world's developing economies. Remember the checkered history of the United States as it grew to global economic power. U.S. panics and depressions in the last part of the nineteenth century make anything that happened in 2008 look tame. Bankers had to move gold by train from their vaults in New York to prevent the default of the U.S. government. Railroad companies went bankrupt with a frequency that makes the takeovers of Bear Stearns, Wachovia, and Washington Mutual look orderly. And the damage handed out to British banks by panic in the United States and in other developing economies of the time, such as Argentina, threatened to bring down the entire global financial system more than once.

And yet this turmoil didn't stop the amazing growth of the U.S. economy. Heck, it didn't even stop the buildout of the U.S. transcontinental railroad system. Trends like the rise of the United States in the nineteenth century and the rise of China, India, and the rest of the gang in the twenty-first century are too strong to be stopped by bubbles and crashes in commodities or real estate.

A 20 percent drop in growth in China seems like a lot, but when the fall is from 10 percent to 8 percent, and it lasts for just a quarter or two, it's evidence that the rise of China, India, and the rest of the gang isn't going to be derailed by a little thing like the near-collapse of the U.S. banking system. So let me say it again: this is the single most important trend for investors today. You've got to be invested in it.

But how, exactly? Do you buy shares of companies in China, India, Brazil, and so on? (And which ones?) Do you buy shares of companies in other countries selling goods and services to China, India, Brazil, et alia? (And which ones?) Do you buy shares in the companies that sell raw materials to these emerging market manufacturers? (And which ones?) How about investing in the companies that build the roads, airports, warehouses, and railroads that make this economic growth possible? (And, of course, which ones?)

To figure all this out, I'm going to break the big growth story into its major parts so that you can understand how each one of the substories plays out on the global stage. That sounds daunting, like something you might need a degree from the London School of Economics to pull off. To capture all—or even most—of the profits from this global economic story, you certainly would. And it wouldn't hurt to have an unlimited travel budget so you could visit each of these economies yourself, and seventy hours of time a week to devote to your research.

Fortunately, you can capture enough of the gains from this global phenomenon to power your portfolio results—and to safely earn a better return than you would investing in U.S. stocks alone—if you understand just four major substories. I'm going to start by laying these four trends out for you. I'll follow that by clarifying the risks of investing in these markets. And then, as I will in every one of the ten stock-picking chapters in this book, I'll end with a list of stocks to buy. In addition, I'll make recommendations for exchange-traded funds, called ETFs, and mutual funds for those investors who don't want to pick individual stocks.

THE FOUR TRENDS FOR PROFITING FROM THE GROWTH OF THE WORLD'S DEVELOPING ECONOMIES

• *These economies have become the world's factories.* Increasingly, the corporations of the developed world use the economies of China, India, Vietnam, and the rest of the gang as low-cost platforms for making their products. About 70 percent of the nonfood items that Wal-Mart sells, for example, come from China.

- *There's big money to be made from selling to the world's factories.* The factories that make everything from auto parts to Barbie dolls need raw materials such as iron ore, copper, oil, and coal. All of these have to be imported by most of the world's factory economies.
- *Getting the raw materials to the world's factories and the finished goods to consumers in the developed economies requires lots and lots of infrastructure.* Someone's got to build the roads, railroads, airports, and warehouses that this logistical system needs. And someone's got to sell the trucks, railroad engines and cars, airplanes, and forklifts that this system needs.
- *All the investment in factories and infrastructure creates millions of higher-paying jobs in the developing world.* This is creating a new or bigger middle class in countries from China to Vietnam. There's a lot of money to be made in satisfying the needs and desires of that new middle class.

Now let's go through each of these subtrends in detail.

#1: You Can Invest in the World's Factories

Ride the train through Trenton, New Jersey, and you will pass an old steel bridge across the Delaware River emblazoned with the slogan "Trenton Makes—the World Takes" in huge neon letters. In 1910, when the Trenton Chamber of Commerce adopted the motto, this slogan was literally true. Trenton churned out steel, rubber, wire, rope, linoleum, and ceramics for markets around the world.

A century later that's no longer true. Today China makes. And so does India. And Vietnam. And Brazil. The developing economies of the world have become the world's factories.

To see China's factory at work, you only have to walk the aisles at Wal-Mart. In 2007, Wal-Mart bought $18 billion of goods from China. About 70 percent of the nonfood items that Wal-Mart sells come from China, according to the China General Chamber of Commerce. If Wal-Mart were a country, it would rank as China's eighth-largest trading partner, ahead of Russia, Australia, and Canada.

But it's not just China.

India's Tata Steel is the fifth-largest steelmaker in the world after its January 2007 purchase of Anglo-Dutch steelmaker Corus Group. But that still leaves the company playing catch-up with ArcelorMittal, which is now the number one steel company in the world. With a production capacity of 120 million metric tons, ArcelorMittal, about 50 percent owned by India's Mittal family, is larger than the entire U.S. steel industry, at 96 million metric tons. ArcelorMittal's 2007 revenues came to $105 billion, compared to $17 billion at venerable United States Steel. China, by the way, remained the number one steel producer in the world in 2006 with production of 420 million metric tons.

And it's not just China and India.

The competition from newcomers with supplies of even cheaper labor is brutal. For example, foreign investment in Indonesia, Malaysia, and Vietnam has picked up as companies look for the next great place to cut costs now that they've wrung all the competitive advantage that they can from moving factories to China and India or sourcing products from them. Here's a recent geographical path for one Taiwanese food company: from Taiwan to Guangdong in southern China in 1995 (cutting production costs by 50 percent) and then in 2004 to Vietnam (cutting costs 35 percent below those in China). Chinese companies themselves are doing much of the moving. In 2006 Chinese companies invested in fifty-seven projects in Vietnam, up from forty in 2005, to build factories where production can be 30 percent cheaper than in China's own Pearl River Delta.

Often the factories that are on the move require less technology and more labor. So, for example, the Chongqing Dongli Manufacturing Company invested $10.3 million in 2001 to build a factory in Vietnam to assemble kits for motorbikes. Low labor costs were key to that move. But even high-technology companies are moving factories to low-cost countries. In 2006 Intel decided to invest $1 billion to build its largest chip assembly and testing plant in the world. In this deal Vietnam's low-cost workforce certainly didn't hurt, but cheap land and long-term tax breaks were even more important.

And finally, it's not just goods.

The developing world's "factories" also include service companies such as India's Wipro, Infosys, and Tata Consultancy Services. India's export of information technology services is growing at about 30 percent a year—more than three times faster than the Indian economy as a whole. India now accounts for about one-quarter of the global pool of information technology talent, according to McKinsey & Company. Other major service exporters based in emerging economies include Argentina's Globant in applications development, the Czech Republic's IBA Group in software development, China's Neusoft in information technology, and India's Polaris Software Lab in application development.

#2: You Can Invest in the Stocks of Companies That Sell to the World's Factories

To invest in this part of the story, you buy shares of the companies outside China, India, Brazil, et cetera, who are supplying the raw materials for the global factory.

Look again at China from this perspective. The country's government planners say they want to shift the source of the country's growth away from the export-oriented industrial sector and toward the domestically oriented service sector. That effort is either failing dismally or was never really serious in the first place. Growth in factory output climbed 18.3 percent in the first quarter of 2007, even faster than growth in the economy as a whole. Those industries that consume the most energy—petrochemicals, coke making for steel, fuel processing and refining, and metal production and processing—are growing at a 21 percent annual rate. So, contrary to what the planners said they wanted, the industrial sector will make up an even bigger share of the national economy tomorrow than it does today, and the steady decline in the service sector's share of the national economy to 39.5 percent in 2006 will continue.

Look at how this affects just a few raw materials.

China's demand for iron ore will grow at an average annual rate of

8 percent from 2007 through 2012, according to Vale, the Brazilian company that is the world's top iron ore supplier. While China makes up about 75 percent of projected global demand growth for iron ore, according to Australia's Macquarie Research, the rest of the developing world is using more iron ore too. Vale (until recently the company was named Companhia Vale do Rio Doce) sees total global iron ore transported by sea—which captures exports to China and India but excludes domestic iron ore consumed in Europe or the United States—growing by 250 million metric tons between 2007 and 2012.

Which might not have a huge effect on prices for iron ore except that the mining industry can't expand production fast enough to meet that demand. In 2007, for example, global demand will exceed global supply by about six million metric tons. The deficit will be met by drawing down global stockpiles.

So you won't be surprised that the price of iron ore is climbing, although you will be surprised when I tell you how fast it's rising. The price of iron ore climbed another 65 percent in 2008 at the first round of annual negotiations that set the world price. In the second round, the price went up 97 percent. That's the sixth consecutive annual increase. The negotiations between Chinese steel companies and the big three iron ore producers—Vale, Rio Tinto, and BHP Billiton—that set the price ended in the biggest increase since the 72 percent jump in 2004.

The picture is remarkably similar for copper. Global copper consumption is projected to climb by 3.5 percent in 2008, according to Corporación Nacional del Cobre de Chile (known as Codelco), the state-owned Chilean company that is the world's largest copper producer. That's despite a slowdown in the U.S. demand for copper as the domestic housing industry slumps, and it would match the 3.5 percent increase in global demand in 2007. The company also didn't see any quick way to expand production, noting that due to rising costs and shortages of everything from truck tires to energy, it now takes up to ten years to bring new production on line. No wonder that copper prices in 2007 stayed stubbornly close to the all-time high of $8,800 a metric ton reached in May 2006 and had only fallen to \$7,621 by August 6, 2008, despite the slump in the U.S. housing market.

I'll have a lot more to say about the global commodities squeeze in Chapter 8.

#3: You Can Invest in the Companies Supplying the Infrastructure That These Factories and Their Raw Material Suppliers Need

Think about what a mining company needs to do to open a new mine and increase production of any of the raw materials that the world's factory in developing economies needs. The company needs engineers and truck drivers. It needs mining equipment to dig out the ore and trucks to transport it to railroads that may in fact have to be built from scratch to ports that also may need to be constructed. Then there are the ships to move the raw material to the processing plants that need it. And let's not forget the power plants that the mine will need to supply its mines with electricity. Sometimes the list seems to go on forever, and one missing item can bring the whole effort to a halt.

Codelco, for example, doesn't have enough electricity to fully develop its new Gaby mine in northern Chile. The mine is slated to start production in mid-2008, but the coal-fired power plants scheduled to supply electricity to the mines and smelters will not be ready until 2011. In the meantime, the company and other copper miners in the region are discussing plans to import liquefied natural gas—which will require the construction of new docking and storage facilities—so they can keep existing gas-fired power-generating plants in operation even as natural gas supplies from current provider Argentina dwindle.

In Western Australia, it's been relatively easy to discover huge new deposits of iron ore. But getting that ore onto ships bound for China requires building new roads, railroads, loading and unloading facilities, and ports.

This infrastructure gap isn't limited to mining by any means, according to a March 2007 report from the World Bank on the Brazilian economy. If Brazil wants to grow faster without a huge increase in inflation, it must increase investment in infrastructure—everything from roads to airports to ports—to 3.2 percent of gross domestic product ($492 billion in 2006) from the current 1 percent rate. The government of President Luiz Inácio Lula da Silva has promised to deliver 5 percent economic growth in the president's second term, which began in October 2006, up from 2.9 percent growth in 2006. The government's plan calls for an additional 0.5 percentage points of GDP—for a total of 1.5 percent—to be spent on infrastructure projects. That's clearly inadequate if you follow the logic of the World Bank report, which says that adding 4 percentage points of annual GDP growth would require infrastructure spending of between 5 percent and 9 percent of GDP. You do the math.

Investors and government planners don't need to imagine what will happen in Brazil if the country doesn't make the investment in infrastructure. They just need to look to India and the damage that decades of underinvestment in roads, ports, airports, and rail lines has done to the country's economy. Somewhere between 30 percent and 40 percent of the country's crops rot in the fields or spoil in transit because of the country's creaky infrastructure. There simply isn't any way to get the food to market in time. What does make it through the supply chain is subject to huge markups at each stage of the process because getting food from warehouse to distribution center to retail store to consumer is so time-consuming and cumbersome. Consumers pay twice as much for wheat, for example, as do wholesale buyers. That adds another layer of inflation to food prices at a time when food inflation doesn't need any help in running wild: wholesale wheat prices jumped 54 percent between April and November 2006.

Agriculture isn't the only sector of the economy paying the price. On overcrowded highways, speeds average less than twenty miles per hour. Major cities in some Indian states cut power to factories one day a week. Ships have to be unloaded manually and cargo manually loaded onto trucks. Getting cars the 900 miles from the factory to the port at Mumbai takes one automaker ten days.

India spends just 4 percent of its gross domestic product on infrastructure, in comparison to the 9 percent spent in China and that disparity has existed for more than a decade. As a result, while China has 25,000 miles of expressways, for example, India has just 3,700 miles.

Facing what amounts to a rebellion by the rural poor over soaring food costs that is likely to cost the ruling Congress Party dearly in elections set for 2009, the government budget released in March 2007 promises to tackle the infrastructure part of the problem by raising government spending on roads, bridges, airports, et cetera, by 40 percent. But the government isn't stopping there: it is promoting public-private partnerships on infrastructure projects that are projected to invest $300 billion to $500 billion in infrastructure over the next five years.

While you're toting up global investment in infrastructure, don't forget Russia. At a summer 2007 meeting in St. Petersburg, the country, then awash in oil and natural resources money, set itself the goal of becoming one of the world's top five economies by 2020. To make the jump from number nine now, Russia's leaders figure they will have to invest $1 trillion over ten years in rebuilding and expanding an outdated transportation and industrial infrastructure. In his last state-of-Russia address, then-president Vladimir Putin said the country would spend $480 billion by 2020 to expand its supply of electricity. Another $400 billion, the president said, would go into the railroad system. Airports would get $30 billion.

That's a lot of money over ten years, but the budgeted $1 trillion will have to climb considerably higher to get the job done. Russia is a country that's almost twice the size of the United States but with half the miles of railroad track and one-tenth the miles of paved roads. And if Russia spends *only* $1 trillion over ten years, it's actually likely to fall even further behind China in the global infrastructure race. China spent $956 billion on infrastructure in 2004–6 alone.

The lesson from all these economies is simple: the faster a country grows, the more it needs to invest in infrastructure. So buying infrastructure stocks is another way to profit from the fast growth of China, India, and company.

#4: You Can Invest in Companies Selling to the Growing
Middle Class of China, India, and Company

We know two things about the middle class in China, India, Brazil, and the rest of the developing world: not so long ago it didn't exist, and it's big.

How big is a matter of intense debate. To start with China again, estimates of the Chinese middle class today range from 100 million to 300 million. Think that range is a bit wide? (Well, what's 200 million people among friends?) It gets even wider once the experts start projecting the size of the country's middle class in the future. Wall Street investment bank Goldman Sachs put the Chinese middle class at 650 million by 2015. The lowball number from other experts is about 300 million.

A big part of the problem is that there isn't any real definition of middle class that you can apply to economies as different as those of Sweden and China, for example. Should the middle class be defined by income level? Or is it a style of consumption? Or does it measure a family's stake in such middle-class goals as a house and car?

The problem doesn't get any easier to solve if you look just at numbers. Goldman Sachs, for example, says that a household income of $9,000 using the official dollar/yuan exchange rate qualifies as middle class in China. That's below the poverty level in the United States. But it qualifies as middle class in China, says Goldman, because prices in China are so much lower than in the United States. Goldman Sachs uses what's called purchasing power parity to correct for the difference. According to one estimate of the difference, $9,000 in China is equal to an annual income of $22,500 in the United States.

Of course, there's just the little problem that because the Chinese don't provide full price data to outside economists, it's very difficult to know what figures to use in calculating purchasing power parity. Recently the Asian Development Bank redid its numbers using what it believes is a better estimate of purchasing power parity based on more complete price reporting. The bank concluded that China's economy was about 40 percent smaller than everyone thought because Chinese prices were higher than the incomplete numbers had indicated.

Whoops.

I think these problems are less important than they seem, however, for three reasons.

First, if an investment makes sense when you conservatively assume a middle class of 100 million, you'll only be overjoyed if the true number turns out to be 200 million. For China, the conservative measure of the middle class is about 100 million to 124 million. According to Arthur Kroeber, editor of *China Economic Quarterly*, these are the Chinese who have incomes high enough so that they can consume instead of merely buying to survive.

Measuring the middle class in India, Brazil, and the rest of the developing world has a similar margin of error. Estimates of the Indian middle class range from 100 million to 300 million (the latter figure representing about a third of the population). A conservative estimate would put Brazil's middle class at 26 million; a high estimate would be about twice that number.

These numbers are nothing to turn up your nose at, even at the lower end of the estimates. At 100 million, the Chinese and Indian middle classes are each twice the size of all of France. Brazil's middle class is either about 50 percent bigger than the population of Florida or one-third larger than the population of California. Certainly if Florida and California are attractive markets for sunglasses, insurance, cars, and oranges, then each of these middle-class populations in the developing world is also big enough to be attractive to companies selling these and other products.

Second, as an investor, once a market has reached a certain takeoff size—and 26 million to 100 million certainly qualifies—you're actually more interested in the rate at which that market is growing than in its size. And for investors the great news is that the middle class in the developing world is growing very fast. In Brazil, for example, between 2002 and 2006, the number of households with annual disposable incomes above $10,000 climbed by 32 percent.

The spending aspirations of this middle class are growing even faster. A 2007 survey by the CLSA brokerage in India found that while only 19 percent of the middle-class households in the survey own a four-wheeled vehicle of any sort, about 21 percent have plans to buy a car. Only 16 percent of these families have taken out a loan of any kind, but consumer credit is growing at a 33 percent annualized rate. Seems like a promising market for carmakers and financial companies—and investors in them.

And third, many people in these developing economies aspire to own one or two products that the developed world normally associates with the middle class even though these individuals are not remotely part of the middle class. So, for example, just about everyone in China wants to own a mobile phone. That's not surprising given the scarcity and poor quality of landline phones in China. And in China a surprisingly large fraction of the population—something approaching not the 12 percent of the country that might be middle class but more like 60 percent of the total population—can afford one, even if they can't afford any of the other trappings of middle-class life as it's defined in the developed economies. If a company can market a product such as a mobile phone at the right price point, the market for this middle-class product isn't limited to the middle class in China or India or Brazil. It's almost everyone.

I wouldn't get too hung up on defining the middle class. It should be clear to anyone who has watched China leapfrog the stages that Europe and the United States followed on their way to economically developed status that the developing world is cutting corners, blazing new paths, and making its own mistakes on its way to joining (or surpassing) the nations that make up the currently developed world. Investors need to factor that into their thinking about where to put money in order to participate in the extraordinary growth in these developing economies.

So, for instance, Kenya, with a population of 34 million, had a grand total of 280,000 landline phone subscribers as of June 2006. That's actually a big drop from 304,000 subscribers in June 2006. But it gives you some indication of exactly how bad service by Telekom

Kenya, until 2004 the country's monopoly phone company, is. The number of people waiting for a landline peaked at about 100,000 in . 2004 before falling to 64,000 in 2006. The entire country had just 7,232 Telekom Kenya pay phones.

About what you'd expect from one of the world's poorest countries, no? Per capita annual income in Kenya was just $580 at the official exchange rate, or $1,300 a year at purchasing power parity.

But if you see Kenya as just another poor country—and one with recent political turmoil to boot—then you're well on the way to missing out on the Kenyan version of one of the most amazing business stories of our time. In the last six years two Kenyan mobile phone companies, Safaricom and Celtel Kenya, have signed up rich, middle-class, and poor Kenyans at a mind-boggling pace until the two companies had 6.5 million subscribers as of June 2006. The capacity of the companies' mobile networks has grown to 10.6 million from just 640,000 in June 2001. At the end of 2006 there were twenty times as many mobile phone subscribers in Kenya as there were landline customers. With a customer base of 6.5 million, about one in five Kenyans subscribes to a mobile phone service.

Now, many of these subscribers aren't especially lucrative to Safaricom or Celtel. They might own a prepaid account and share a phone. Such a subscriber might use a few minutes of calling time a week. Resellers of mobile services might be what are called "umbrella ladies" in some parts of Africa, where the business consists of a single phone and a table shaded by an umbrella where customers can make a call. But rates per minute are high—far higher than in neighboring Uganda and Tanzania—and Safaricom is remarkably profitable. In the year that ended in June 2007 it made a profit of $259 million on revenue of $731 million.

And while the company is following a very developed-world model by building a data network that will let it sell more expensive data and Internet services to its customers, it's also pursuing strategies suited to the needs of the average Kenyan. So the company is developing new rates designed to pull in more of the key sixteen-to-twenty-five-year-old user group—a fast-growing population in Kenya but one without much income. And it has launched M-Pesa, a low-cost, mobile-phone-based money transfer service. Customers get a cash storage account on their mobile phone's SIM card and can collect or pay in cash at any Safaricom agent and then send money to any mobile phone in Kenya. The service seems dead-on for a country with just 400 bank branches and only 600 ATMs.

It's hard for a developed-economy company to match a developing-world strategy such as this one. Of course, that hasn't stopped companies such as Motorola from trying. Most of the time these companies have found themselves engaged in an unwinnable tug-of-war. Cut prices low enough so that you can sell to developing-world consumers who haven't yet made it to something like a middle-class income and you wind up savaging your profit margins. Keep prices high enough to make a decent profit margin and you price yourself out of the developing market. On the other hand, it's not impossible to tap this market: Nokia, for example, is one developed-world company that has been able to create a winning developing-world strategy.

Adding It All Up

The Opportunities

What's the effect of a middle class that has hit take-off size, that is growing at high and sustainable rates, and whose buying power is amplified in some markets by purchases of middle-class goods and services by non-middle-class customers?

• *An explosion in intracountry travel.* Domestic air traffic is projected to grow by 8.1 percent a year in China from 2007 through 2026. A market that is now one-fifth the size of the domestic North American market will climb to half the size of that market by 2026. The country will need a total of 3,400 new planes over the next twenty years. A projected 22 million new consumers will buy travel products and services over the next two decades. In India the number of passenger miles flown a day climbed by 46 percent from April through December 2006. Six new airlines have entered the domestic market.

- *An expanding market for "affordable" luxury goods.* Take one industry, eyeglasses, as an example. Luxottica manufactures and sells glasses and sunglasses under its own brands (such as Ray-Ban and Oakley) or licensed brands (such as Versace, Chanel, and Prada) through a network of 4,611 branded stores including LensCrafters in the United States and Canada. And now here's the future: in the last two years the company has acquired Modern Sight (28 stores) in Shanghai, Ming Long (113 stores) in Guangdong, and Xueliang (79 stores in Beijing) to bring its total in China to 270 stores, and in September 2006 the company opened a flagship LensCrafters store in Beijing, the first of a planned 90 stores in China. Sales outside the United States and the company's home market of Italy are projected by Banca Caboto in Milan to grow by 25 percent in 2007. In the third quarter of 2007, same-store sales in China grew by 17 percent from the year earlier quarter.

- *A wave of buying of traditionally middle-class financial products such as life insurance and credit cards.* Only 3.1 percent of India's population of 1 billion has any life insurance, up from a mere 1 percent in 1990. Insurance premiums amounted to just $13.6 billion in 2006, according to Swiss Re. That lags South Africa—population 45 million—with penetration of 10.8 percent and premiums of $20.7 billion. India also lags China with premiums of $32 billion and South Korea at $42 billion. Just for context, life insurance premiums hit $584 billion in the United States in 2006. But if you're an investor, forget the small size of the market now and focus on the growth rate. Within the next five years, premiums in India are expected to hit $60 billion. That's a doubling and doubling again in five years. This is a market that's taken off.

- *The real estate market in China and India is full of speculative froth, sure, but prices will climb in the long term on rising demand for better housing as incomes rise.* Local real estate operators in India hooted when Farallon Capital Management, a U.S. hedge fund, paid $54.5 million an acre for an eleven-acre plot in central Mumbai in

March 2005. At the end of that year, Farallon bid $95.5 million an acre for a nearby property—and wound up losing the auction to a higher bidder. I think it's safe to say that real estate was—and will be again—a hot investment in India. Merrill Lynch forecasts that the Indian realty sector will grow from $12 billion in 2005 to $90 billion by 2015. And India is one of the last developing markets to catch fire. China is far enough along that the Macquarie Group, the Australian financial company that is the world's largest private manager of infrastructure, is in serious discussions with the Beijing government to create an investment market that would let foreign money buy and sell real estate in China. Macquarie isn't dissuaded from its long-term goals by China's short-term efforts to cool off real estate speculation either. China raised interest rates five times from March through September 2007 in a moderately successful effort to deflate a real estate bubble in Shanghai and other big cities.

THREE BIG RISKS

Risk 1: Profitless growth. It's so easy in any situation—like this one—where growth is so rapid for an investor to become mesmerized by fast growth in revenue and to forget about profits. That fascination with top-line revenue growth is what sucked so many investors into the U.S. dot-com boom that went bust in 2000. And it's a real danger—perhaps an even bigger danger—in the current emerging market boom.

So many of the developing economies that are growing so fast and so many of the most attractive growth industries aren't fully open to market forces, and it's quite possible to generate profitless or nearly profitless revenue growth across an entire economic sector.

Steel is a great example. Remember that I told you that China was the largest steel producer in the world? Well, that doesn't mean it's the most profitable or even very profitable at all. Steel production in China grew by 23 percent in 2004 to 273 million tons, then grew by 20 percent in 2005 and another 15 percent in 2006, and tacked on another 18 percent jump in 2007. Total 2006 production of 419 million tons rose to 492 million tons in 2007.

Just one problem for steel companies intent on making a profit: steel capacity jumped even faster, to 530 million tons by the end of 2006. It's hard to make much of a profit when the industry is capable of making 530 million tons of steel and actually producing just 419 million tons. A steel company in an industry with that much idle capacity will sell steel at just about any price to prevent its steel mills from joining that 110 tons of idle capacity.

In a market economy you'd expect that this much excess capacity would cause some steelmakers—ideally the least efficient ones—to go out of business or to file for bankruptcy. Not in China, however. Banks are only too willing to lend to even technically bankrupt companies at the order of local leaders who are rewarded by the system—either officially through promotion or unofficially through cash payments under the table—for producing jobs and raising production in the local economy.

The Chinese government in faraway Beijing has had an official policy for years aimed at shutting the most inefficient of the country's 1,500 steel producers. In 2005, when the steel industry produced 348 million tons of steel from its production capacity of 470 million tons, the official goal was to cut annual production capacity by 55 million tons in the coming five years. Instead capacity climbed to 530 million tons by the end of 2006.

Some small producers have indeed been forced out of business or pressured to merge with larger companies, but China's bigger steel companies have more than compensated by building new plants. For example, Baosteel, China's biggest steel company, planned to add 25 million tons in new capacity in 2007. Investment in the steel industry in 2007 was running at an annual rate of $35 billion a year. Demand for steel is exploding in China as the country rushes to build twenty new cities a year to accommodate the 12 million people expected to move to urban areas from the countryside over the next two decades. But even with all that demand, and even with a government trying to force inefficient makers out of business, capacity will still exceed production and production will exceed consumption in 2010. In that year, Chinese steelmakers are projected to produce 63 million tons of steel more than the domestic economy demands.

Risk 2: You can't believe the numbers. A reasonable investor might expect that a steel industry with 100 million tons or so in excess production capacity might be in the red, right? But not according to the official numbers issued by Chinese companies and then compiled by the Chinese government. In 2005, when the industry produced 348 million tons but had an annual capacity of 470 million tons, the steel industry as a whole made a profit, according to Beijing's figures. Sixty-six of China's largest steelmakers realized profits of $9.5 billion, according to official figures reported by the *People's Daily*. I'd guess from that phrasing that the country's 1,434 other, smaller steel companies collectively lost money—although less than the $9.5 billion in profit recorded by the 66 biggest players. That's possible since the spread between big players and small in the Chinese industry is huge. Only 55 of the country's 1,500 steel producers have annual production capacity of more than 1 million tons. The country's biggest steel company, Baosteel, by contrast, produced 28 million tons of steel in 2006.

But while possible, a profit across the industry in 2005 would have been remarkable considering all the bad things that happened that year. Production costs—driven by the soaring price of iron ore— climbed 65 percent in 2004 and 2005. All that excess production capacity drove domestic steel prices down by 16 percent from March to August 2005. And yet somehow the industry as a whole made a profit, according to official figures.

Skeptical? You've good reason to be. Those "profits" are based on below-market-rate loans: It's much easier to make money when you can book your interest expense at close to zero because your board of directors is made up of the same local officials that control the bank that lent you money. There are no costs for pollution control since these same local officials control who can pollute and how much. And when it comes to selling that steel, who says that you can't get a higher-than-market price, even with excess capacity run amuck? Those same local officials control the building contract for the new local hospital and can tell management at that new motorbike factory what steel company to buy from and how much to pay.

It's not that every set of books in China is cooked. It's just that investors can't tell which ones are cooked and which aren't.

Let's take the case of LDK Solar, a Chinese maker of the silicon wafers used to produce solar cells. The company was a darling from the moment it listed its shares on the New York Stock Exchange at $27.20 on June 1, 2007, until September 26, 2007. That day the shares closed at $73.95 for a gain of 172 percent in a little less than four months.

By October 19, 2007, shares of LDK Solar were selling at $35.73, a drop of 78 percent in less than a month.

What happened? Charley Situ, a financial controller who had been fired by the company, claimed that the company's inventory numbers were fraudulent and that 250 million metric tons of silicon being carried in the company's inventory at the purchase price were actually worthless. His accusations were picked up by financial publications such as *Barron's* and the *Wall Street Journal* and by investment analysts at CIBC and Goldman Sachs.

But was Situ telling the truth? Investors who own the stock—called longs—saw a conspiracy by short sellers to profit by driving the price into the ground. (Short sellers borrow shares of a company's stock from other investors with a promise to replace the shares at a future date. They then sell those borrowed shares on the open market. They make a profit if the share price goes down, as they can replace the original borrowed shares by buying shares at a lower price on the open market, and they lose if shares go up, since they have to buy at a higher price to replace those borrowed shares.) And they might have had a point. While LDK has issued 104 million shares of stock, almost all are locked up by the terms of the company's June 1 initial public offering. Only about 4 million shares are available for trading. That makes it relatively easy for shorts—or longs, for that matter—to stampede the stock higher or lower.

By the longs' analysis, even if *all* the silicon that Situ flagged is worthless, the impact on earnings would only be about 56 cents a share. That would work out to a drop in share price of $7.60, not the drop of $40 that took place.

But there are holes in the conspiracy theory. The CIBC analyst that the longs see as a tool of the shorts actually downgraded LDK on valuation before Situ's charges: the stock had climbed 50 percent in a month and the shares were fairly valued. The analyst, Adam Hinkley, also noted that aggressive expansion of silicon production in China will lead to overcapacity and pricing pressure in the market in 2009. The history of the Chinese steel industry suggests that's a reasonable worry.

LDK didn't do a good job at putting the story to rest either. After initially affirming its inventory practices in a press release, the company then raised questions in a conversation with another analyst about the way it accounted for inventory. LDK announced an external audit—a move designed to increase management's credibility—and then undermined that credibility by appointing an outside auditor instead of its normal audit firm, KMPG. That raised questions about why LDK had changed auditors in midcrisis. Did KMPG know something about the inventory issues Situ raised that management wanted to bury? That was one question I saw in Internet discussions of LDK.

Can you figure this one out? Go ahead, I dare you. At the time you could certainly form an opinion—both the longs and the shorts had done that. But while the crisis was unfolding, you couldn't get the facts you needed to feel confident saying this stock was a buy or a sell.

Certainly accounting problems aren't unique to developing-country companies and stock markets. Some U.S. companies—Enron and Tyco come to mind—have produced global hall of fame financial lies in their day. But I'd argue that the run-of-the-mill company in a developing market leaves the investor with questions that the average developed-market stock does not. Who actually owns the company? An individual, a family, a group of local officials, managers from a supplier or a customer, the army? Are transactions conducted at arm's length and at fair market prices? Are all costs showing up on the books? Is cash flowing into the company at below-market rates or out of the company through theft and bribes?

It's tough, sometimes impossible, to tell. And when you can't tell, you shouldn't invest your money.

Risk 3: If you don't know who owns the shares, it's just about impossible to accurately value the stock. Let's take a look at PetroChina, a Chinese oil company that became the most valuable company in the world by market capitalization on November 5, 2007. With a market capitalization of $1 trillion, PetroChina at the end of 2007 was worth more than BP and Chevron combined. The company's stock market value passed that of General Electric on October 15 and the company took over the number one slot from ExxonMobil at $507 billion on November 5.

But remember how market cap is calculated. You start with the price per share on the public market (or for privately owned companies the price of the most recent sale of shares to private investors)—$6 a share in the case of PetroChina on November 5—and then multiply that price by the number of shares issued by the company.

That calculation works reasonably well if most of a company's shares trade in the market. Then the price for the shares that do trade is a reasonable stand-in for the price of those shares that don't trade—say, the ones locked up in a company's treasury to pay for employee stock grants, or the ones held by some investors, such as the Chinese government in this case, that never sell. But it doesn't work very well when so few shares trade that a good deal of the price of the publicly traded shares results from the scarcity of shares. In this case, the public shares trade at a premium value because there aren't enough to satisfy market demand. If more shares traded, that premium would diminish and might even vanish. Certainly when a majority of a company's shares don't trade, investors should consider the possibility that in buying the stock they're paying for its scarcity value. If the owners of the shares that don't trade suddenly decide to sell them on the public market, that could send the price of shares and the company's market cap tumbling.

Well, guess what? As of the end of 2006, China National Petroleum owned 88 percent of the shares of PetroChina. Since China National

Petroleum is itself a state-owned company, that means that almost 90 percent of the shares of PetroChina are owned by the Chinese government. The Chinese government has announced an official policy of reducing its ownership stake in state-owned companies. To what level? Well, it probably depends on the Chinese government's willingness to part with stakes in strategic sectors such as oil and aviation. In those sectors I don't think the Beijing government will be selling big stakes soon.

But wait, the calculation gets even more suspect. PetroChina's initial public offering was limited to just 4 billion shares, about 2.18 percent of its existing shares. The underwriters received bids of $456 billion for those shares, initially priced at about $14.7 billion by the underwriters. Why so much demand? Because this was going to be the first time residents of China—aside from residents of Hong Kong—could buy PetroChina shares. The company's stock has traded on the Hong Kong stock exchange and on the New York Stock Exchange (as an American depository receipt) for years, but by law investors from mainland China couldn't buy those shares. With that much demand for such a limited number of shares, you can imagine what happened to the share price on the first day of trading—it climbed 163 percent from the IPO price.

Even in 2008 shares in Shanghai traded for 150 percent more than shares in Hong Kong, and because investors can by and large invest in one of these markets and not the other, there's little chance that normal arbitrage will quickly reduce the price in Shanghai. And, then, of course, there's the little matter of the 88 percent of the company's stock that never trades and is held by the Chinese government.

And that's how PetroChina got to be the world's first $1 trillion company.

You can argue that the Chinese government will never sell these shares and that it would never do anything to reduce the stock market value of PetroChina, but you really can't be sure of that. The Chinese government created PetroChina in 1999 by transferring assets from China National Petroleum to PetroChina. The state then bolstered PetroChina's reserves in 2005 by transferring overseas oil and gas reserves from a wholly owned subsidiary of China National Petroleum to PetroChina. That should serve as a reminder that outside investors have no say over what happens to PetroChina's assets. China National Petroleum elects PetroChina's entire board of directors, so in effect the Chinese government decides who is going to run PetroChina, where the company will put its money, and what assets it will pursue.

And what the government gives, it can take away. In 2008 the Beijing government decided to increase competition in China's wireless industry, now dominated by China Mobile. The government will transfer wireless networks operated by China Unicom, an increasingly weak rival to China Mobile, to fixed-line phone operators China Telecom and China Netcom. Shares of China Mobile, which has about 70 percent of the wireless market in China, fell by 8 percent on the day in May 2008 when the plan was announced.

So the Beijing government could decide to sell, say, a quarter of its current shareholdings in PetroChina in pursuit of a policy designed to control a stock market bubble in China. It could decide that PetroChina should invest in some uneconomical oil projects as a matter of national energy security. The party members in charge of China National Petroleum and PetroChina could decide to spin off some of the company's assets into a new company in order to line their own pockets. Who knows?

We do know that the Chinese government intends to lower and then eliminate the wall keeping mainland investors out of the Hong Kong market. At the least, that would reduce the huge price difference between Shanghai and Hong Kong shares. At the Hong Kong share price PetroChina was worth about $412 billion and ExxonMobil was still, at the end of 2007, the most valuable stock in the world by market capitalization.

How the Trends Play Out for Investors

- Economies in the developing world are growing at 8 percent, 9 percent, even 11 percent a year. A good growth rate for a developed economy is 3 percent or 4 percent.

- Money will flow to the economies—and stock markets and stocks—that can deliver those higher growth rates.
- Remember that any stock market is still a market of stocks. In developing markets it's very hard to tell if revenue growth at any individual company is real or how much profit growth it translates into.

You have four themes to follow to invest in the stock markets of the developing world:

- You can invest directly in the companies that have turned the developing economies of the world into the global factory.
- You can invest in the companies, often in developed economies, that sell to the companies that make up the global factory.
- You can invest in the companies that will build out the infrastructure that these developing economies need to keep developing.
- You can invest in the companies that sell to the still small but rapidly growing middle class of these developing economies.

TREND BREAKERS AND TREND MAKERS RIPPED FROM THE HEADLINES

TREND BREAKERS

- *Signs of runaway inflation in China and India.* In February 2008 inflation was running at a very fast 7 percent in China, for example. But that's still below the 25 percent inflation rate in Vietnam in April 2008. The traditional way to fight inflation is by raising interest rates—and that can slow an economy. If inflation runs out of control in either China or India, central banks in those countries will be forced to raise interest rates. Any slowdown in those big economies would be enough to slow the global economy too.
- *Political turmoil that makes investors demand a higher return for putting their money at risk in these economies.* In India the current government and its opposition are having a hard time putting together

legislative majorities. In Brazil, the government has shied away from the political pain of reducing a bloated government bureaucracy. Russia has backed away from the rule of law both in its election and in its treatment of contracts with foreign investors. In China the Beijing government is having an increasingly hard time getting local officials to follow its policies.

• *Signs that the theory of decoupling—the belief on Wall Street that developing economies won't slow down much if the U.S. economy slumps—is just wishful thinking.* That theory got a spanking in 2008.

• *Watch out for central bank missteps in developing economies as these banks try to slow inflation or end real estate speculation.* The U.S. Federal Reserve finds it hard enough to manage the developed financial markets of the United States. Imagine the difficulty in managing financial markets in developing economies that don't have nearly the transparency, timely data, or stability of the U.S. economy. Developing country stock markets crash from time to time as central banks and governments impose utterly reasonable textbook solutions that turn out to have unpredictable results in the reality of developing financial markets. Crashes like these are painful and costly to investors and can be extremely frightening, but they come with the territory and they actually represent good buying opportunities. It's better to buy when everyone is running in fear than when everyone believes that already astronomically high prices are headed to the moon and beyond.

Trend Makers

• *Announcements by more developing countries of huge infrastructure investments.* China led the way. Russia has jumped on board. Brazil and India are lagging but thinking about it. More ports, roads, airports, and so on are good for the infrastructure stock picks at the end of this chapter, certainly, but they also mean that higher growth doesn't have to lead to runaway inflation in these developing economies.

• *A continued shift in developing economies, especially China's, from manufacturing for export to manufacturing for domestic consumption.*

Governmental policies in the developing world have been designed to stunt domestic demand so that savings rates would stay high, providing lots of money for investment, and so that export earnings would pile up, providing the kind of currency cushion that developing economies learned they needed after the Asian currency crisis of the late 1990s. As countries get richer, though, it becomes harder and harder to prevent the average guy and gal from spending. Look for numbers out of China and elsewhere that show consumption accounting for a bigger part of the economy.

• *A continuation of the extraordinary increase in the stability of developing world markets and economies—especially relative to the stability of U.S. markets.* For example, in 2008 Brazil earned an upgrade from Standard & Poor's to investment grade, a recognition that Brazil has implemented fiscal policies that have produced government budget surpluses and a stronger currency. Slower growth in the developed world and more risk in developed world financial markets is a formula for rising stock markets in Mumbai, Shanghai, Singapore, and Hong Kong. I'll have more on the "stability premium" awarded by investors to economies and markets that show reduced volatility in Chapter 12.

Stock Picks That Put the Wind from Those Trends at Your Back

Accor (OTC: ACRFF) is the world's fourth-largest hotel operator by rooms, with 4,000 hotel properties in ninety countries. Accor has targeted its high-end Sofitel brand for divestiture in 2010, but that sale doesn't mean the company is getting out of the hotel business. In fact, Accor is on track with plans to add 200,000 rooms worldwide from 2006 to 2010. Instead the Sofitel sale is part of the company's effort to redeploy assets and capital from high-end brands and Europe to budget hotel offerings in the United States and Asia. Accor, already the global leader in budget hotels, sees its biggest opportunities in that segment in Asia and the Middle East. In 2008 those regions accounted for 14 percent and 5 percent of company revenue, respectively. According to a sum-of-the-parts valuation by Deutsche Bank, this international hotel and travel-service company sold at a discount of about 30 percent in late 2007. The biggest reason for that discount, according to Deutsche Bank: investors undervalue the company's potential for growth in the developing world. The company's operating profit from its budget hotels outside the United States climbed 20 percent in 2007 and is projected to climb 12 percent in 2008.

Central European Distribution (NASDAQ: CEDC) is the largest producer of vodka in Poland and is the leading importer of spirits, wine, and beer in Poland and Hungary. When we think about the developing world, we tend to overlook countries such as Poland, but Poland's economy is growing at a rate that more closely resembles that of India than that of the more developed economies of Western Europe. In the scheme of things, Poland isn't China, but it's definitely a member of "the rest of the gang." I like Central European Distribution shares as a way to participate in the very strong growth of the Polish economy and the resulting improvement in consumer incomes in Poland. In addition, with Poland's entry into the European Union, Central European Distribution can use its solid base in the country to build exports to the rest of Eastern Europe. But the big prize is Russia. Central European acquired the Parliament brand, the third- or fourth-fastest-growing vodka in the subpremium vodka segment in 2007, as its initial entry into the Russia market. Parliament sales were up 19 percent in the first quarter of 2008 from the first quarter of 2007. Another acquisition, of importer Whitehall, in 2008 moves Central European even further into a Russian market that is just starting to shake out relatively inefficient state producers. Sales grew by 79 percent in 2007 and are forecast to increase by 75 percent in 2008 and 2009. Earnings per share climbed 37 percent in 2007 and are forecast to climb 37 percent in 2008 and 30 percent in 2009.

Coach (NYSE: COH). First Japan and now China. Coach has successfully learned how to translate "accessible luxury" from the U.S. market to Japan. Beginning in 2000 with just 2 percent of the Japanese market, by 2008 the company had grabbed a 12 percent market share going up against such heavyweights in the luxury business as Louis Vuitton, Prada, and Gucci. (Coach now has a bigger market share in Japan than the last two of that trio.) China is next. In 2008 Coach bought out its Hong Kong joint venture partner and opened a new flagship store in the city that is its biggest outside the United States. The company plans to open fifty more stores in China in the next five years to go with the thirty it already operates in the country. The target, says Coach CEO Lew Frankfort, is China's emerging middle class. Right now the handbag market in China is about $1.2 billion in sales. And, as in Japan in 2000, Coach has just a tiny sliver of that, about 3 percent.

General Electric (NYSE: GE) is the one-stop shop for industrial infrastructure. Need a locomotive, steam turbines, a power plant, a nuclear reactor, or just something mundane like a hundred jet engines? General Electric can sell it to you. Infrastructure—35 percent to 40 percent of revenue in 2008—is the fastest-growing part of GE's business. Current growth rates of 15 percent to 20 percent in the infrastructure business will be sustainable for ten to fifteen years as developing economies continue to build railroads, power plants, and airline service. The company's huge financial business has been a drag on the share price thanks to the company's big exposure to the meltdown in the financial markets set off by the subprime mortgage crisis. That makes it possible for investors to pick up one of the world's premier infrastructure stocks at a relatively bargain price. The other big emerging-economies story, health care, has just started to show up in the revenues of the company's medical equipment business.

Jacobs Engineering (NYSE: JEC). This California engineering services and construction company recycles U.S. dollars. The company's largest market is Europe, but its fastest-growing is the Middle East, where dollar-rich oil producers are spending to build up their energy infrastructure and to diversify by investing in refineries and chemical plants. With projects diversified across industries from transportation to petroleum to pharmaceutical to defense, Jacobs isn't vulnerable to a downturn in any one sector. The company's backlog grew by 50 percent in the second quarter of 2007 from the second quarter a year earlier.

Joy Global (NASDAQ: JOYG). Milwaukee's Joy Global is one of the three big suppliers of mining equipment to survive the twenty-five-year industry slump—which means that the company doesn't have a whole lot of competition now that mining is enjoying boom times again. (The company's predecessor, Harnischfeger, went bust in 1999 at the bottom of the cycle.) Original equipment makes up about 35 percent of sales; the other 65 percent is aftermarket products and services. (You shouldn't be amazed to discover that mining equipment shows lots of wear and tear.) About 70 percent of Joy Global's equipment goes into the coal mining industry, with copper and iron mining making up the company's number two and number three markets. Overseas markets make up about half of Joy Global's sales. Of the emerging markets where the company operates, China has shown the fastest growth in recent years, with much of the demand coming from the country's coal industry.

Luxottica (NYSE ADR: LUX). Today the story is North America. Tomorrow the story is China and the rest of Asia. For example, most of the company's 1,970 Sunglass Hut stores are in the traditional North American and European markets. But in May 2008, the company opened its first stores in Thailand and now has 220 Sunglass Hut stores in Australia, New Zealand, Hong Kong, Singapore, and Thailand. Globally, Milan-headquartered Luxottica manufactures and sells glasses and sunglasses under its own brands (such as Ray-Ban and Oakley) or licensed brands (such as Versace, Chanel, and Prada) through a network of 4,611 branded stores such as LensCrafters, Pearle Vision, and Sunglass Hut. In the last two years, the company has acquired Modern Sight (28 stores) in Shanghai, Ming Long (113 stores) in Guangdong, and Xueliang (79 stores in Beijing) to bring its total in China to 270 stores. In September 2006, the company opened a flagship LensCrafters store in Beijing, the first of a planned ninety stores in China.

Suntech Power Holdings (NYSE ADR: STP) is already the number three producer of silicon solar cells in the world. But Suntech Power is unusual for a Chinese company: management actually emphasizes profits and not just revenue growth. That's critical for any company in the solar industry right now because solar cell makers are in a race to drive down costs faster than selling prices fall in this highly competitive market. Investors can actually see the technology path that will produce higher yields and increased profits at this Chinese solar cell maker. It's called Pluto, and the proprietary technology is scheduled to move from pilot line to full production line by the end of 2008. According to company management, Pluto will add one full percentage point to the conversion efficiency of Suntech's solar cells, which now show conversion efficiency of 16.5 percent for monocrystalline silicon. Upping the efficiency with which the cells turn sunlight into electricity is key to driving down the cost of solar-generated electricity and driving up sales and profits at solar cell makers. Pluto couldn't be coming on line at a better time, since the average selling price for modules of solar cells is projected to drop by 13.4 percent in 2009 from 2008, according to Wall Street investment banker Cowen and Company. Despite that decline in selling price, Cowen is projecting that gross margins at Suntech will climb to 24 percent in 2009 from 22.8 percent in 2008.

Additional Stocks for Building an Overweight Position in this Sector

• **BHP Billiton** (NYSE ADR: BHP). This mining company produces just about every commodity that China needs, from metallurgical coal to copper to iron ore from nearby Australia.

• **Burlington Northern Santa Fe** (NYSE: BNI). Let's not forget about the need to get stuff to and from the global factory in the world's biggest economy, the United States. Among its competitors, Burlington Northern Santa Fe gets the highest percentage of its business from coal, agricultural products, and intermodal, the three freight groups where I expect to see the biggest long-term growth.

- **Caterpillar** (NYSE: CAT) is the world's largest producer of earthmoving equipment. Think the Peoria company could be a global infrastructure player? (Oh, and Caterpillar also makes electric power generators and engines used in the oil industry.)
- **Cemex** (NYSE ADR: CX) has used free cash flow from its protected and highly profitable home market in Mexico to build itself into the third-largest player in the global cement industry.
- **Fortescue Metals Group** (OTC: FSUMF) is the new kid on the Australian iron ore scene. The company shipped its first load of iron ore in May 2008 to—where else?—China.
- **Infosys** (NASDAQ: INFY) is one of the four horsemen of Indian information technology outsourcing. To thrive in this industry, Infosys has had to win over global clients that now include 113 members of the Fortune 500. And since these companies can do business with anyone in the world, the fact that they're doing business with Infosys should give an investor confidence in the company's management. Projected earnings per share growth is 22.6 percent on average over the next five years.
- **Komatsu** (OTC ADR: KMTUY) is Japan's answer to Caterpillar and a big player in the Asia market for construction equipment.
- **LAN Airlines** (NYSE ADR: LFL). Based in Chile, LAN Airlines flies passengers in that country, Argentina, Peru, and Ecuador. Freight operations, which include a trucking hub in Miami, account for more than 30 percent of revenue.
- **Macquarie Infrastructure** (NYSE: MIC) is a portfolio of infrastructure investments run by the Australian investment bank that is the world's largest private manager of infrastructure.
- **Nokia** (NYSE ADR: NOK). The big growth in wireless phone sales is in the markets of the developing world. But these markets demand a cheap, entry-level phone, and most wireless phone companies can't make an entry-level phone cheaply enough to keep profit margins as high as they are in their slower-growing developed markets. Nokia can.
- **Vale** (NYSE ADR: RIO). This Brazilian company is the largest producer of iron ore in the world and owns about 23 percent of the Chinese market for iron ore.

MUTUAL FUNDS AND ETFs (EXCHANGE-TRADED FUNDS)

- **iShares MSCI Brazil Index** (NYSE: EWZ). Brazil is a commodities powerhouse. Thanks to its decades-long dedication to developing sugar-cane-based transportation fuels, the country leads the world in biofuels. In recent years it has become a major grain producer, adding that stream of exports to its huge position in soybeans. Mining company Vale is the world's leading producer of iron ore and a major producer of nickel and other base metals. Petrobras, the state oil company, has recently found reserves with more than 30 billion barrels of oil off the country's coast. That's not so much good luck as a reflection of the company's world-class skills in deep-water exploration and production. You can get exposure to all this with one trade through iShares MSCI Brazil (EWZ). The ETF's biggest holdings include Petrobras and Vale.

- **iShares MSCI Singapore Index** (NYSE: EWS). Owning a piece of Singapore's economy through this ETF gives you a stake in China and other developing economies in Asia. For example, the fund owns a piece of Singapore Telecommunications, which owns 21 percent of Thailand's Advanced Info Service, with 17 million wireless subscribers and a 52 percent market share; 31 percent of India's Bharti Group, with 42 million wireless subscribers and a 29 percent market share; and 35 percent of Indonesia's Telkomsel, with 29 million wireless subscribers and a 55 percent market share, among other Asian assets. Collectively, what Singapore Telecom calls its "associates" saw pretax profit grow by 16 percent year to year. The fund also owns a stake in Singapore Airlines, whose wholly owned subsidiary SilkAir is a regional airline targeting secondary cities in the fast-growing markets of China, India, Thailand, Indonesia, Vietnam, Malaysia, the Philippines, and Cambodia. About 60 percent of the fund is invested in financial services, including such Singapore banks as DBS Group and United Overseas Bank. These banks have long run international networks that tie together Singapore and Hong Kong. In recent years, those networks have gone regional. United Overseas now has subsidiaries in Malaysia, Thailand, Indonesia, and the Philippines. And it looks like they're expanding aggressively into the commercial real estate markets of Singapore's fast-growing neighbors, especially India. Singapore Telecom and Singapore Airlines are, respectively, the ETF's second- and seventh-largest holdings.

4

GLOBAL BLUE CHIPS

Great Companies from Developing Economies

A NEW GENERATION OF GLOBAL BLUE CHIPS IS EMERGING FROM the developing economies of the world. This new generation of global blue chips is growing faster than traditional U.S. blue chips such as Coca-Cola and IBM, and these new global companies are safer than you may think. Over the next decade you'll crush the returns of investing in either U.S.-based blue chips or established global blue chips by investing in this new generation of emerging global companies. The financial crisis that nearly overwhelmed the developed economies of the United States and Europe in 2008 just makes this outperformance more likely. The debacle that began in the U.S. mortgage sector has left many developing-market blue chips able to raise money at a lower cost than their developed-world competitors, and with less highly distracting restructuring to do to repair the damage caused by that crisis.

To find these stocks, you'll need to put a couple of dangerously shortsighted perceptions about emerging economies and their stock markets behind you. These days we all recognize the investment potential of an India, China, or Brazil, or of smaller but fast-growing markets in Vietnam, the Philippines, or Poland, and we all want a piece of the action. I gave you my best ideas for doing that in the last chapter.

But we still tend to think of the home-grown companies in these emerging economies as, well, emerging, primitive, or underdeveloped. These companies are good enough to play and win in their domestic economies, the unexamined common opinion holds, but they don't measure up to the global giants headquartered in the United States, the United Kingdom, Germany, or Japan. We're willing to buy the stocks of these companies because they're a great way to get a piece of a fast-growing domestic market, but we don't think of them as competitors in the global economy. Maybe someday, we think, they may make the big leagues after they've grown up and learned how to compete from the Procter & Gambles and Toyotas and Nokias.

Well, consign that idea to the dustbin of history, where it can keep company with such quaint notions as "Japan will never be anything but a maker of cheap tin toys" and "Who would ever buy a flat screen TV or a cell phone from Korea?"

There's a new generation of emerging economy companies that have cut their teeth in their domestic markets, sharpened their skills by moving out to neighboring regional markets, and are now setting their sights on even more distant horizons. These are companies that dominate a local or regional market as thoroughly as PepsiCo and Coca-Cola dominate the U.S. market. They've got as much savvy about how to sell in the new global world as Nokia or Toyota—and perhaps more because they live closer to the new customers of the world's emerging economies. Plus these companies have the kind of competitive advantage that provides safety for investors from the ups and downs of the global economy and from shifts in individual sectors.

Want an example? Well, take a look at the global telephone industry. In 1998 a list of the top five global telephone companies, valued by stock market capitalization, read like this:

1. NTT (Japan), $132 billion
2. AT&T (United States), $93 billion
3. BT (United Kingdom), $79 billion
4. Deutsche Telekom (Germany), $75 billion
5. SBC (United States), $74 billion

All were companies from the developed economies of the world, as were the rest of the top ten: Bell Atlantic, GTE, BellSouth and World-Com (United States) and France Telecom (France).

All those are (or were, in the case of WorldCom, BellSouth, Bell Atlantic, and GTE—all companies that for one reason or another are no longer with us) familiar blue chip stocks. AT&T, for example, has long been known as the quintessential "widows and orphans" stock: safe, reliable, and paying out a decent dividend.

Fast-forward ten years to February 2008. The list is a bit different.

1. China Mobile (China), $300 billion
2. AT&T (United States), $224 billion
3. Vodafone (United Kingdom), $175 billion
4. Telefonica (Spain), $134 billion
5. Verizon (United States), $107 billion

The number one telephone company in the world is a mobile phone company? From China? The rest of the top ten has its own surprises. Yes, it is still dominated by developed-world stocks: France Telecom, Deutsche Telekom, and NTT and NTT DoCoMo from Japan take four of the next five slots. But coming in at number ten in the world? America Movil, a wireless phone company that dominates the Mexican market with 130 million wireless phone subscribers in Latin America and the Caribbean. Its Mexican subsidiary, Telcel, has 80 percent of the Mexican market.

You would have done well by investing in the developed-market blue chip phone companies on this list. From 2003 to 2007 you would have seen a 14.5 percent annual return if you'd put your money in blue chip Deutsche Telekom and just a tad less if you'd put your money in AT&T (well, actually if you'd put your money in SBC, which acquired AT&T in 2005, BellSouth in 2006, and then changed its name to AT&T). AT&T has returned 13.4 percent on average for each of those five years.

But you would have done spectacularly better if you'd put your money into America Movil or China Mobile. The average annual returns for these two stocks from 2003 to 2007 were 68.7 percent and 50.3 percent, respectively.

If you'd invested $10,000 on the last trading day of 2002, by the last trading day of 2007, you'd have had $125,603 if you'd put your money into America Movil and $18,313 if you'd put your money in AT&T.

Now, you may be comfortable looking at that $107,000 discrepancy over five years and saying, "Well, that's the price you pay for investing in safe developed-market blue chips instead of in risky emerging-market companies." But I'm not. I think there is a new generation of emerging-market blue chips that offer better safety than the average stock in their market and industry. And they offer much, much, much higher returns than developed-economy blue chips. Companies such as these deserve as much of a place in your portfolio as do the developed-market blue chips I cover in Chapter 12.

U.S. investors have long bought familiar U.S.-based blue chips such as PepsiCo and Johnson & Johnson because their history of delivering steady 8 percent to 12 percent earnings growth year in and year out gives them a good chance of beating the stock market indexes with very low risk. For example, PepsiCo shares have returned an average annual rate of 9.3 percent over the last ten years (1998–2007), with Johnson & Johnson at 9.7 percent. Both are well above the 4.2 percent average annual return on the Standard & Poor's 500 Stock Index over that period.

Great market-beating returns. But not as great as they could be for two reasons. The first is that U.S. blue chip stocks are relatively expensive and relatively slow-growing, at least in comparison to emerging global blue chips. And second, in the fastest-growing parts of the world economy, it's developed-market blue chips that are playing on unfamiliar turf.

1. U.S. blue chip stocks are relatively expensive and relatively slow-growing in comparison to emerging global blue chips. Because these U.S.-based blue chips are so familiar, they aren't especially cheap. They're so well known that they're a fixture of individual investors here in the United States and of institutional portfolios at in-surance companies, pension funds, and banks around the world.

And because U.S.-based blue chips don't call the fastest-growing parts of the global economy home, their growth inevitably lags. While these global companies are *exposed* to the fastest-growing parts of the world economy, they still get much of their sales from the more slowly growing, if bigger, economies of the United States, Europe, and Japan. With that geographic distribution of sales, these companies can't take full advantage of the phenomenal growth rates of China, India, and the rest of the developing world.

For example, U.S. investors looking for international growth from a U.S.-based blue chip are often steered to a stock such as PepsiCo be-cause the company gets such a large percentage—60 percent—of its sales from outside the United States. But the company's exposure to the fastest-growing economies of the developing world isn't nearly as large as that number suggests. Much of those non-U.S. sales come from relatively slow-growing developed world economies such as Canada, the United Kingdom, and the countries of continental Eu-rope. Break down the company's sales into developed economies ver-sus developing economies and the percentages show why the global growth game is stacked against even an internationally oriented U.S. company such as PepsiCo: only about 24 percent of the company's sales come from the developing economies of Latin America, the Mid-dle East, Africa, and Asia. The rest come from the developed economies of the world.

I'm not saying that U.S. blue chips such as PepsiCo and Cisco Sys-tems don't deserve a place in your portfolio. These developed-market blue chips—along with other bastions of predictability—still do de-serve a role in your portfolio, as you'll see in Chapter 12.

I am saying, however, that if you're looking for solid revenue and earnings growth from a low-risk blue chip, you can find more growth at a lower price in the stocks of the blue chip companies now emerging from developed economies.

Contrast two U.S. blue chips with two emerging global blue chips. In May 2008, investors were paying a price-to-earnings ratio of 21.4

for PepsiCo's projected five-year annual earnings growth rate of 10.8 percent and a price-to-earnings ratio of 17.3 for Johnson & Johnson's projected 9.8 percent annual earnings growth rate. Using what's called the PEG ratio (PE ratio to growth rate) to measure how much an investor is paying for earnings growth, the two U.S. blue chips come out at 1.8 and 1.9, respectively. That's expensive. (Investors who look for growth at a reasonable price target a PEG ratio of 1 or so.) And only the predictability of these companies justifies that ratio.

Now look at what you'd pay for growth in the case of two of the emerging global blue chips I name at the end of this chapter, Indian software leader Infosys and Latin American airline Lan Airlines. Infosys sold at a price-to-earnings ratio of 22.6 in May 2008 and showed a projected five-year average annual growth rate of 24.3 percent. Lan Airlines sold at a PE ratio of 13.2 and showed a projected five-year average annual growth rate of 23.5 percent. That gives the stocks PEG ratios of 0.93 and 0.56, respectively. Now that's cheap growth—at least, it is if the projected earnings growth rates turn out to be reasonably accurate. You're paying such a low price for earnings growth because the growth isn't considered very predictable, and unpredictability is exactly what you don't want in a blue chip, domestic or global.

Which brings me to my second reason for thinking that the returns from developed-economy blue chips won't be as great as the returns from these emerging global blue chips. This second reason bears directly on the question of how reliable earnings will be from these emerging global blue chips.

2. **In the fastest-growing parts of the world economy, it's developed-market blue chips that are playing on unfamiliar turf.** As great as developed-economy blue chips such as PepsiCo, Johnson & Johnson, and Cisco Systems are at keeping their fingers on the pulse of the market, they are inevitably less familiar with the fastest-moving trends in developing economies than are the companies that call those markets home. To develop and market successful new products, developed-country companies have got to learn to think in cultures

that are profoundly different from their own. It's not just chance that Korean mobile phones and Korean software for mobile phones are way cooler in Korea than competing products from Motorola and Nokia, for example. Korean companies such as Samsung and LG live in that market. Their employees and their families use phones in the startlingly innovative ways other Koreans do. And that's a huge advantage when you're talking about a country, Korea, that's at the cutting edge of a wireless phone society.

To take another example, Microsoft, a huge supplier of software to mobile phone companies, employs ethnographers to prowl the shops and homes of China. One of their big discoveries: in an emerging economy with occasionally uncertain power supplies, a wireless phone with a flashlight has a big marketing edge over phones equipped with even the greatest software. If you live in that economy every day, that's knowledge that comes with the turf.

That local knowledge in turn leads to a better understanding of the zigs and zags of the local economy and a more predictable stream of earnings. So for example, Chinese athletic shoemaker Li-Ning signed on to sponsor the U.S. Ping-Pong team for a fraction of the $100 million that competitor Adidas spent to become an Olympic sponsor. Why the U.S. Ping-Pong team? Because while the U.S. team had almost no chance of winning a medal in Beijing, Li-Ning understands that China is Ping-Pong-mad and the audience that tunes in to see the Chinese team trounce the world will see foreigners wearing Li-Ning gear. And as anyone who has counted the Chanel, Prada, and Louis Vuitton logos on the main shopping streets of Shanghai knows, foreign brands have huge cachet among Chinese middle-class consumers. In addition, by sponsoring a whole team, not only did Li-Ning get a bargain, but it avoided the problem that confronted Nike. That company's key endorsing athlete in Beijing, hurdler Liu Xiang, pulled out of three big races in the months running up to the Olympics. That raised the possibility in the months before the games that Liu Xiang, named most popular athlete in China in 2007, wouldn't run up to expectations. (He did actually pull out, with an injury.)

From an investor's point of view Li-Ning's local knowledge enabled the company to cut marketing costs, gain more exposure for its product than a Western company might imagine, and reduce the possibility that some "accident" could seriously diminish the return on those marketing bucks. All that adds predictability to a company's earnings stream.

As investors, we are increasingly accustomed to thinking about putting money into China, India, and the rest of the developing world to take advantage of the extraordinarily fast growth of these economies. We're on the lookout for developed-market companies such as Italy's Luxottica that will let us tap into the growth of the Chinese middle class, for example. You'll find that perspective well represented in the stock picks in Chapter 3.

But we're not used to thinking of these developing markets as the source of a new generation of global blue chips. That stands the logic of Chapter 3 on its head. We're certainly interested in these companies because of the growth in their home markets, but the ultimate long-term value of these stocks is that they have shown signs of transcending their home markets. They're using the growth of their home economies and their dominance of part of that economy as a springboard to become a player in the global economy, competing successfully along with the General Electrics, the Unilevers, the PepsiCos, and the IBMs of the developed economies.

For example, in 1984 China's Haier Group was a state-owned enterprise—then known as the Qingdao General Refrigerator Factory—that made shoddy refrigerators for local customers. The company was on the edge of bankruptcy, kept afloat only by loans from Chinese banks more concerned about the loss of local jobs than about ever getting their money back. Production was a tiny eighty refrigerators a month, and many of those came back to the factory from disgruntled customers.

The turnabout came in 1985 when a customer returned one of those defective refrigerators to the factory. Zhang Ruimin, an assistant city manager who had been hired the previous year to save the factory, searched through the company's inventory of four hundred refrigerators looking for a replacement for the customer. Nearly 20 percent of the machines headed out the door for sale, he discovered, were defective. So the new boss had the seventy-six faulty refrigerators lined up on the factory floor and then passed out sledgehammers to workers and ordered them to destroy them. The demonstration was effective: imagine the impact in your place of work if your boss told you to destroy one of your company's products that cost the equivalent of two years of your pay. One of the hammers now hangs in the company's headquarters.

That began an amazing turnaround at the company. Today Haier dominates the Chinese market for washing machines with a 23 percent market share in 2007; it is also a leader in other white goods, the category of consumer durables that includes washing machines, refrigerators, microwave ovens, and air conditioners. The company operates twenty-two factories in its hometown of Qingdao.

Haier, however, isn't just a domestic company. It is now the third-largest (well, I've seen it ranked second, third, and fourth, to tell the truth) seller of white goods in the world, with annual revenue of more than $16 billion. Haier opened its first overseas factories in Indonesia in 1996 and then expanded production into the Philippines and Malaysia in 1997. The company opened its first factory in the United States in Camden, South Carolina, in 2000.

By now Haier has a well-honed approach to entering a new market. It will start with niche products—in the United States the entry points were compact refrigerators (suitable for college dorm rooms) and electric wine cellars—in order to establish a brand presence.

That's followed by the purchase or construction of a local factory—the company bought a factory in Italy as part of its drive to enter the European market—and partnerships with local brand owners and retailers to build volume and distribution. Then Haier uses its combination of good quality at low cost to expand that initial penetration.

That's exactly the strategy that Haier is using, for example, in its attempts to crack the very, very tough Korean market for white goods. The company began its challenge to consumer giants Samsung and LG on their home turf with small domestic appliances—it is now the number one seller of electric wine cellars in Korea—sold through online retailers in 2003 and is now moving up in size and distribution. Haier opened its first store in Seoul's mall-heavy Yongsan area in 2007.

In the process of moving from failing local company to global giant Haier has developed its own corporate culture under Zhang, who is now the company's chairman and CEO. Haier's "OEC model"—the term is an abbreviation of the slogans "Overall," "Everything, everyone, everyday" and "Control"—has echoes of General Electric's Six Sigma performance system with a dollop of Mao's collective philosophy, with everyone from design to marketing responsible for a product's success or failure.

The global economy is dotted with companies rooted in emerging economies that are a lot like Haier. In Mexico, cement maker Cemex has shown that the conventional wisdom that held that the high transportation costs of cement would keep it a locally produced commodity was wrong. By the time Cemex acquired European cement maker RMC in 2005, 80 percent of Cemex's revenue was already coming from outside Mexico. In the process of building an $18 billion business by acquiring local companies, Cemex has developed what it calls the "Cemex way," which quickly integrates new acquisitions into a standardized system of production, marketing, and distribution built around centralized information technology systems.

The examples of Haier's OEC model and the Cemex way show exactly how wrong it is to pigeonhole and then dismiss these companies as simply successful exploiters of low-costs in their home market. The brutal truth of these economies—as hundreds of local and multinational companies have learned to their sorrow—is that anyone can become the low-cost leader of the moment, but since the supply of low-cost labor is so large and the barriers to entry so low, it's tough in China or India or Brazil to build more than a few years of success just on low costs. Companies with the decade- or two-decade-long track record of a Haier or Cemex (the latter has been the largest producer of cement in Mexico since 1976) have been built on more than just low costs. Success comes from low costs plus some other competitive advantage.

So for a company such as Brazil's Embraer, now the world's leading maker of regional jets and the third-largest manufacturer of aircraft in the world, the key combination has been low costs and cutting-edge research and development. At China's Johnson Electric, which owns half the world's market for tiny electric motors used to power external rearview mirrors in cars, for instance, the combination is low-cost manufacturing and a production system that caters to customers' desire to buy motors designed specifically for their products. At India's Infosys and Wipro, the combination is low-costs and a highly skilled workforce of computer science engineers.

This isn't to say that these developing-economy emerging blue chips come without their own set of risks peculiar to the group. And investors accustomed to investing in companies from developed economies are especially unlikely to know exactly what questions to ask about who owns the company, what rights a shareholder actually has, the conflicts of interest between majority family or government owners and private shareholders, and the interplay between national governments and the companies those governments regard as "national champions."

Take Haier Group, for example. The company's stock does trade on the Hong Kong stock exchange, but you shouldn't assume that means that buying a stake in Haier is like buying a piece of General Electric. The company is officially owned by its employees, but since they receive no dividends, have no ability to sell their stake, and in fact don't even know how much they own, effective ownership and control remain with the Chinese government. As a state-owned enterprise, Haier has had to jump through hoops to raise capital on China's stock markets. A subsidiary, Qingdao Haier Refrigerator Company, has been listed on the Shanghai Stock Exchange since 1993. The mother company got a public listing on the Hong Kong Stock Exchange when it acquired a controlling position in a publicly listed joint venture. It's not at all clear to me what an investor who owns shares of Haier through any of these vehicles actually owns. But "ownership" in this situation is certainly not equivalent to what "ownership" usually means in developed-economy stock markets.

Outside China, many of these emerging blue chips are tightly con-trolled by a single family even if they are public companies. That can often be a competitive advantage for a company since the tight control by a limited circle of family members can enable it to make and exe-cute strategic decisions more quickly than one that needs to win agree-ment from a board of directors representing disparate interests and backgrounds. So the Mittal family, for example, has been able to move with speed that has left rivals gasping for breath in its successful drive to build ArcelorMittal into the largest steel producer in the world.

But this tight family control also means that minority public share-holders are simply along for the ride when a company violently changes direction. For example, until 2007 one of my favorite emerg-ing blue chips was San Miguel, despite a history as a pot of gold fought over by the great families of the Philippines such as the Soriano, Zobel, and Cojuangco clans. In the last decade San Miguel had used its domination of its Philippine home market (90 percent of the na-tional beer market, 85 percent of the soft drink market, 70 percent of the processed meat market, etc.) as a base for expanding into a con-glomerate with businesses outside of beer and soft drinks with big stakes in China and Australia. By the end of 2006 San Miguel had started or acquired eighteen businesses and increased revenues by 266 percent. Recent buys had included National Foods, Australia's largest dairy manufacturer, Berri Limited, an Australian juice brand, and Del Monte Pacific.

But in 2007, San Miguel abruptly changed direction. The com-pany announced that it would sell about 10 percent of its domestic crown jewel, San Miguel Brewery, in a public offering in 2008. I think that's a reasonable way to turn the company's domination of its do-mestic market into capital that can be invested in other businesses. But at the same time the company announced that it would sell off its stake in the recently purchased National Foods for an estimated price that would give San Miguel a 5 percent return on its 2005 investment with, again, the intention of investing in other businesses.

And what other businesses? Power generation, property develop-ment, and mining, the company said. One target was the 40 percent stake of PNOC Energy Development that the government sold off in November 2007. PNOC Energy is the world's second-largest producer of geothermal power. Another target was the National Transmission Corp., holder of a government concession to operate the country's electric power grid. San Miguel lost out in the bidding for these assets, although the company says it will pursue other opportunities in the energy sector.

Success or failure in the bids aside, the sudden change in direction is enough to make any investor's head spin. A stake in San Miguel has turned from ownership in what seemed to be a rising regional food and beverage power into ownership in a food, mining, and power generation conglomerate. I'm convinced that in the food and beverage business San Miguel had the scale and the experience to build a blue chip company. In power and mining? In its region the company is going up against some of the biggest companies in the mining world without much more of an edge than strong support from the Philippine government encouraging a national champion to go for it.

Contrast that with Embraer, the Brazilian company that divides the world market for regional jets with Canada's Bombardier. Embraer started life as a state-owned champion designed to get Brazil into the high-prestige—and strategically important—aviation industry. The company was privatized in 1995 and the government still owns a big stake designed to prevent any foreign company from acquiring Embraer. But the company has gradually worked its way into alignment with international standards of corporate governance. So, for example, the company has recently converted preferred shares into common shares and redistributed voting rights so that shares carry equal voting weights. The retirement of longtime CEO Mauricio Botelho also signals the company's maturity. New CEO Frederico Curado, formerly in charge of the commercial aviation group, earned his promotion for his success in building up Embraer's share of the commercial market to just below 50 percent. He knows the company's engineering, manufacturing, procurement, contract, and sales structure because he's worked with all those functions during his career at Embraer. The company's strategy is extremely transparent. Its newest planes—the 100-seat Embraer 190, on the market since 2006, and its 120-seat Embraer 195, which hit the market in 2007, stretch the range of regional jets to 2,500 miles without refueling and provide more cabin room than traditionally cramped regional jets. Both the extended range and the roomier cabins are aimed at helping the company grab more of the booming global market for intracountry air travel in the developing world.

Doing the research to discriminate between a San Miguel and an Embraer will be a lot of work. Investors won't exactly find themselves tripping over information on these emerging global blue chips. For example, on February 25, 2008, I did a search on the Thomson Reuters Research on Demand database of global investment research for Embraer (Embraer-Empresa Brasileira de Aeronautica S.A., to use the company's full name), which went back to September 2007, about six months. Even through Embraer is the world's third-largest manufacturer of planes and is traded as an ADR (an American depositary receipt), which allows investors to buy shares on the New York Stock Exchange, I found research reports from only one U.S. investment company, Standard & Poor's, and from only one global investment company with a big U.S. footprint, Deutsche Bank. According to Zacks Investment Research, only eight analysts in their database put out earnings estimates for Embraer, compared to eighteen for Boeing. Embraer is a big deal in its home market—there's lots of good coverage in the Reuters database from companies such as Banco Fator Corretora—but it's still under the radar for analysts and stockbrokers sitting in New York.

And that's for an established industry leader with a New York Stock Exchange ADR. If you want to really see what virgin territory this can be, take a look at the Reuters offerings for BYD, the biggest battery maker in China (and a company planning to produce its own hybrid car). Going back almost a year on February 25, 2008, I didn't find research from a single U.S. investment company, although there was decent coverage from Japan (Nomura and Daiwa), Hong Kong (Auerbach Grayson), and Deutsche Bank again.

But an investor willing to dig *can* find information on these emerging blue chip companies thanks to the wonders of the Internet. Searching on "Haier" and "refrigerators" or "washing machines" in February 2008, I came up with stories on the company's entry into the Korean market for home appliances (the *Korea Herald*), on the company's background and plans for India (the *Hindu Business Line*), rising washing machine and air conditioner sales in China (Xinhua News Agency), brand building in China *(China Daily)*, and the rise of emerging-market multinationals (the *Economist*). The Wikipedia entries on the companies I researched for this chapter were uneven, but in the best—such as the one on Haier—you could find great information on who actually owns the company's shares. And then, of course, there was the company's own Web site, Haier.com, that gives you an archive of company press releases, product lineups and descriptions, and company background. That's more than enough to make an informed decision on buying or selling the stock.

And since the Wall Street big boys don't follow the stocks of emerging global blue chips very carefully, this research will pay off for your portfolio. In this group of stocks you really do have a chance to discover real gems before the rest of the stock market does. So do the work and then sit back and watch your shares rise in price as other investors discover what you already know.

How the Trends Play Out for Investors

- Get over the notion that only developed economies and developed stock markets produce blue chip stocks.
- Efficient, battle-tested competitors are emerging from the world's developing economies to take on first regional and then global markets.
- Buying earnings growth by buying the shares of these emerging global blue chips is cheaper than buying earnings growth at established developed-world blue chips.

- Emerging blue chips have a real edge over their developed-economy kin because these companies have better intelligence about what's happening on the ground in emerging economies.
- The best emerging blue chips have developed their own cultures and technology base. Factors such as that, and not the transitory advantage of lower wages, are the foundation for success at these companies.
- Figuring out who actually owns an emerging blue chip and what rights a shareholder actually has can be the most daunting task facing an investor in emerging blue chips.
- Because Wall Street doesn't follow these stocks very deeply, you'll have to do your own digging to get the information you need, but you can find what you need on the Internet.
- Since Wall Street isn't researching these companies to death, a hardworking individual investor can get ahead of the herd and earn the profits that come to smart pioneers.

TREND BREAKERS AND TREND MAKERS RIPPED FROM THE HEADLINES

TREND BREAKERS

- *Beware of meddling by politicians.* China Mobile, for example, is now facing a restructuring of the Chinese telecommunications industry by officials in Beijing that would create two new strong competitors for the wireless industry leader.
- *Macroeconomic trends such as runaway inflation,* a big rise in home-country currency versus the euro, yen, and dollar, or a surge in interest rates in a company's home economy that make its products less competitive.
- *A big upswing in protectionism.* These emerging blue chips need an open global economy in order to prosper as much as established blue chips such as IBM and PepsiCo do—perhaps more so, since

they're at a much earlier stage of their growth and more easily stunted if they're shut out from a big national market such as the United States or Japan.

• *A rise in the volatility of emerging-country financial markets.* In 2008 we're in the midst of a period when many developing markets and economies actually seem less volatile than developed markets in the United States and Europe. (Who's in the middle of a housing bust and a credit crunch, the United States or Brazil?) But this isn't an irreversible trend, and a return of emerging market volatility would raise the cost of capital for emerging global blue chips.

Trend Makers

• Headlines showing that *inflation, government deficits, and currencies continue to be in better shape in developing economies than in the developed economies.*

• *A stable or increasing gap in economic growth between developing economies* such as China and India and developed economies such as the United States and the European Union.

• *Improvements in financial transparency* as shares of emerging blue chips move from trading solely on local stock exchanges to additional listings in New York, London, and Frankfurt.

• *New emerging blue chips take their first steps onto the global financial stage.* Some of my favorite companies in this category—such as Indian wind turbine maker Suzlon and Indian wireless phone leader Bharti Airtel—still trade only on restricted local markets that are, for all intents and purposes, closed to overseas investors. If you can find a way to buy in now—in India you have to open an account with an Indian brokerage company—great, but keep an eye on companies such as these for future wider listing.

• *Announcements of new acquisitions* by these emerging blue chips in their home and regional markets that then actually go through rather than being blocked on political grounds. Most of these companies do business in extremely fragmented industries where the opportunity for the best run, best capitalized company to gain market share is huge—as long as politicians don't decide to protect all the smaller players.

STOCK PICKS THAT PUT THE WIND FROM THOSE TRENDS AT YOUR BACK

Cemex (NYSE ADR: CX) has used free cash flow from its protected and highly profitable Mexican home market to build itself into the third-largest player in the global cement industry. In 2005 Cemex bought London-headquartered RMC Group to continue its attack on the European cement market. In 2007 the acquisition of the Rinker Group gave the company a bigger footprint in Australia and a substantial premixed concrete business in Tianjin and Qingdao, China. Cemex still sells for only roughly half the price-earnings ratio of U.S. cement and aggregate competitors. I expect that discount to close over time as the investors gradually catch up with the company's global stature.

Embraer Empresa Brasileira de Aero (NYSE ADR: ERJ) is one of the world's two dominant producers of regional jets and a growing presence in the business jet market. Embraer is a major beneficiary of the boom in in-country travel in developing economies. In these countries, it's often cheaper to link cities by air than to connect them with roads or rail lines. Aircraft deliveries climbed to 169 in 2007 from 130 in 2006, and the company's target is 195–205 aircraft in 2008. The company's new longer-range and roomier regional jets, the Embraer 190 (on sale in 2006) and the Embraer 195 (on sale in 2007), are the key to the company's plans to grab more of the growing market for regional jets from the world's developing economies.

Infosys (NASDAQ: INFY). One of the four horsemen of Indian information technology outsourcing (along with Wipro, Tata Consultancy, and Cognizant Technology Solutions), Infosys combines fast growth with proven management. Infosys has proven that it can manage its way through challenges. The stronger Indian rupee and rising competition for the best Indian talent in information technology have pushed up costs, but Infosys has been able to raise prices, increase efficiency in India, and move work to markets with lower salaries in Eastern Europe and Latin America. In the fiscal 2008 year that ended in March 2008, the company was able to hold operating margins at 27.6 percent in spite of an 11 percent appreciation in the rupee against the U.S. dollar. Of course, the reason to own Infosys remains growth. Projected growth in earnings per share is 15 percent for fiscal 2009 (which ends in March 2009), 12 percent for fiscal 2010, and 22.6 percent on average over the next five years.

LAN Airlines (NYSE ADR: LFL). Based in Chile, LAN Airlines flies passengers in that country, Argentina, Peru, and Ecuador. Freight operations, which include a trucking hub in Miami, account for more than 30 percent of revenue. Earnings-per-share growth for 2007 was 22 percent, but under the impact of higher fuel costs and other expenses, earnings are projected to decline in 2008 before rebounding to 23 percent growth in 2009. Revenue, however, is projected to grow at a blistering pace even through the earnings drought. According to Deutsche Bank, revenue will grow by 18 percent in 2008, up from 13 percent growth in 2007. Investors used to money-losing U.S. airlines take note: this isn't your average airline. The Chilean airline's return on equity, a measure of profitability, was almost 50 percent in 2006, compared with the airline group average of 40 percent, and only dropped to 37.5 percent under the impact of higher oil prices in 2007. Chile's financial and fiscal policies have made the country one of the least risky among emerging markets.

Petroleo Brasileiro S.A. (NYSE ADR: PBR), aka Petrobras, isn't just discovering a lot of oil and natural gas. It's discovering them in tough geologies and then drilling for them in extremely challenging environments. That combination shows the company's emergence as an oil company with cutting-edge technology, and that makes the Brazilian oil giant a very attractive partner for national oil companies that don't want any piece of the Western oil majors as partners. Two

2007 discoveries, the Jupiter and Tupi oil and gas fields, exemplify the company's new stature. Either of these fields alone would be the biggest find since the 2000 discovery of the giant Kashagan oil field in Kazakhstan. But getting to that oil will be a huge challenge. The oil lies under 4.5 miles of ocean water and then under as much as another 17,000 feet of sand, rock, and salt. That salt is an especially tricky problem since it takes 3-D imaging developed only in the last ten years to even see oil underneath salt layers. Developing Tupi and Jupiter won't be cheap. Tupi alone could cost between $50 billion and $100 billion to develop. At the end of that process, though, Brazil's proven reserves could equal those of oil powers Nigeria or Venezuela. And Petrobras could have earned itself a place among the few global oil companies with the technology and the cash to tackle the excruciating complexities of a world in which all the easy oil has already been pumped.

Stocks for Building an Overweight Position in This Sector

- **Bharti Airtel** (trading only on the Mumbai exchange at this time) has 24 percent of the Indian wireless market, one of the fastest-growing in the world
- **BYD** (Hong Kong: 1211.HK) is the third-largest rechargeable battery maker in the world. The Chinese company combines low-cost labor with state-of-the-art battery technology.
- **Haier** (OTC: HRELF), which is number three (or so) in the global white goods market, has been eating up market share in the United States, India, and Korea.
- **Johnson Electric** (OTC: JELCF) owns 50 percent of the market for tiny electric motors used in everything from cars to home appliances to power tools. It's hard to imagine a more diversified global footprint.
- **Suzlon** (trading only on the Mumbai exchange at this time) has with the acquisitions of Hansen Transmissions and REpower moved from the biggest supplier of wind turbines in India to the fifth-largest and most integrated wind turbine manufacturer in the world.

Mutual Funds and ETFs (Exchange-Traded Funds)

It's difficult to get exposure to emerging blue chips through a sector or a country fund. A few actively managed mutual funds do specialize in finding little-known companies in exactly the developing economies I've flagged in this chapter. As always with mutual funds and ETFs, check out commissions and management fees before you buy. But since you're paying for intensive management in order to find these emerging blue chips, it's okay to pay more than you would for a fund that mimics a plain-vanilla index such as the U.S. Standard & Poor's 500. I'd recommend:

- **Matthews China** (MCHFEX), Matthews Pacific Tigers (MAPTX), Matthews India (MINDX), and Matthews Korea (MAKOX).
- **Templeton BRIC** (TABRX)—BRIC stands for Brazil, Russia, India, and China, by the way, Templeton Developing Markets (TEDMX), and Templeton China World (TCWAX).

5

A WEALTHIER AND OLDER WORLD

Who Will Manage All That Money?

THE FINANCIAL SECTOR GOT HAMMERED IN 2007 BY THE COL-
lapse of the subprime mortgage market, by rising defaults on commercial loans and credit cards, and by the tumbling prices in derivatives so
complex, it turned out, that nobody understood them. Shares of
Washington Mutual, the biggest savings and loan in the country,
plunged 70 percent. Countrywide Financial dropped 78 percent. Citigroup fell 47 percent in 2007, Merrill Lynch (MER) 41 percent, Bear
Stearns (BSC) 45 percent, Bank of America 23 percent, and American
International Group 17 percent.

The first four months of 2008 weren't any better. Washington
Mutual fell another 19 percent, Citigroup another 5 percent, Merrill
Lynch another 9 percent, and Bank of America another 6 percent.
Bear Stearns tumbled another 88 percent and was bought by JP
Morgan Chase. Countrywide Financial dropped another 44 percent, raising the possibility that Bank of America, which had decided to buy Countrywide, would either cut the price or drop the
deal entirely. And just in case investors were starting to think the
worst was over, on August 6, American International Group announced that it would take another $5.6 billion loss from the falling

value of its portfolio of mortgage derivatives. That brought total writedowns from mortgage-related investments to $26 billion. On September 24, the company agreed to an $85 billion bailout loan from the federal government.

And finally, on October 3, after watching five European banks get bailed out in a single day, after witnessing the disappearance of Wachovia and Washington Mutual, and after watching the meltdown of the U.S. stock market, Congress voted to approve a $700 billion rescue for the financial system.

Want to buy a financial stock?

You should. Centainly not right away. The mortgage crisis isn't over. Banks are still hoarding cash. And there's a better-than-good chance that bad credit card debt, bad car loans, and bad commercial loans will take another bite out of the sector.

But someday. Maybe in late 2009 or in early 2010.

The financial crisis of 2008 destroyed individual companies, damaged franchises, and even left some survivors expending all their energy to dig out from the wreckage. But hard as it may be to believe, the long-term reason to buy financial stocks is intact. The reason, or maybe better yet, reasons to buy financial stocks aren't going to be reversed because of some little globe-shaking, financial capital-rocking market crisis. They're too strong for that. Each is based solidly on the fundamentals of an increasingly wealthy global economy and on the aging of the global population.

First, in the developing economies rising global incomes are creating huge new markets for financial products such as credit cards and life insurance that we in the United States take for granted. Second, an aging global population of hundreds of millions of baby boomers in the world's developed economies and hundreds of millions of newly comfortable Indians, Chinese, Vietnamese, Russians, and Brazilians are socking away money for retirement and need somebody to manage it. The meltdown in the financial sector gives investors a chance to get in on one of the most important of the ten trends in this book at bargain prices.

To understand why you want to own this sector for the long term, take a look at one of the companies whose stock was hammered in the 2007–8 meltdown in the financial sector. HSBC Holdings, the global banking giant once known as Hong Kong Shanghai Bank, saw its shares fall 29 percent from the October 31, 2007, high to their February 11, 2008, temporary low. The problem? An aggressive entry into the U.S. market home loan business through the acquisition of Household International for $15 billion. That 2003 deal came just in time for the bank to get slammed by the subprime mortgage disaster. The company's Household unit was one of the biggest originators of subprime mortgages, and the bank also aggressively bought mortgages from a network of 280 unaffiliated mortgage lenders. In 2007 the bank had to add $12.2 billion to its loan loss reserves—which means the company had to take money out of its profits and put it aside in a reserve fund to pay for anticipated future losses on loans that will have gone bad—for its North American operations as defaults climbed on mortgages and other loans.

Weigh that short-term carnage against the long-term potential, though, and you'll see why, despite the bank's demonstrated ineptitude in the U.S. market, you want to own these shares long term. For example, take a look at its credit card business in developing economies such as India. In 2006 the number of credit cards HSBC had in circulation in India grew by better than 60 percent. Yep, at the end of 2006, more than 2 million Indians carried an HSBC credit card—impressive until you realize that India has a population of about 1 billion people and HSBC's market penetration rate is roughly 0.2 percent.

Or look at China. Its banking market is one of the fastest-growing in the world. From 2001 to 2006 total yuan deposits with the country's financial institutions rose at a compounded average annual growth rate of 18.5 percent, according to Daiwa Investments.

Total yuan loans climbed by 14.9 percent compounded annually. And that's just the tip of the trend. In the United States personal loans add up to about 105 percent of national gross domestic product. In the United Kingdom they're 85 percent, in Japan 35 percent, and in

China just 15 percent. Despite fast growth in personal loans, the market has barely been tapped by U.S.—or even Japanese—standards.

But the real growth is in personal financial products and services beyond personal loans. The country has no pension system to speak of. No scheme to provide health care in retirement. And, because of an aging population and a decades-long commitment to one child per family, the country will have very few children to take care of hundreds of millions of aged parents.

So guess what the fastest growing financial product is in China? (Well, after brokerage accounts, that is—20 million Chinese opened new brokerage accounts in the first five months of 2007, and by year's end the country had 115 million brokerage accounts. A red-hot bull market in stocks will have that effect in a nation that loves to gamble.) It's life insurance. It's one way to put together a modest inheritance that will give ungrateful children a reason to exercise their family duties.

Life insurance penetration, the total of life insurance premiums written as a percentage of the country's gross domestic product, in China trails both the world average and the Asian average. According to Swiss Re, life insurance density is 13.1 percent in the United Kingdom (the most penetrated market in the world), 11.6 percent in Taiwan, 8.3 percent in Japan, 4 percent in the United States, and just 1.7 percent in China. The gross life insurance premium per capita in China is just $34 a year compared to $1,790 in the United States and $155 on average in Asia.

Personal accident and casualty insurance shows the same pattern. Penetration in China is just 1.2 percent and the per capita premium is just $19. But as the country's population of automobiles and other insurable goods increases, premiums are projected to grow by a compounded average of 10 percent a year for at least the next five years, Daiwa Investments calculates. The per capita premium for this type of insurance in the United States is $2,134 a year.

Think there's room for growth there?

You'll find the same combination of higher incomes and higher consumption of financial services and products in India, Russia, and . . . well, pretty much anywhere that economic development is giving people some money to save and at the same time weakening the traditional family-based system for care of the elderly.

In India the total premium collected for life and other types of insurance soared by 83 percent from 2001 to 2004. That huge increase represents a very small part of the potential growth in this market since the penetration for life insurance increased in those years to just 2.88 percent from 2.32 percent. There's still a way to go before India catches up with penetration in South Korea, for example, at 7.9 percent.

In the Middle East, a region with some of the highest economic growth rates and youngest populations in the world, insurance premiums are growing at a 12.5 percent compounded average annual rate.

Back in the United States (and the rest of the developed world) the market for credit insurance and credit cards is more mature, although specific markets in individual countries can be exceptions. A developed country such as Japan, for example, has by U.S. standards a radically low percentage of credit card carriers.

But just because the markets for credit cards, personal loans, and insurance is mature in the developed economies doesn't mean that there's no room for growth in those markets. In these markets the fastest-growing business—and the most profitable—for banks and brokerage firms is managing money for folks who have a bit of it.

What makes the prospects for the financial sector so positive in countries as different as Japan, France, and the United States? Similar demographics.

WE LIVE IN A RAPIDLY AGING WORLD

You may be familiar with the situation in the developed economies. By 2040—just over thirty years from now—45 percent of the population in Japan, Spain, and Italy will be sixty or older, according to the

Center for Strategic and International Studies. Makes the United States, where only 26 percent of the population will be sixty or older by 2040, seem positively childlike.

Still, that 26 percent figure for the United States represents a huge increase from 16.3 percent in 2000.

And the problem is that each of those oldsters will have a smaller working-age population to support him or her. By 2025 the number of people age fifteen to sixty-four will fall by 10.4 percent in Spain, 14.8 percent in Italy, and 15.7 percent in Japan. By 2040 there will be one retiree for every worker in Japan, Spain, and Italy.

But the problem—and the opportunity for the financial industry—isn't limited to the developed world. Developing countries are aging just as fast or faster than developed economies. By 2025 the median age in the "Asian Tiger" economies of South Korea, Taiwan, Thailand, Singapore, and Hong Kong will hit forty. The United States, in contrast, won't hit a median age of thirty-nine until 2030. Also aging fast are Indonesia, India, Brazil, Mexico, Iran, Egypt, Russia, and, most surprisingly China. By 2020 China will have a population with 265 million sixty-five-year-olds. By 2020, the United Nations Population Division projects, China's labor supply will be dropping as its population ages and the median age of China's population is likely to be higher than in the United States. India, among the youngest of the developing economies, will see the median age of its population hit 37.9 in 2050. That's about as old as the U.S. population is today.

None of these economies, developed or developing, is prepared to finance an aging population. The United States is in the best shape. Social Security delays full retirement benefits for anyone born after 1960 until age sixty-seven, and 80 percent of workers save for retirement.

Best, however, isn't too great. The Social Security trust fund goes into the red in 2042 unless there are changes to benefits or taxes, and the average worker saves only about $700 a month toward retirement, according to a 2007 survey by AXA Equitable. That adds up to about half the maximum annual contribution of $15,500 a worker can make to a 401(k) plan in 2008.

But the situation in the rest of the world is absolutely dismal. Europe's historically generous government retirement plans are cutting benefits and delaying retirement. European workers aren't used to saving much for retirement either. In France, Germany, and Italy the average is just $300 a month.

Japan faces the heaviest burden in the developed world. Already 17 percent of its population is over sixty-five, and from 2005 to 2012 the country's workforce is projected to shrink by 1 percent every year. A 2005 plan by then Japanese prime minister Junichiro Koizumi estimated that even an increase in pension taxes to 18 percent from the current 14 percent by 2017 would still require that benefits be slashed to 50 percent of average pre-retirement wages from 59 percent now.

But in many ways the situation is worse in the developing economies, and it will require a much bigger effort by both government and the private sector to prevent an absolute disaster as these economies age. Traditionally in many of these countries parents could count on their children to take care of them in retirement, and that duty constituted the only "retirement plan" for much of the population. That tradition is under attack from demographic trends that have reduced the number of children in a family just as the number of old people is soaring. In China, the country's one-child policy has led to adult couples as the sole support for two sets of grandparents. The tradition is also being eroded by a growing unwillingness among some upwardly mobile younger workers to take on this responsibility.

This family-based solution to retirement has also meant that very few workers are covered by any pension plan at all. For example, only 11 percent of Indians have any pension at all. In China the percentage is a higher but still stunningly low 20 percent.

The efforts in developing economies to shore up underfunded and inadequate public pensions, where they exist, have recently focused on privately managed savings accounts. Chile led the way on this approach when it replaced its public system with retirement accounts funded by worker contributions and managed by private firms. The Chilean plan did indeed fix a huge government budget deficit, create a pool of pension assets in the local currency for local businesses to tap through debt and equity issues, and expand the number of workers with some retirement benefits. Eleven other Latin American nations have adopted the Chilean model, and it has spread to the developing economies of Eastern Europe as well.

Time has shown that these plans have major weaknesses. Workers at the low end of the pay scale don't contribute much. What's worse, workers in the informal economy don't contribute at all. Of Brazil's 70 million workers, for example, 56 percent work in the informal economy and don't contribute to these plans.

But even with these drawbacks, and well-justified protests about fees that can run as high as 25 percent of a worker's contributions, plans along the Chilean model do work to familiarize a new mass audience with some of the financial products and services that the U.S. middle class takes for granted. That promises a growing market in these countries for financial products and services as their populations age and as national incomes rise.

These two trends, operating in both developing and developed economies, add up to a formidable global tide that will lift financial shares around the world. In a nutshell, I like the financial sector for the long run because

- Rising global incomes and an aging world put more and more assets in the hands of asset managers, who then earn fees on that larger base of assets
- Rising global incomes and an aging world create a demand for more complex financial instruments—life insurance rather than a savings account, or baskets of stocks (exchange-traded funds or ETFs) rather than purchases of individual stocks—that earn higher fees on that larger base of assets

You can see those trends in the revenue growth being posted by financial companies in both developed and developing economies.

In the developed economy of the United States, one beneficiary of these trends is State Street, the Boston-based company that specializes in services for pension and mutual funds, investment managers, and individual investors. Standard & Poor's projects that revenue will grow by 28 percent in 2008, despite turmoil in the financial markets. Over the long term, Standard & Poor's notes, the company will benefit from "the outsourcing of custody services, growth in worldwide pension systems, the development of more complex investment vehicles, consolidation among financial processing providers, and increasing pressure on public retirement systems." Couldn't have put it better myself. Although the company suffered $3.2 billion in unrealized losses from the decline of the value of its portfolio in 2007, assets under management finished the first quarter of 2008 up 6 percent from the first quarter of 2007, at $1.96 trillion. Fees for managing these assets climbed 7 percent. Assets under custody climbed 34 percent from the first quarter of 2007 to $14.9 trillion, and fees for servicing these assets climbed by 34 percent from the first quarter of 2007. (Assets under custody are stocks, bonds, cash, and other financial instruments owned by other companies but for which State Street provides custody services for a fee, such as managing mutual fund shareholder buys and sells.) Growth in the last decade has been spectacular. In 1996 assets under management were just $292 billion and assets under custody were $2.9 trillion.

In the developing economies of India and Brazil, investors can see the same trends producing the same kinds of growth at Mumbai's HDFC Bank and Sao Paulo's Itau Bank Financial Holding. As incomes rise and as people become more accustomed to new financial products, HDFC Bank has increased fee income an average of 55 percent annually over the last five years as it originates more mortgages and opens more credit card accounts. Itau Bank Financial Holding has grabbed 25 percent of the new market for credit cards and consumer—mostly auto—loans. And there's plenty of room for growth because the loan-to-GDP ratio in Brazil—called loan penetration—is just 30 percent. It's 65 percent in Chile and 105 percent in the United States.

The financial sector won't be risk-free, however, even after the mess of 2007–8 gets cleared away. The world faces a fundamental problem that makes it likely that we'll see a rerun of the recent debacle every five years or so.

GETTING HIGH RETURNS WITH LOW RISK IS THE GOAL—BUT IT'S IMPOSSIBLE

To capture the tremendous upside of the financial sector over the next ten years and avoid some or all of the downside, you have to make sure you understand the problem that caused the financial crisis that began in 2007.

Maybe the easiest place to start to understand why the financial markets suffered a near-meltdown in 2007–8 and why so many individual financial stocks took such hits is with the U.S. corporate bond market. This market once provided investors—and pension funds and insurance companies—with an amazing combination of safety and yields that were higher than those on U.S. Treasury bonds. In 1992, 72 percent of all the companies issuing bonds rated by Standard & Poor's earned an investment grade. A bond rating is based on an assessment by one of the rating companies—Standard & Poor's, Fitch's Investment Services, or Moody's—of how likely a company (or country, state, city, or sewage authority) is to meet its obligation to pay regular interest on its bonds, and how likely it is to be around in good financial health and able to redeem its bonds for full face value when they mature. At the top of the scale, from AAA to BBB– in Standard & Poor's system, you'll find investment-grade debt. This is, according to the ratings companies, debt issued by companies that are financially strong enough, come hell or high water, to pay their obligations. Below these ratings are the non-investment-grade levels, ranging from BB to the increasingly speculative CCC, CC, and C. An investor in a non-investment-grade bond expects to get paid more in interest than the holder of an investment-grade bond because there's a larger chance that the company won't be around—or at least, not in sufficient financial health—to pay its obligations.

But a very telling thing has happened in the world of U.S. corporate bonds since 1992. The number of issuers of investment-grade corporate bonds has shrunk, and the number of speculative-grade issuers has climbed. Forget about finding an AAA rating—once the gold standard in the corporate-bond sector—among today's issuers. Just seven nonfinancial U.S. companies earned that rating at the start of 2008. The overall median credit rating of an issuer declined in the same period from A– in 1992 to BBB– by the end of 2006. BBB– is the lowest credit rating that still qualifies as investment-grade. Everything below that is junk. The number of B-rated issues, according to Standard & Poor's, has doubled in the past decade, and the number of CCC-rated firms has more than tripled.

This decay in the credit quality of corporate bonds couldn't come at a much worse time for the managers of pension funds, insurance company portfolios, and, indeed, any portfolio designed to cover the huge costs of retirement in a rapidly aging world where folks are living longer after retiring from the workforce. Investment-grade bonds were once ideal for these investors since they paid relatively high interest rates and were issued with maturity dates far in the future. In a world where longer life spans mean that pension funds and other retirement vehicles have to pay out longer and more for each retiree, investment-grade corporate bonds hit the mark.

But as credit quality declined and as more and more corporate bonds lost their investment-grade ratings, there simply weren't enough of these bonds to go around.

Faced with this rising tide of retirement obligations, managers of retirement money in one form or another found themselves between a rock and a hard place. They needed safe assets. Some of them are required by the rules of their portfolios to invest in only investment-grade assets. They needed long-lived assets that matched the dates in the future when obligations to issue retirement payments materialize. And they needed assets that delivered high returns while still meeting the requirements of safety and long maturity.

Managers of retirement money could make up for the shortfall in supply of safe corporate bonds by buying even safer government bonds, but those high-quality government bonds came with lower yields. That's a huge problem for the folks who sponsor pension funds, such as state and city governments, and those companies that still offer traditional pensions. If the yield earned by a fund's assets goes down, the sponsor has to put in more money to keep future obligations in line with future assets. That's money that cities, states, and corporations either don't have or don't want to spend on pension benefits.

And that was the moment when Wall Street walked in the door with an amazing deal. Investment bankers could spin speculative-grade credits—whether corporate debt and loans from a buyout deal or mortgages from financially challenged home buyers—into investment-grade credits. By bundling together groups of credits, or pools of loans, corporate debt, or mortgages, the investment banks said, you'd lower the risk that an investor would take a hit if any one loan or mortgage went bad.

And then, by cutting up those pools and putting the riskiest deals together in one segment, called a tranche, and the less-risky deals in other tranches, you could make sure the less-risky tranches wouldn't suffer any losses—even though they were made up originally from risky ingredients. The riskiest tranches might get wiped out, which is why investors who bought them got a higher yield, but they created a kind of buffer for investors in the less-risky tranches, the investment banks said. Investors in those less-risky tranches wouldn't take a hit until the riskier tranches were wiped out, the banks promised. And it follows, the banks argued, that the less-risky tranches met the standards for investment-grade credit ratings.

Voilà! From pools of risky speculative-grade credits, Wall Street could manufacture the investment-grade credits that the retirement industry desperately needed.

The managers of retirement money wanted to believe that Wall Street and other centers of financial engineering could manufacture investment-grade, long-term, higher-yielding debt. Because the need for this kind of financial instrument was so great, its potential buyers were willing to suspend belief. They might have known in their heads that investment-grade debt couldn't be manufactured like this. But in their hearts they wanted to believe. They needed to believe. They had to believe.

Except the magic didn't work. More accurately, it worked only until the real world threw something at the financial markets that wasn't in the computer models that had designed these new forms of debt. When more borrowers with lousy credit ratings and inadequate incomes started to default than the computers had predicted, and when the risky tranches proved too small to protect the risk-free tranches from big losses, the real world effectively shattered the dream. And then the whole carefully built structure came tumbling down.

History is full of instances where Wall Street inventions haven't behaved as advertised. And it's just as full of instances where investors decided to overlook what they knew of the history of other Wall Street miracles of financial engineering. Five years from now enough people will have forgotten the pain of 2007 and the need to fund global retirement will be even more pressing. We'll go through some version of this all over again. Remember, history may not repeat itself, but it sure does rhyme.

The financial sector, in short, is a place with plenty of opportunities in the decade ahead for making money—and for losing it.

There's no better example of the difference between buy-and-hold and my Jubak Picks strategy than what happened in the financial sector in 2007–8. And there's no better example of why my Jubak Picks strategy beats the stock market without gimmicks or extra risk than what happened in the financial sector.

Until I bought shares of U.S. Bancorp on April 4, 2008, I hadn't owned a U.S. financial stock in my online portfolio since I sold American International Group on July 20, 2007. I haven't owned a financial stock from anywhere else on the globe since I sold Brazilian bank Unibanco (Uniao de Bancos Brasileiros) on November 15, 2007. U.S. Bancorp is the only bank stock I own in this portfolio as of July 10, 2008.

That let my portfolio escape the worst of the 2007 and 2008 meltdown in the financial sector as problems rippled out from the mortgage sector to overwhelm banks from San Francisco to Switzerland.

Because financial stocks made up about 25 percent of the value of the Standard & Poor's 500 Stock Index in 2007, my avoidance of the sector was one of the major reasons that Jubak's Picks returned 25 percent in 2007 and the S&P 500 returned just 5.5 percent. The Dow Industrials (2007 return 8.8 percent) and the NASDAQ Composite (2007 return 9.8 percent), while better than that of the S&P 500, were still dragged down by the burden of the financial sector to a comparable degree.

I owned so few or no financial stocks even though I still liked the sector for the long term. I hadn't and haven't changed my opinion of the power of the trends that I've outlined in this chapter. But after doing the kinds of fundamental and technical analysis I explain in Chapters 13 and 14 of this book, I decided that the odds were that the stocks in the sector would suffer big damage in 2007–8. Not 10 percent damage—that's the kind I'm perfectly willing to suffer through—but the 40 percent to 80 percent damage that I cited at the beginning of this chapter. I'm not willing to take that kind of punishment, especially because I think that there's a good chance that you can see it coming if you use some very basic fundamental and technical tools.

You can't hope to avoid all risk in the stock market. But you can protect yourself from the worst damage much of the time. And I think you should.

Now that it's the fall of 2008, I'm starting to poke around in the wreckage of the financial sector again. As I write this, it's October 2008, and I'm not buying anything quite yet. There's still bad news on home mortgages, credit card debt, auto loans, and corporate bonds to come in 2008 that will hit the financial sector like Godzilla hit Tokyo. Someday this year or next, though, I'll start buying banks, insurance companies, and money management companies again. The stocks will be cheap. They'll be ready to bounce back. Owning this sector—and the huge opportunity that trends in this sector represent—will give me a great chance of beating the market indexes in 2009 and onward.

How the Trends Play Out for Investors

- The financial sector suffered a meltdown in 2007 because banks thought they could make up for lax lending standards by using Wall Street financial engineering and because money managers, desperate for safe, higher-yielding debt, were willing to believe Wall Street when it said it could turn risky paper into AAA-rated credits.

- Instead Wall Street built rickety mountains of debt out of dubious financial insurance, and the result was that nobody knew who owed who what or what anything was truly worth. A mess like this takes time—2008 and probably most of 2009—to clean up.

- But the long-term trends are definitely blowing at gale force in the sector's direction. Rising incomes in the developing world will create a huge market for financial services and products from auto loans to life insurance to credit cards. The aging of the developed and developing economies will mean lots of fees for money managers, custody banks, and wealth advisors—anybody who can help the world pay for its retirement.

- The danger here is that so much opportunity will result in relatively frequent replays of the crisis of 2007. Banks have a nasty habit of chasing business even when that business comes from customers with bad credit ratings and terrible odds against paying off their loans on time. What you want more than anything else in this environment is company management that knows how to say no.

- Fortunately, in the financial sector it's relatively easy to identify management that can say no by tracking such fundamental measures as the rates at which loans go delinquent or lenders default. In the picks section at the end of this chapter, I've tried to highlight that and similar numbers so you can get an idea of what fundamental measures to watch.

- In the developed markets, look for the stocks of companies that gather and manage assets. That's where the growth is coming from as an aging population gets more and more anxious about funding its retirement.

- In the developing markets, look for the stocks of companies that are bringing financial services and products that are already mature in the developed world to new markets. The growth to capitalize on here comes from credit cards, consumer loans (especially for autos), home mortgages, life insurance, and increasingly brokerage accounts.

TREND BREAKERS AND TREND MAKERS RIPPED FROM THE HEADLINES

TREND BREAKERS

- *Headlines announcing the next asset bubble.* The giveaway for the 2007–8 debacle was a boom in housing prices that went to extremes. If you're a bank, you can't make enough bad loans to really get you into trouble unless you've got runaway demand for loans fueled by a boom in prices of the asset that people are buying with that loan. That kind of feedback loop—in the run-up to the 2007 crisis, rising home prices created more demand for mortgages, which pushed home prices higher—is essential to creating the ensuing bust. I don't have the foggiest idea where the next asset bubble will break out. But I'm positive there will be one and that banks will get in trouble again.

- *Interest rates go up.* Financial companies don't, all things else being equal, like rising interest rates. Higher rates do two bad things from a bank's perspective. First, they decrease the value of existing debt. If you can get 6 percent on a newly issued bond, an old bond paying 5.5 percent drops in value. Second, and this is more important, rising interest rates slow the economy and increase stress on borrowers. Some borrowers won't be able to pay interest on their debt or pay off the debt when it matures. Higher interest rates increase defaults in a bank's loan portfolio, and news of rising default levels is never good for a bank stock. (This is why the U.S. Federal Reserve lowered interest rates in 2007 and 2008 to help banks and decrease pressure on borrowers when default rates were rising.)

- *Stories that show inflation is on the rise.* Inflation erodes the value of existing debt (and equity and houses and . . .). Higher inflation is especially hard on bank stocks because investors, rightly, see rising inflation leading to an increase in interest rates as central banks fight to lower inflation by raising rates and slowing the economy.

Trend Makers

- *News that the yield curve is getting steeper.* Just kidding: you won't see this in any headline. But you will find stories on this critical topic buried back in the business section or in the markets coverage of the *Wall Street Journal* or the *Financial Times.* The yield curve— the difference in yield between short-term debt (say, three-month Treasury bills) and long-term debt (say, ten-year Treasury notes)—is much more important for bank profits than the absolute interest rate. That's because banks make money by borrowing in the short term themselves (most bank loans at most banks even these days aren't funded with depositors' money but by bank debt sold in the financial markets) and lending in the long term. Banks are in clover when short-term rates plunge—as they were doing in early 2008 as the Federal Reserve tried to revive economic growth—and long-term rates stay stable or even rise.
- *Headlines about the opening of markets in China, India, and the rest of the developing world* to let foreign companies sell credit cards or life insurance or other investment products. Most developing markets have restrictions on who can own how much of a domestic company selling into that market and limits on how much market share an overseas company can grab. India, for example, has very strict rules on overseas market share in the life insurance business. Any liberalizing of these restrictions will be a boon for global sellers of these services and products.
- *Stories about innovative solutions to the distribution problem.* ICICI Bank has the biggest branch network of any of India's private banks. But that network still numbers just a thousand branches. JP

Morgan Chase operates more branches in New York City's borough of Manhattan alone. A lack of branches—and an even bigger shortage of ATMs—makes selling financial services and collecting everything from deposits to loan payments a challenge in developing markets. Implementing a solution that relies on something as cheap and ubiquitous in developing economies as a cell phone will give institutions a huge edge over those who have to build expensive brick and mortar branches.

• *Developed economies may be "mature," but that doesn't mean that innovation has stopped or that innovators can't steal market share and profits from slower-moving competitors.* The invention of the exchange-traded fund (ETF) proves that. These now represent a huge challenge to the existing mutual fund giants who will either join the trend, cut fees for their existing funds, or lose market share. Or perhaps all three. When you read stories about innovators, see if one company's name appears repeatedly. Journalists go with the trend just like investors, and if they start to tout one company repeatedly, it's an indicator that a company may be using technology to rejuggle the competitive landscape. (Or that journalists have jumped on another hype bandwagon.)

Stock Picks That Put the Wind from Those Trends at Your Back

HDFC Bank (NYSE ADR: HDB). It is only the third-largest bank in India, but under managing director Aditya Pura, the former head of operations for Citibank in Malaysia, it is the best-run. Because HDFC's base of retail deposits—from a network of 746 branches in 329 cities serving 10 million customers—provides about 40 percent of the capital it lends out, the bank has been able to maintain a healthy net interest margin (2.32 percent in the fourth quarter of the fiscal year that ended in March 2008) even as the Reserve Bank of India raised interest rates. (The net interest margin is the difference between the interest rate a bank pays to depositors and in the financial markets for the money it raises to lend out and the interest rate it receives on those loans. The higher the net interest margin, the more profitable a bank can be.) A conservative approach to credit quality kept nonperforming loans to just 0.83 percent of all loans in the fourth quarter of fiscal 2008. (It doesn't hurt, certainly, that bouncing a check remains a felony in India.) Noninterest income—most of it from fees—is forecast to grow by 30 percent annually over the next five years. In the United States the stock trades as an ADR (American depository receipt), with each ADR equal to three Indian ordinary shares.

HSBC Holdings (NYSE ADR: HBC). The financial crisis of 2007–8 hasn't been kind to HSBC. In 2007 the bank had to add $12.2 billion to its loan loss reserves for its North American operations as defaults climbed on mortgages. All in all the bank is looking at a $17 billion loss from its ill-fated entry into the U.S. mortgage market. The bank has reacted by aggressively reaffirming its presence in Asia. In December 2007, for example, HSBC bought the financially distressed Chinese Bank in Taiwan, adding thirty-nine branches in the country to the eight that it already owns. The deal will also bring HSBC a million new customers in Asia's fourth-largest banking market. The company has a lot of strength to build on in Asia too. It's the largest bank in Hong Kong, the source of about 20 percent of its profits, and owns a 60 percent stake in Hang Seng Bank, the third-largest in the city. In India it is one of the biggest corporate lenders and a pioneer in wealth management for India's growing middle and upper classes. Worldwide the private bank group had $333 billion under management at the end of 2006. Overall, the bank is the world's biggest collector of deposits, with $1.1 trillion in deposits, and serves more than 125 million retail customers. North America accounted for 27 percent of assets in 2006, Europe for 45 percent, Hong Kong for 15 percent, the rest of Asia for 9 percent, and Latin America for 4 percent. The bank has never come right out and said that the deals to enter the United States were a huge mistake and that it doesn't know that market very well, but I think its repositioning is a tacit admission that the future for HSBC is in Asia and Europe. I think that's spot on, as the English say, and the reason that you want to own this bank for the long term.

ING Groep (NYSE ADR: ING). This Dutch bank and insurance company is positioned to pick up the pieces dropped by Citigroup and American International, both internationally and inside the United States. To give you just one glaring example of the way that ING is expanding into markets where challenged competitors are pulling back, in July, Citigroup announced the sale of its German consumer-loan business, with 340 branches and 3.2 million clients. In contrast, just two months earlier, ING announced that it would buy German online mortgage broker Interhyp for about $644 million.

Before the current crisis, I would have identified Citigroup, American International, and HSBC as the leaders in the race to build dominant global financial brands. Stumbles by Citigroup and American International have thrown the race open to new players.

Now, thanks to the crisis, I think ING is likely to bump one of these from its place in the global top three. The company already has 75 million customers around the world, and it's making all the right moves to expand that number. About half of ING's business is in insurance where ING has been busy shifting capital from mature West European markets to faster-growing markets in Central Europe and Asia. For example, on July 9, the company received regulatory approval to enter the insurance market in Ukraine.

In the banking part of its business, ING has stepped up its penetration of the U.S. market through its online ING direct business. ING is an aggressive accumulator of online deposits, with more than $300 billion in online deposits worldwide. In the post-crisis world, raising funds for making loans from relatively low-cost deposits instead of in the capital markets will be a huge competitive advantage. The company is also going after the lucrative and fast-growing market for managing retirement money. On July 1, the company acquired CitiStreet, a retirement plan and benefit service and administration business. The deal makes ING the third-largest defined-contribution pension business in the United States, with $300 billion in assets under management.

Itau Bank Financial Holding (NYSE ADR: ITU). The second-largest bank in Brazil is the most profitable bank in Brazil—and also one of the fastest-moving. The bank recently bought Bank of America's operations in Chile and Uruguay and is expanding into Argentina. The Brazilian market for auto loans and credit cards is still in its infancy, but Itau Bank already owns 25 percent of both markets to go with its 9 percent share of Brazil's bank deposits. None of these moves has diluted the bank's profitability. Even as higher interest rates and an appreciating currency were cutting into banking sector profits in 2007, Itau Bank still managed a net interest margin of 11.4 percentage points. Neither have these trends eroded the bank's emphasis on credit quality. Nonperforming loans fell to 4.7 percent in the third quarter of 2007 from 5.2 percent in the third quarter of 2006. Return on equity has averaged 29 percent annually during the last six years. In the United States the stock trades as an ADR with each ADR equal to one preferred share.

State Street (NYSE: STT). Stability and innovation are not a bad combination in any company in any sector. But it's especially valuable in the financial sector, where innovation is so hard to come by and all the more valuable for its scarcity. First, stability. State Street is one of the largest global custodians and asset managers in the world. Clients such as mutual funds or insurance companies use State Street for their back-office bookkeeping in exchange for a fee, and you can bet that the fees on $15 trillion in custodial assets add up to a decent penny. Plus, since clients don't want to muck up their bookkeeping and alienate their customers, custodial clients don't tend to move from one institution to another with great frequency. In fact, the usual way to get a new custodial client these days is to buy one with the acquisition of another custodial firm. That's why State Street bought Investors Financial Services in July 2007. The company came along with a stable of hedge fund and other alternative investment managers and gave State Street a bigger presence in what was—and what will be again—one of the fastest-growing parts of the financial industry in the developed world. On the asset side, where State Street directly manages $2 trillion in assets, the company has shown its talent for innovation. State Street is now one of the biggest players in the fast-growing market for exchange-traded funds, the most serious threat to traditional mutual funds since the rise of the modern mutual fund in the 1960s. State Street got burnt badly in the subprime mortgage debacle. I think it's fair to say that the company thought it understood the risk of the new generation of debt instruments better than it did. As of May 2008, the company faced pressure to put a $29 billion structured investment vehicle on its books, which could lead to losses. I think that worry, which has depressed the stock's price for 2007 and well into 2008, should be largely over by 2009, however, letting the long-term strengths of the company reassert themselves to drive the stock price higher.

Stocks for Building an Overweight Position in This Sector

• **Banco Santander** (NYSE ADR: STD) has grown from its Spanish roots to become the seventh-largest in the world on the back of one of the industry's best information technology systems. In 2007, 48 percent of revenue came from Europe (14 percent from the United Kingdom) and 38 percent of revenue from Latin America.

• **DBS Group Holdings** (OTC: DBSDF) gives you exposure to consumer banking in China, Thailand, and Indonesia, and the Indian life insurance market from its base in Singapore. That makes these shares a lower-risk way to invest in these markets than the shares of domestic banks in China or Indonesia.

• **ICICI Bank** (NYSE ADR: IBN). I like this more as a bank that sells insurance than as a bank qua bank. The company's insurance business, when it reaches full speed, has huge potential.

• **Middleburg Financial** (NASDAQ: MBRG) is a community bank in the very wealthy northern Virginia horse country outside of Washington, D.C. The bank has a 16 percent share of deposits in fast-growing Loudon County. I'd expect earnings to be roughly flat in 2008 with 2007 but growth to resume in 2009.

• **Northern Trust** (NASDAQ: NTRS). Think of this as a smaller but more conservatively run version of State Street. Northern Trust's private banking business serves roughly 20 percent of the Forbes 400 superrich. I'm expecting that problems at competitors will lead to new business wins at Northern Trust. According to Standard & Poor's, revenue will grow by 12 percent in 2008.

- **SEI Investments** (NASDAQ: SEIC) manages about half the assets it administers for private banks and money managers. That's an incredibly lucrative business, at least the way that SEI runs it. Operating margins were 43 percent in 2007 and 2006. The company's new Global Wealth Platform is going to bring in a lot of wealthy U.S. clients with money to manage.

- **United Overseas Bank** (OTC: UOVGF) is another Singapore bank that gives investors a way to play China's growing financial market with less China risk.

- **U.S. Bancorp** (NYSE: USB) shows how one of the best-run banks in the United States can take advantage of the turmoil in the rest of the banking sector to build market share. Compared with the fourth quarter of 2007, average interest-bearing deposits climbed by 3.3 percent in the first quarter of 2008, and the net interest margin climbed by 4 basis points (100 basis points equal 1 percentage point). The bank did announce a $253 million charge related to structured investment vehicles, but the bank continues to show less exposure to the debt market crisis than its peers.

- **Wilmington Trust** (NYSE: WL) owns a network of about fifty branches in Delaware and Pennsylvania and shows $8.4 billion in deposits. But it's the trust and wealth management business that the company has built through acquisitions that makes this a stock to own for the long term. Because of this business, noninterest income accounts for an unusually large 50 percent of total revenue, with wealth advisory services alone contributing 57 percent of that noninterest income.

MUTUAL FUNDS AND ETFs (EXCHANGE-TRADED FUNDS)

It's easy to get broad exposure to the U.S. financial sector, but it's much harder to fine-tune that exposure.

• On the broad end, investors seeking exposure to the entire U.S. financial sector have three good choices in the Financial Select Sector SPDR (XLF), Vanguard Financials ETF (VFH), and iShares Dow Jones U.S. Financial Sector (IYF).

• After these, the fine-tuning gets tougher. The iShares Dow Jones U.S. Financial Services (IYG) concentrates on big U.S. banks, such as Bank of America and JP Morgan Chase, with exposure to credit card companies such as American Express. You can buy Wall Street's biggest financial companies with the KBW Capital Markets ETF (KCE). The iShares MSCI Singapore Index (EWS) will give you three of Singapore's biggest banks, and the iShares MSCI Brazil Index (EWZ) will give you three of Brazil's biggest banks. I haven't been able to find a mutual fund or an ETF that will give you significant exposure to the wealth management banks of the United States, however.

6

Higher Inflation

The Decade of Our Discontent and the Dawn of a New Era

I

T'S THE END OF AN ERA, ALTHOUGH YOU MAY NOT BE ABLE TO see it because of all the dust kicked up by the financial crisis of 2008. The stumble in the global economy set off by a global constriction of credit led the world's central bankers to stop worrying about inflation. Who can worry about rising prices when banks are failing and unemployment is rising? But make no mistake, the hundreds of billions in cash pumped into economies from China to the United States to the European Union to Russia will come back to haunt us all in the form of higher inflation in the decade to come. It truly is the end of an era.

Inflation peaked at an annual rate of 13.3 percent in 1979 in the United States, and it's been pretty much headed downhill ever since. To tame the high inflation, Paul Volcker, chairman of the Federal Reserve from 1979 to 1987, had to induce a major recession—the U.S. economy shrank on an annual basis in both 1980 and 1982—by cranking interest rates up to double-digit levels; for example, the average business loan in 1981 carried an interest rate of 19.54 percent. But that broke the back of the raging inflation of the 1970s and set us on a downward course that lasted almost thirty years.

That thirty-year cycle is now over. We're not headed back to the double-digit inflation of the 1970s—in the United States, inflation as measured by the Consumer Price Index (CPI), what's called headline inflation, hit 12.2 percent in 1974 and 13.3 percent in 1979—but the trend has reversed. At the end of 2007 and continuing into 2008, the Federal Reserve and the European Central Bank, the two most important inflation fighters in the world, were both worried that inflation was too high, and headed higher. Headline inflation, the number the European Central Bank watches, was a record annual 3.6 percent in March 2008, way above the 2 percent top of the bank's target range. In the United States, the Consumer Price Index climbed at an annualized rate of 4 percent in March. The Fed's preferred measure of core inflation—that's headline inflation minus any increases in volatile food and energy prices—was a lower 2.0 percent. (Energy prices were up an annualized 17 percent in March, so leaving them out of the inflation calculation helped.) But even that's pushing the limits of the Fed's comfort zone of 1.8 percent to 2 percent.

That's not high in comparison to inflation at the last peak in the 1970s and 1980s, and it's not high in absolute terms either. Inflation from 1926 to 2006 ran at a compounded annual rate of 3 percent, according to the *Stocks, Bonds, Bills, and Inflation 2007 Yearbook*.

But it's the direction of the long-term trend that matters to investors. And after a decade—from 1991 through 2000—when headline inflation never broke above 3.4 percent, the recent trend is clearly upward. From an extraordinarily low annual rate of 1.6 percent in 2001, inflation climbed to 2.4 percent in 2002, dipped back to 1.9 percent in 2003, and then climbed to 3.3 percent in 2004, 3.4 percent in 2005, dropped back to 2.5 percent in 2006, and closed out 2007 at 4.3 percent.

If you pay attention to the economic news right about now, you're about to yell, "Stop. How can you be talking about the return of higher inflation when inflation came to an abrupt stop in the fall of 2008. In September what's called headline inflation, which includes the cost of everything we buy, was exactly zero. Core inflation, which excludes food and energy prices, was just 0.1 percent. How can you talk about the return of inflation?"

Well, as with every other trend in this book, while the bear market of 2007–8 and the economic slowdown of 2008–9 felt like a big deal while we lived through them, those periods weren't long enough to reverse decade-long trends in the economy and the stock market. And to figure out those long-term trends, you have to average the data to avoid being misled by short-term and temporary shifts.

So, for example, when I say that inflation peaked in 1979 and it's been downhill since then, I'm speaking about a trend that is, of course, punctuated by years when inflation spiked upward. In 1986 inflation ran at just 1.1 percent, a big drop from 3.8 percent in 1985. But in 1987 inflation climbed to 4.4 percent, on its way to a temporary peak at 6.1 percent in 1990.

But the key point is that if you graph all these years and draw the trend line that best fits these points, it will point clearly downward. Ten years from now, if you do the same exercise with that decade of data, I think the line will point clearly upward, in spite of the temporary downturn in inflation caused by the economic slowdown of 2008–9.

The great puzzle of the last fifteen years has been why inflation has remained so low even as global growth accelerated. Before the housing market crash of 2007, in the United States the economy grew at a real rate (that's after subtracting for inflation) of 3.6 percent in 2004, 3.1 percent in 2005, and 2.9 percent in 2006. That's above the 2.5 percent to 3 percent speed limit for low-inflation growth in the economy calculated by the Federal Reserve; growth above the speed limit should lead to higher inflation. In that period China's economy, which had been speeding along at a 10 percent annual growth rate, actually accelerated to more than 11 percent growth. India and Russia haven't lagged far behind. And even such growth laggards as Europe and Brazil have moved, if not to the fast lane, at least out of the breakdown lane on the shoulder of the global economy.

All that growth should have produced inflation. It certainly did produce big increases in the prices of raw materials ranging from oil to copper, soybeans, and iron ore. But when it came down to measured inflation at the consumer or wholesale levels? Nada.

As the U.S. and global economies recovered from the stock market crash of 2000, economists were left sucking for explanations like a miler about to be lapped by the field. In the early stages of the search for explanations, then Federal Reserve chairman Alan Greenspan said surprisingly strong productivity growth in the United States was the reason why the U.S. economy could grow faster than the Fed's speed limit without producing an increase in inflation. Increases in productivity kept unit labor costs down as workers turned out more stuff and services per hour worked. That, plus more efficient use of raw materials, made it possible for companies to pay higher prices for raw materials without raising the prices they charged to customers. That explanation became less and less satisfactory as the amount of missing inflation kept climbing.

Explanation two focused on what came to be called the Wal-Mart effect and the increasing globalization of the world economy. As globalization brought new workers into the global workforce, this explanation said, these lower-paid workers exerted downward pressure on global wages as companies moved to low-cost manufacturing regions or used global wage rates as leverage to exact pay cuts from their domestic labor force. Wal-Mart and other global distribution channels used their extraordinary scale and cutting-edge logistics to distribute these lower costs to consumers around the world. The result? China and other low-cost manufacturing regions exported deflation to the rest of the world.

I'd add a third explanation to these two, one that mainstream economists, especially those who work for one of the world's central banks, don't talk about much. Inflation is so low because it is not being measured correctly. Part of the problem is in the details of how prices are measured in the various national inflation numbers. In the United States, for example, the inflation numbers include not the cost of a house but of housing. The inflation in home prices is calculated using something called the rental equivalent, or how much the cost of renting a comparable home rises and falls. Economists at the St. Louis Federal Reserve Bank have calculated that because housing rental prices actually fall when the economy is in the middle of a housing boom and home prices are rising fast, this statistical method alone led to the official inflation rate being understated by as much as 0.5 percentage point in the years of the housing boom.

The bigger problem, though, is in the way that we conceptualize inflation as limited to the prices of the things and services we buy and don't include inflation in asset prices, that is, in the prices of things such as houses or technology stocks. Now that money flows so freely from one asset class—from real estate to commodities, for example—and one national market to another, fast growth in the money supply in one country, which in the past would produce price inflation in that country, can now produce a bubble in asset prices in that country or somewhere around the world. If, however, you include asset price inflation in your definition of inflation, then much of the problem of why inflation was so low disappears. It wasn't low, in fact. Inflation was showing up in asset prices for houses and technology stocks but not in consumer prices for lawn mowers and garbage bags, that's all. The bubbles in the stock market in 2000 and in the housing market in 2006 were signs of global inflation that were not reflected in the official rates of inflation.

THE TREND: UP

No matter what explanation you buy in to, the global trend in measured inflation is up. Unfortunately, higher inflation is coming from every direction you care to look. It's coming from commodity prices: the price of wheat was up 64 percent in the twelve months that ended in April 2008. Energy prices: gasoline prices climbed 22 percent from April 2007 to April 2008. The price of drugs will go up in 2008 by 10 percent, U.S. health insurers estimate. College costs are expected to climb by 8 percent to 9 percent in 2008.

Normally, the Federal Reserve and the European Central Bank would move to stomp out inflation by raising interest rates. But thanks to a weakening U.S. economy and turmoil in the debt markets, the Federal Reserve and other central banks initially lowered rates and expanded the money supply instead. The short-term measures enacted to prevent the financial crisis of 2007–8 from getting worse guarantee that inflation will be far higher and far more entrenched by the time the central banks decide it's safe to tackle the problem.

For example, even as inflation was creeping upward, the Federal

Reserve was lowering interest rates because of the near-meltdown on Wall Street caused by the subprime mortgage market. From June 2006 through April 2008 the Federal Reserve cut interest rates seven times. The central banks of Canada (an economy that catches cold when the United States sneezes) and the United Kingdom (which is fighting its own real estate bust) also cut interest rates. The European Central Bank, which takes a much tougher stance on inflation than the U.S. Federal Reserve, could normally be counted on for an interest rate increase even if European economies are slowing and a strong euro is creating problems for European exporters, but the debt market crisis put even that central bank on hold in early 2008.

At the same time, central banks in the United States and Europe flooded the financial markets with short-term cash beginning in August 2007 and continuing into 2008. The U.S. Federal Reserve has made extra short-term cash available to stressed lenders through special auctions of first $20 billion, then $30 billion, then $50 billion, and then on May 5 $75 billion of short-term loans, bringing the total to $175 billion. The European Central Bank trumped that figure when it lent out $502 billion in its own special auction. In December 2007 and January 2008 the central banks were worried that banks would stop lending in the critical end of the year period in order to dress up their own balance sheets so the Federal Reserve and the European Central Bank decided they had to supply the liquidity that banks wouldn't. In the first half of 2008 the central banks kept pumping money into the system because banks had started to hoard cash rather than lend it.

While the central banks are the high-profile lenders of last resort, other financial agencies are contributing their own river of cash to the flood. For example, while the Federal Reserve and the European Central Bank were getting the headlines, it was the little-known Federal Home Loan Bank system—a group of twelve private banks funded by thousands of financial institutions, set up in 1932 during the Depression—that kept the U.S. mortgage market from imploding. Data from the Federal Reserve show the home-loan banks made new loans to stressed mortgage lenders in 2007 of $235 billion.

Much of this money was called short-term—the Fed's special auctions offered loans for just 28 days, for example. The idea was that the central banks would sop up much of this extra cash when the short-term loans matured. By removing the money from the economy so quickly, the central banks would minimize the possibility that all this money would increase inflation. But as 2008 progressed short-term loans turned into long-term loans because the central banks just kept rolling over the loans every month. A good part of this cash was quickly becoming part of the long-term money supply.

Which turns this short-term money into a long-term inflation problem. First, since the economy can't quickly ramp up production to meet higher demand once the recession ends in 2009 or so, inflation results as a larger supply of money chases a limited supply of goods. And second, an increased money supply without a real increased demand for that extra money drives down the value of money. And then it takes more money to buy the same goods. Voilà—inflation.

It didn't help the long-term inflation picture that these developed economies or the global economy in general weren't exactly strapped for cash even before this crisis led Federal Reserve chairman Ben Bernanke and his peers at the world's other central banks to open the short-term floodgates. (Fed chairman Bernanke will quite possibly never live down his remark that all you needed to do to fight deflation was to have helicopters drop cash on the financial markets. Yes, not so long ago, back in 2001–2003, the big fear was that deflation, falling prices, would savage the world economy. That comment earned Bernanke the moniker "Helicopter Ben.")

In the first quarter of 2008, the U.S. money supply (as measured by M2, the broadest measure of money supply), for example, grew by an annualized 10.8 percent. Economic orthodoxy these days holds that a money supply growing faster than the economy produces inflation. U.S. economic growth in the first quarter of 2008 was an annualized 0.9 percent. Second quarter growth was 1.9 percent.

The European Central Bank added 20 percent to the money supply in the twelve months through April 2008, according to *Grant's Interest Rate Observer*. The European Union economy has grown by 2.6 percent in that time period.

But it's not just the developed economies of the world that have been pursuing inflationary monetary policies. In fact, the cash added by the Federal Reserve and the European Central Bank looks like small change compared to the money supply growth in the fastest-growing global economies. In China, money supply grew by an annual 16.7 percent rate in March 2008. That's down from an annual 18.5 percent rate in November 2007. In Russia the money supply grew by 50 percent in 2007, estimates Goldman Sachs, and in India the money supply was up 24 percent. By Goldman Sachs's estimate the average growth in money supply in developing economies was 21 percent in 2007.

Growth in the money supply at those kinds of rates exceeds even the growth rates for the fastest-growing of these economies. China's economy grew by 11 percent in 2007 while its money supply grew by 18 percent. Russia: 50 percent money supply growth and 6.2 percent economic growth. India: 24 percent money supply growth and 9 percent economic growth. That's inflationary.

Once inflation is loose in an economy it can take a long time to get it back under control. Inflation in China hit 6.5 percent in October 2007 and then kept right on climbing. In March 2008 inflation rose to 8.3 percent in China. The Russian Economic Development and Trade Ministry projected 2007 inflation of 7 percent to 8 percent, but actual inflation for 2007 came in at 11.9 percent, up from 9 percent in 2007. In the first quarter of 2008 inflation was running at an annualized rate of 12.5 percent. Inflation in India has come down to a 4.1 percent annual rate in January from a 7.3 percent annual rate in August. But that improvement looked more and more temporary as 2008 unfolded. In March wholesale prices, usually a good indicator of where consumer prices are headed, climbed at an annual 7 percent.

It increasingly looks as though what we're seeing in these countries isn't a onetime spike in inflation caused by a sudden increase in the price of rice or pork, but instead a long-term trend toward higher inflation that will take years to reverse.

I find additional support for that conclusion from the fact that these countries—well, China and India, anyhow—have actually been trying to fight inflation and failing to make much progress. If a government is putting reasonable inflation-fighting measures in place and yet inflation is barely budging, it's a pretty good indicator that inflation has got a grip on that economy for the long term.

China, for example, has been trying, and trying hard, to fight inflation. The People's Bank of China raised interest rates six times in 2007 to a one-year lending rate of 7.47 percent, the highest official rate since 1998. The central bank has also raised reserve requirements, the amount of capital that a bank is required to keep in reserve and that it therefore cannot lend, to 14.5 percent of deposits. The 1-percentage-point increase in reserve requirements announced on December 8, 2007, was the biggest jump in four years. The government also set tighter and tighter lending limits as the year progressed. In November 2007, seven banks, including the big Agricultural Bank of China, were prohibited from making any more new loans at all for the rest of 2007.

WHAT'S WORKED? NOTHING, REALLY

But nothing worked. Money supply kept growing. Inflation was surging.

Why not? When push comes to shove, the folks who run developing economies in China, Russia, Saudi Arabia, and elsewhere will risk almost anything to keep their economies growing. A growing economy means more jobs, fewer protesters in the street, and more years in power for the current leadership.

The best way to ensure continued fast growth is to make sure that your currency, whether yuan, rubles, or whatever, stays undervalued against the currencies of the countries that make up your big export markets. The last thing any of these governments want is for a falling U.S. dollar to set their own currencies appreciating and to make their exports more expensive. That would slow growth at home and result in fewer jobs. And that would be asking for political disaster.

Here's how a fall in the U.S. dollar is supposed to work. When the U.S. is running a big trade deficit, our trading partners wind up holding a larger number of U.S. dollars every month. A trade deficit means we're importing more goods and services than we export, and we wind up exporting dollars in order to pay for the excess goods. As those dollars build up overseas, governments, companies, and individuals recycle them by buying U.S. bonds and stocks and other assets. This increases the exposure of these overseas owners of dollars to the risks of the U.S. currency and U.S. asset markets. If the value of the dollar declines, their dollar-denominated investments will lose value as well.

At some point, these overseas owners of U.S. dollars start to demand higher returns—higher interest rates on Treasury bonds, for example—to offset that currency risk. Some may sell off a portion of their dollars, producing exactly the kind of fall in the currency that they had worried about in the first place, which leads again to a demand for higher returns. The higher interest rates demanded by overseas dollar holders finally start to slow economic growth in the United States. That slowdown, plus the higher prices consumers have to pay for imported goods because of the weak dollar, starts to take a painful bite out of the export revenue of our biggest trading partners.

Though a weaker dollar might be great medicine to reduce the U.S. trade deficit, it confronts our trading partners with a rather stark choice: they can let their currencies rise relative to the U.S. dollar or intervene in the currency markets to keep the value of their own currency relatively stable against the dollar.

Canada, our biggest trading partner, has let its currency rise. The Canadian dollar, the loonie (so called because it has a picture of a loon on it), reached parity with the U.S. dollar in 2007 and on some days exceeded its value by a few cents. That's a huge upward move—a 61 percent gain—for the Canadian currency, which was worth just 62 U.S. cents in 2002. That's a boon for Canadians who want to go on a shopping spree in the United States, but it's not such great news for the Canadian economy. Exports accounted for about one-third of Canada's $1.4 trillion GDP in 2007 with the U.S. taking about 80 percent of those exports, according to the *CIA World Fact Book.* But with the U.S. dollar falling against the Canadian dollar, everything that Canada exports to the United States has become more expensive. That has sent some U.S. customers scurrying to look for cheaper sources of supply, perhaps inside the United States. Canada's exports to the United States fell 2 percent in 2007.

Economic growth in Canada, which came in at 2.6 percent in 2006, climbed to 2.7 percent for all of 2007 but started to show signs of slowing in the second half of the year. By the fourth quarter of 2007 growth had dropped to an annualized 0.6 percent. No wonder that the Bank of Canada cut Canadian interest rates by one-quarter of a percentage point in January 2008 in order to keep the economy from slowing further. That month the bank lowered its projections for Canadian GDP growth in 2008 to 1.8 percent.

China has taken the opposite course and has opted to intervene in the financial markets to keep its currency stable. In July 2005, when China reformed its exchange-rate system to let the yuan move in a bigger price range against the U.S. dollar, it took 8.28 yuan to buy a dollar. On October 2, 2007, it took 7.51 yuan to buy a dollar. That's a move of just 9.3 percent. Over the same period, the Canadian dollar gained 23.5 percent against the U.S. dollar, and the euro gained 18 percent against the U.S. dollar.

Why did the Chinese currency stay so cheap relative to the dollar (and get cheaper versus the euro and Canadian dollar)? The Chinese central bank conducted massive dollar-buying sprees to keep the value of the dollar up versus the yuan.

Without intervention, the huge influx of U.S. dollars into the Chinese economy due to China's trade surplus with the United States would have depressed the value of the U.S. dollar against the yuan. Dollars would have been in such great supply relative to demand that the price of the currency would have dropped.

But the People's Bank of China took steps to make sure the drop was orderly and relatively minor. The bank bought U.S. dollars in China for yuan, removing some of the huge supply of dollars and keeping the price of the yuan from rising too rapidly against the dollar.

Just as choosing to let its currency rise cost the Canadian economy growth, trying to stabilize its currency came with its own set of costs for China. By buying dollars for yuan, the People's Bank was injecting huge amounts of yuan into its domestic economy. The bank tried to remove as much of that injection as it could—central bankers call this operation "sterilization"—by selling government bonds for yuan. That had the effect of removing yuan from the economy.

But it's just about impossible to run a completely successful sterilization: you never manage to sop up all the extra money. And in China that extra money has contributed to runaway growth in China's money supply. When money supply grows faster than a country's economy, the result is inflation, which is exactly what happened to China's economy.

Consumer inflation grew at a 4.4 percent annual rate in June 2007. Food was the big culprit, with the prices of eggs and pork jumping 20 percent from last year's prices. In response, the People's Bank ordered its fifth interest-rate increase since April 27, 2006. The 0.27-percentage-point increase on one-year bank-deposit interest rates and on commercial lending took the rate paid on deposits to 3.33 percent. The one-year lending rate climbed to 6.84 percent.

That didn't work. In August, the bank raised rates again. In September, the government reported that inflation for August had come in at a 6.5 percent annual rate. So on September 14, the People's Bank raised interest rates again, to 3.87 percent on one-year bank deposits and 7.29 percent on commercial loans. This interest rate hike and the final one of 2007 in December did start to slow inflation by mid-2008. Inflation in July fell to 6.3 percent. But that improvement is likely to be temporary. China's leaders started to talk of the need for more growth in August and actually cut rates in September.

In late 2007 and early 2008, in an attempt to tackle the underlying cause of China's inflation problem, the government allowed the yuan to appreciate much more quickly against the U.S. dollar. From January 1 through May 6, 2008, the yuan had climbed 4 percent against the U.S. dollar. That's a glacial rate of adjustment for many currencies, but for the Chinese yuan it's an extraordinary rate of appreciation. The inflation numbers in early 2008 showed that degree of currency appreciation is enough to make a difference in inflation. But by mid-2008, Beijing had reversed course on the yuan too.

Countries make economic decisions for all kinds of reasons. Few of

them are economic in the narrowest sense, and most of them are political in the largest sense. Canada has decided to sacrifice a bit of growth
and concentrate on fighting inflation, which has been stubbornly
above the 2 percent target set by the Canadian central bank. That's
politically feasible in Canada, where unemployment stood at 5.4 percent in February 2008, high by U.S. standards but the lowest in
Canada in thirty-three years, according to Lloyds TSB Bank.

China's government has apparently decided to sacrifice inflation to
growth. A 2 percent GDP growth rate in China would be regime sui-
cide. Millions of jobless workers would riot in the streets of Chinese
cities. A rate of growth near 8 percent would be ideal, Beijing's planners said at the beginning of 2007, because that is high enough to generate the jobs the country needs to stay even with its population
growth and low enough to keep the economy from further overheating. And if it's a question of erring on the side of more growth, rather
than gambling with the uncertainties of the effect of a stronger yuan on
exports—and jobs—then full steam ahead.

China isn't alone in deciding to sacrifice inflation to growth. Russia intervenes in the financial markets to prevent the ruble from appreciating too much against the dollar, for example. Countries such
as Kuwait and Saudi Arabia that peg their currency to the dollar are
pursing the same policy. (The Reserve Bank of India, which has a
tradition of independence, has been almost alone in letting its currency appreciate and aggressively using higher interest rates to slow
inflation. As a consequence, India has one of the lowest inflation
rates among developing economies—and an economy that is showing the most strain as the Indian rupee appreciates against the dollar.
The unfavorable shift in exchange rates has created a growth crisis
in the Indian information technology industry as companies such as
Infosys, Tata Consultancy, and Wipro find themselves hard-pressed
to compete with the prices offered by companies in Eastern Europe
and Vietnam. The Reserve Bank of India is facing increasing political pressure to do something about the rupee. The new head of the
bank, appointed in August 2008, is expected to be less vigilant
about inflation.)

This decision to trade high inflation for high growth has consequences that aren't limited to the national economies of China, Russia, and the rest of the developing world.

Faster growth in these developing economies creates more demand for commodities and drives up the global price for oil, corn, iron ore, soybeans, coal, cotton, nickel, and more. For example, China will import 415 million metric tons of iron ore in 2008, an increase of 11 percent from 2007, according to the China Iron and Steel Association. That comes on top of the 17.3 percent increase in iron ore imports in 2007.

The big three iron ore mining companies, BHP Billiton, Rio Tinto, and Vale, which produce 75 percent of the world's seaborne iron ore, are projected to increase production by 50 million tons in 2008. Assuming that other iron ore miners can increase production comparably, the global industry will increase production by about 62.5 million metric tons in 2008. But increased demand from China will eat up 65 percent of that new production. That leaves the steel industries in the rest of the world's growing economies to fight over a mere 22.5 million tons of new production. See why iron ore prices negotiated by Japan, Korea, and China increased another 70–97 percent in 2008?

The story isn't very different in any other globally traded commodity. As I point out in Chapter 7 on oil, Chapter 8 on natural resources, and Chapter 9 on food, global supply is stretched tight in most of these markets by soaring global demand. In a market as tight as this, global commodity producers have all the pricing power, so they are able—and more than willing—to pass on any increase in their costs to customers. That creates the kind of automatic inflationary loop that economists fear so much when they see it developing in the labor markets. But this time it's the producers of nickel, coal, oil, and wheat that are hiking prices to pass through their forecasts of future inflation.

This just about guarantees that those forecasts of higher inflation will be self-fulfilling prophecies.

How the Trends Play Out for Investors

- *This inflation in the developing markets—and its spillover into the global market—is intentional.* Inflation in China, Russia, and elsewhere isn't a policy mistake; it's the inevitable fallout of a policy decision to go for the growth. That means a key driver of global inflation—the huge increase in global money supply coming from developing economies—will cease only when policy changes in these countries. I don't know about you, but I wouldn't bet that any government in the developing world is ready to sacrifice growth—and its own hold on power—to the battle for lower inflation anytime soon. (Look back at U.S. history. In the nineteenth century that developing economy was more than happy to grow as fast as it could and was constantly looking for ways to escape the monetary discipline imposed by a global gold standard. The United States was perfectly willing to see international creditors pay the costs—in bankruptcy and depreciating currencies—for its manifestly destined growth.)

- *Rising global commodity prices are a major consequence of this decision to trade higher growth for lower inflation.* Higher prices for oil, soybeans, nickel, and so on are a major mechanism for turning local developing-economy inflation into inflation in the global economy. The pricing power developing-economy growth gives to commodity producers creates a commodity price spiral that gives inflation strong momentum.

- I haven't even talked in this chapter about *the influence of an aging world on inflation.* See Chapter 5 on demographics and finance for a full discussion of that topic. Suffice it to say here that inflation is perhaps the only way that developed economies have to pay the massive obligations they've built up to their retired populations. The need to pay those obligations just about guarantees huge domestic budget deficits in those economies that will be an additional source of global inflation over the coming decades. Of course, courageous politicians could decide to tell an aging electorate that there's no money to pay the bills and that retirees will have to get by with lower benefits and less health care instead, but I wouldn't hold my breath. There's no reason to think that developed-economy politicians are any less able to see their own self-interest and act on it—long-term consequences be damned—than developing-economy politicians are.

• *Higher inflation, for the three preceding reasons, is a long-term trend.* I don't know if this cycle toward higher inflation will last as long as the previous thirty-year cycle of lower inflation, but I think it's a good bet that we're looking at a trend more likely to run ten years than it is to run five.

TREND BREAKERS AND TREND MAKERS RIPPED FROM THE HEADLINES

TREND BREAKERS

• *Watch Europe's economies,* especially Italy and France, for signs that developed-economy politicians are showing signs of anti-inflationary zeal. An outbreak of fiscal discipline in these countries would be a sign that inflation might not gallop ahead as fast as I've projected here. Italy and France have some of the most generous retirement benefits in the world—in Italy, even after a recent decision to add a year to the deadline, the retirement age in 2008 is fifty-eight—and neither can afford to actually pay these benefits without a big increase in budget deficits that are already pushing against European Union limits. I expect the governments will keep running the printing presses; but, hey, it's unlikely, but politicians could find some backbone and slow down my projections for the growth of inflation.

• *China could get serious about inflation* now that the world's spotlight has shifted from the Beijing Olympics. Remain skeptical, however, until you see the People's Bank of China raise bank deposit rates high enough so that Chinese savers actually earn a yield above inflation for keeping their money in the bank. Only a move like that will take the heat out of the overinflated asset markets in China.

• *Signs that the U.S. economy is slipping into an extended honest-to-goodness recession in 2008–9* rather than the two-quarter slowdown or short recession Wall Street was expecting as late as mid-2008. A big enough slowdown in the United States would take pressure off global commodity prices. On the other hand, a U.S. slowdown might not take as much pressure off global prices as economists project because a weaker U.S. dollar would give emerging-economy exporters even more incentive to suppress appreciation in their own currencies.

• Could we get *a serious rally in the U.S. dollar?* Some currency experts see a real dollar rally—as opposed to seasonal blips such as those the dollar sees in January of most years or the fight-to-the-dollar rally of the third quarter of 2008—as possible in 2011 or so. A turn in the dollar would likely mark a correction to a falling market that has pushed the dollar down too far and too fast. Markets always move too far to the upside in the rally and too far to the downside on a plunge. A dollar rally after a fall of the recent magnitude has historically resulted in a 25 percent or better jump in price in the first year of the rally. That's enough to put an end, temporarily at least, to the rally in gold prices.

TREND MAKERS

• *Japan's government is likely to be the first of the developed economies to give up on all budget restraint and adopt inflation as an unofficial policy for solving their demographic crisis.* Japan is the fastest-aging of the developed economies, the country with the biggest budget deficit as a percentage of gross domestic product, and the one where individuals have the least saved for retirement.

• *Signs that the Federal Reserve and the European Central Bank have moved goosing economic growth ahead of fighting inflation.* The Federal Reserve by law is supposed to worry about both employment and inflation; the European Central Bank's mandate is more narrowly focused on sound money. The odds are that the Federal Reserve will cave first. But if the European Central Bank follows suit, inflation could kick up to higher levels than anyone now expects.

• *Pressure from Congress and the White House on the U.S. Federal Reserve to use higher inflation as a way out of the home mortgage crisis in the United States.* A rise in nominal home values, even if it is only due to inflation, would increase the odds that stressed home owners could refinance their adjustable-rate mortgages before they reset at higher interest rates. Of course, higher inflation would mean higher home mortgage rates, but a refinancing would at least buy home owners a couple of years' grace before the roof fell in again. The move wouldn't fix the problem, merely spread it out over more years, but it's politically attractive nonetheless.

• *Signs that the Democrats' recent rhetoric about budget restraint and "pay-as-you-go" turns out to be only rhetoric* if they get real operational control of the Senate in the 2008 elections. Nobody expects much in the way of sound fiscal policy from Washington, but it would still ratchet up inflationary expectations to see nobody in Congress trying to hold any budget line.

STOCK PICKS THAT PUT THE WIND FROM THOSE TRENDS AT YOUR BACK

BHP Billiton (NYSE ADR: BHP) is an Australian mining company with a finger in everything from copper to uranium. With this one pick, you can give your portfolio exposure to most industrial commodities and to a natural-resource economy that's likely to make the Australian dollar one of the world's best currencies over the next decade or more. In fiscal 2007 BHP (the company's fiscal year ends in June) got about 27 percent of its revenue from copper, silver, zinc, gold, and lead mining. Iron ore and other metals used in stainless steel (nickel, for instance), two other key inflation commodities, made up 26.3 percent of revenue. The company's Australian base gives it a natural platform for exports to the fast-growing inflation leaders China and India.

Goldcorp (NYSE: GG). Goldcorp has got the two qualities that you're looking for in a gold mining company and its stock. First, it's a low-cost producer; in fact, by my calculations, it's *the* low-cost producer among big gold companies. Cash costs of production at the Canadian company have been steady or actually falling in recent quarters thanks to the high-grade ores in the company's mines. It costs less to produce gold when there's more gold in each ton of rock and you have to refine less ore to get at it. Cash costs in the company's gold operations—that's costs net of sales of copper and silver—were $240 an ounce for the first quarter of 2008. Not bad when gold is selling for $850 an ounce. Second, the company is expanding production. The company has a solid pipeline of new mines with high-grade ore set to go into production in 2008 and 2009. Goldcorp's big Penasquito mine in Mexico remains on schedule for the first gold pour from ore in 2008. The company has upgraded proven and probable reserves for the mine to 13 million ounces of gold and 864 million ounces of silver. Gold production is projected to climb by 30 percent in 2008, according to Canadian investment dealer Canaccord Adams, and to increase further in 2010 as other new mines go into production or older mines expand.

Kinross Gold (NYSE: KGC). Kinross Gold has merged its way from junior to senior status. The Canadian company has a higher cash cost of production—an estimated $365–$375 an ounce in 2008—than Goldcorp. But Kinross Gold makes up for that with big gains in production in 2008 and 2009. According to Canaccord Adams, those new operations will push gold production at Kinross Gold to 1.92 million ounces in 2008, up from 1.6 million ounces in 2007. That's a 20 percent increase in gold production. In 2009, predicts Macquarie Research, the research arm of the Australian investment bank, production will climb by more than 30 percent from 2008 levels as expansion at the company's Brazilian mine Paracatu and new mines in Russia (Kupol) and Chile (Cerro Casale) add to gold output.

Rayonier (NYSE: RYN) owns, controls, or leases about 2.7 million acres of timberland in the United States and New Zealand. About 400,000 acres in the United States are what's known as higher-and-better-use land more valuable for development than it is as timberland. Rayonier owns about 200,000 acres of higher-and-better-use land in the Georgia-Florida coastal corridor. Recently—even in the middle of the home building crash—the Florida-headquartered company sold

3,100 acres of that for about $15,000 an acre. But you can pick it up for way less by buying shares of Rayonier. At a December 30, 2007, price of $47 a share, my estimate of 400,000 higher-and-better-use acres means that by buying Rayonier shares, you can buy an acre of Rayonier's land holdings for $9,300. See the potential for some real estate appreciation here? The deal is actually even better than that since my calculation didn't give any value to rest of the company's operations— the production of lumber, pulp, and fibers. And it's the company's other business that are generating the cash to pay investors a 4.25 percent dividend (as of the end of 2007). That's important because it means you get paid better than 4 percent on your money while you wait for the end of the housing bust and recovery of the land market in 2009 or so. Rayonier's timber-to-wood-products businesses are themselves good plays on the rising demand for paper, wood products, and timber as economies such as China's and India's accelerate.

Tejon Ranch (NYSE: TRC). Raw land, despite the 2007 meltdown in the housing market, is a great way to profit from inflation. As they say, God isn't making any more land, so the world has got a limited supply and increasing demand. And you know what that does to the price of a commodity over time. But that saying is even more true if we're talking about land within commuting distance of Los Angeles. California-based Tejon Ranch owns about 270,000 acres sixty miles north of Los Angeles and within spitting distance of Interstate 5. The company raises cattle, grapes, almonds, and pistachios on the land but has plans to turn some of it into commercial development and three residential communities. In May 2008, Tejon Ranch and a coalition of environmental groups announced an agreement that would conserve 240,000 acres of the company's 270,000 acres but permit development to go ahead on the remaining 30,000. At the stock's closing price on May 8, investors were getting an acre of developable land for about $23,800 when they bought shares in the company. No dividend with this one. You'll just have to be patient and let time—and inflation—work for you.

Stocks for Building an Overweight Position in This Sector

- **Deltic Timber** (NYSE: DEL) is an Arkansas timber-to-real-estate player that's a smaller Rayonier. The company owns 436,000 acres of timberland—and two sawmills—in Arkansas and northern Louisiana with real estate development centered on Little Rock and Hot Springs. The company's land also overlays part of the Fayetteville Shale natural gas formation, and the company started to receive royalty payments from gas wells on that land in 2007.

- **Freeport McMoRan Copper and Gold** (NYSE: FCX) recently announced plans to increase copper production by 25 percent and molybdenum production by 42 percent by 2010. The Phoenix-headquartered company expects to sell 1.4 million ounces of gold in 2008.

- **Plum Creek Timber** (NYSE: PCL) is another timberland-to-real-estate development opportunity. The Seattle-headquartered company owns 8.2 million acres of timberland. As of May 2008 the shares paid a 4 percent dividend.

Mutual Funds and ETFs (Exchange-Traded Funds)

- **Central Fund of Canada** (CEF), a passively managed closed-end fund that invests in gold and silver bullion, gives you the ability to buy gold and silver bullion without the worry of where to store the metals. Since this is a closed-end fund—which means the fund issued only a limited number of shares at its initial public offering and no more are created even as money flows into the fund—it can trade at either a premium or discount to the value of the gold and silver the fund holds. The premium and discount reflect the temporary popularity of gold and silver bullion with investors. Buy at a discount if you can.

- **StreetTracks Gold** (GLD) is an ETF that, like the closed-end Central Fund, aims to track the price of gold by holding gold bullion. No worries about premiums or discounts to asset value when you buy this one, but never a bargain either.

7

ENERGY

As the World Runs Out of Cheap Oil

In THE WEEK OF APRIL 14, 2008, RUSSIA, THE WORLD'S SECOND largest oil producer, announced that its oil production had declined by 1 percent in the first quarter of 2008, and Mexico, the second-largest source of oil imports by the United States in 2007, reported that its oil production had tumbled by almost 8 percent in the first quarter of the year.

And the problem isn't limited to Russia and Mexico. The International Energy Agency estimates that production from existing oil fields is declining annually by about 4.5 million barrels a day. Just to stay even, the world needs to find that much new oil.

But global demand for oil is also growing. Recently world demand for oil has grown by about 2 percent annually—that means the world needs to produce about 1.75 million barrels a day more each year than last. So staying even really requires new production of about 6.25 million barrels a year.

If you understand why the world's oil companies are finding it increasingly difficult to meet that goal, you understand why oil hit a record $147 a barrel in July 2008, up more than 100 percent from

April 2006, and why I think that oil could well hit $180 a barrel within two years of the publication of this book.

You'll understand why even near recession in the United States, an economic slowdown in Europe, and a return to recession in Japan have only temporarily dented oil prices. Even with all that economic slowing taking place, on October 1, 2008, oil still traded at $100 a barrel. That's a 40 percent increase from the price just a year earlier. Imagine what will happen to oil prices when those economies recover and the oil industry suddenly has to ramp up the new production that it shut down when oil prices were *just* $100 a barrel. Remember, when you track a volatile commodity such as oil, it's the long-term trend in prices rather than the monthly ups and downs that's important.

And you'll understand why owning the right kind of energy stocks—the shares of companies that are fighting to expand global oil production—is essential if you want your portfolio to beat the stock market indexes over the next ten years.

Let's start by looking at the story of a single oil field. If you understand the continuing crisis at Mexico's giant Cantarell oil field, the second-largest by production in the world, you'll understand about 75 percent of what you need to understand to make money from the continuing climb in global energy prices.

The Cantarell Oil Field Is Dying

Production from Cantarell fell by 12 percent in 2006 and another 15 percent in 2007, and Pemex, Mexico's national oil company, has warned that production could drop another 20 percent in 2008. Even if Pemex radically steps up its investment in the field, production from Cantarell will fall by 10 percent annually until it hits just 700,000 barrels a day by 2012, a level significantly below the 2 million barrels a day that the Cantarell field produced in January 2006.

Replacing the oil from Cantarell from other fields in Mexico is an almost impossible task for Pemex. According to Pemex, production at the country's second-largest field, Ku-Maloob-Zaap, one of the twenty largest fields in the world, will climb to 800,000 barrels a day by 2009 from 500,000 barrels a day now. That's not enough to offset the 600,000 barrels a day in production that Pemex believes it will lose from Cantarell during those years—and remember that estimate depends on Pemex getting all the capital it needs for new technology to slow the decline at Cantarell. Ku-Maloob-Zaap itself will go into production decline by 2011, and by 2021 production will have fallen by about 300,000 barrels a day from the field's peak.

Any oil that Pemex finds to replace Cantarell's declining production will be much more expensive to produce. For example, developing the massive Chicontepec onshore field in eastern Mexico, according to Pemex, will require the drilling of 13,500 to 20,000 wells at a cost of $30 billion to $38 billion over the next fifteen years—or about a thousand new wells a year, about 33 percent more wells than Pemex drilled in all its oil fields in 2007—in order to tap the oil found in isolated pockets below 14,000 square miles of surface. In contrast, Cantarell's oil is in a concentrated reserve that takes up just 70 square miles. Fully tapping Cantarell required just 208 wells.

All that investment would expand production at Chicontepec to 600,000 barrels a day from 30,000 barrels a day now.

Mexico's oil production, which peaked at 3.4 million barrels a day in 2004, fell to 2.9 million barrels in 2007. Proven reserves have tumbled to 14.7 billion barrels in 2007, which the government reports is just 9.2 years of production. At current levels of investment in production, Mexico, the tenth-largest oil exporter in the world, exporting 1.7 million barrels a day in 2008, could become a net oil importer within the next ten to twenty years.

Cantarell and Mexico aren't isolated examples. In 2004 Indonesia went from being a net exporter of oil to a net importer. Kuwait announced a cut in forecast peak production in November 2005 at its Burgan oil field, the second-largest in the world by reserves, to 1.7 million barrels a day from the previous forecast of 2 million barrels a day. In 2006 oil production fell by 6.9 percent in Norway and 10 percent in the United Kingdom, which shares declining North Sea oil fields with Norway. The United Kingdom went briefly from net exporter to net importer in the second quarter of 2006 before returning to the net exporter column. By the end of 2007, though, the Oil Depletion Analysis Center expected the country to slip permanently into the importer column in the near future. In 2006 production declined an estimated 5 percent in Venezuela, according to the International Energy Agency. Global oil supply was static or actually fell in the first three quarters of 2007 before rebounding in the fourth and then falling in the first quarter of 2008 in both Mexico and Russia.

In July 2007, the International Energy Agency, in its *Oil Market Report*, projected that a tight oil market would get even tighter over the next five years. In the year since the report the problem has worsened. Supply from such non-OPEC oil producers as Mexico, the United Kingdom, and Norway is falling even faster than predicted a year ago.

The agency was counting on production increases from Russia, Nigeria, and Saudi Arabia to pick up the slack and keep growth ahead of demand. But that doesn't seem to be happening. Russia, which the agency projected would be able to increase production by 5 percent by 2012, reported a decline in early 2008. Russia's a good indicator of the likely shortfall in oil production from oil-producing countries outside of OPEC. Total non-OPEC production is projected to climb by just 1 percent annually from 2007 to 2012. That's a significant comedown from the 1.4 percent annual growth in non-OPEC production from 2000 to 2007.

The supply situation isn't any brighter inside OPEC. In Nigeria, a third of the country's oil output by 2015 is at risk, energy advisors to Nigerian president Umaru Yar'Adua have warned, because the government hasn't been paying its share of the costs of joint ventures—about $3 billion to date—with Royal Dutch Shell, ExxonMobil, and Chevron. If the government's failure to pay puts the joint ventures in jeopardy, Nigeria can kiss plans to double its current production goodbye. Instead total oil and gas production will fall by 30 percent by 2015. And Saudi Arabia announced in April 2008 that it sees no need to invest in expanding production further after new fields come into production in 2009.

The best case, the International Energy Agency calculates, will leave supply growing at about 1 percent annually from 2007 to 2012. Even that might be optimistic, though, since global oil production grew by just 0.4 percent in 2006.

Which creates just a teeny-weeny problem, since the agency projects that demand will grow by 2.2 percent a year during that 2007–2012 span. If that strikes you as a sure recipe for higher and still higher oil prices, even from the current painful levels, I think you're dead right.

So How Did the World Get to This Latest Stage in the Oil Squeeze?

Let's go back to Cantarell to see. When the Mexican fisherman Rudesindo Cantarell discovered the field named after him in the shallow waters of the Gulf of Mexico in 1971, the first well drilled was an actual gusher. The oil in the field was under so much pressure that this first well produced 36,000 barrels of oil a day instead of the 200–300 barrels a day at the average well. By 1980 Pemex had sunk more than two hundred wells and Cantarell was pumping more than 1 million barrels a day. Production peaked at 2.3 million barrels a day in 2004.

But serious problems were building up under the surface. As Pemex pumped more and more oil out of the superconcentrated Cantarell field, pressure in the field began to drop. Beginning in 1998 Pemex injected nitrogen gas into the rocks in an effort to keep pressure up. Still, Pemex has to pump the oil to the surface now. But that wasn't the big problem. Even with the extra pressure, more and more water began to seep into the field and find its way into Pemex's oil wells.

That's a common problem in older oil fields, and oil companies have learned to deal with it by buying and installing expensive pumping and separation equipment to divide the water from the oil in the flow from a well. Some of the oldest wells still producing in Texas can deal with flow that's 99 percent water.

But Pemex didn't have the money to invest in this basic technology.

In Mexico Pemex is not only a sacred cow, a symbol of the country's economic independence from the United States, but also a cash cow. The capital budget of the national oil company is set by politicians in Mexico City eager to grab as much of the company's revenue as possible for the national budget. Pemex right now provides about 40 percent of total government income. Without the cash to invest in water separation technology, Pemex simply shut any well in the Cantarell field as soon as water content climbed to 5 percent.

In response to the crisis, the Mexican government has upped Pemex's capital budget. In 2007 Pemex invested $2.3 billion in Cantarell, and in 2008 it plans to invest $5 billion more. A new water separation plant will let Pemex handle well output with as much as 9 percent water. The company began drilling its first horizontal wells in 2006 in an effort to get more oil out of the Cantarell formation. In 2007 Pemex drilled five new development wells at Cantarell and repaired nine major wells. In 2008 the company will complete a nitrogen recovery plant at the field that will make it easier and less expensive to inject nitrogen gas to increase pressure in the field. All that should slow the decline of production at Cantarell. Pemex projects that production will decline by only 200,000 to 300,000 barrels a day in 2008, about half the decline projected without these steps. But that will still leave production on track to fall to 700,000 barrels a day by 2012 from 1.5 million barrels a day in 2007.

To make up for that decline Pemex will spend $2.4 billion on its second largest field, Ku-Maloob-Zaap, to increase nitrogen injection and water separation. That boosted production to 500,000 barrels a day by the end of 2007 from 496,000 barrels a day at the beginning of the year. Why so little bang for those pesos? Because Ku-Maloob-Zaap is itself on the edge of a decline that will begin in 2011, according to Pemex.

To offset the decline of the two fields Pemex will turn to Chicontepec, an onshore field discovered in the 1920s. Pemex hasn't exploited that find to date because, unlike the concentrated oil of Cantarell, the oil in Chicontepec is scattered in smaller pockets spread over thousands of square miles.

But the most damaging underinvestment may be in new oil discovery technology. For example, in November 2007 the company announced the discovery of what may be a new reserve in the deep water of the Gulf of Mexico with as much as 200 million barrels of oil. Confirming that discovery would require seismic studies and test wells drilled at the edge of current deep-water drilling technology. Outside industry experts doubt that Pemex has the in-house expertise to perform and analyze those studies and to drill the required test well.

So why doesn't Pemex farm out the work?

Because despite revenues of nearly $105 billion in 2007, Pemex may simply not have the money. The national oil company pays out 60 percent of its revenue as royalties and taxes to fund the national budget, and so in 2007 Pemex showed a loss of $1.5 billion on that $105 billion in revenue. Consequently, Pemex has been forced to borrow to fund its capital budget, and the company now owes $43 billion. With so much money going to the national coffers, some debtors are already worried about the company's ability to service that debt. In November 2007 Fitch, one of the three major debt rating companies, raised a red flag about Pemex's debt levels.

Pemex also can't strike a partnership with one of the major Western oil companies to trade a share of its oil flow for capital and technology. Pemex is constitutionally prohibited from taking on other oil companies as joint venture partners in oil exploration and production. Relatively minor changes to the law that would allow Pemex to form partnerships with outside experts in deep-water drilling bogged down in Mexico's Congress after opponents of Mexican president Felipe Calderón charged they amounted to a backdoor giveaway of the country's patrimony.

Pemex faces estimated capital needs of $70 billion to $100 billion in the remainder of this decade.

The issues facing Pemex at Cantarell are facing other oil companies in oil fields from the North Sea to Kuwait to Siberia. While the details vary, the basic situation is similar across the global oil industry. It's why oil prices are so high now and why they're headed still higher.

THE BIGGER PICTURE HAS TWO PARTS

One part of the picture is called "peak oil," a theory put forward by American oil geologist King Hubbert, who accurately predicted in 1956 that U.S. oil production would peak in the late 1960s or early 1970s. It begins with the straightforward premise that easy-to-find oil reserves are found first, and easy-to-produce oil is produced first. As global oil production matures, oil becomes harder to find; discoveries are smaller and in less accessible regions or geologic formations. Producing oil from these new discoveries costs more.

At the same time as global oil production matures, producing oil from existing fields also gets more difficult and more expensive. Cantarell, for example, may start off gushing oil to the surface, but as any field ages, producing oil requires increased pumping, the injection of water or nitrogen gas to add pressure to the reservoir to make up for the drop in pressure as oil is removed from the reservoir, and then finally, as water seeps into the oil deposits, increasing separation of water and oil. Peak oil theory stresses that recovering the last oil also requires more technology, more equipment, and more dollars than recovering the first barrel, and that it's never possible to recover 100 percent of all the oil in a field. Primary recovery, the easy part, extracts a quarter of the original oil. The technologies called secondary recovery—which most commonly involve pumping water into the field to increase pressures and then separating the water from the oil—still leaves about 50 percent of the oil in the ground.

The newest techniques of enhanced recovery—replacing water with nitrogen, carbon dioxide, polymers, solvents, or steam—still leave 30 percent to 40 percent of the original oil in the ground.

And, peak oil theory notes, much of that oil will stay in the ground. The water floods of secondary recovery—and in some fields water is used in even primary production—isolate the oil remaining in the rock into droplets. Even the newest techniques of enhanced recovery can't do much with oil that's been dispersed in this way.

Look around, say the proponents of peak oil theory. Doesn't it describe what you see? Cantarell, the world's second largest field, is in decline. Kuwait's Burgan field, another top-five field, is showing signs of maturity. The world's biggest field, Ghawar in Saudi Arabia, either already is in decline or is likely to start to decline within a decade. Since 1990 only one new field, Kahagan in Kazakhstan, has been discovered that might pump more than 500,000 barrels a day at its peak. Peak oil believers say conventional global oil production has already peaked or will do so soon.

Well, sometimes you see only what you want to see, the opponents of peak oil theory often retort. Peak oil theory doesn't want to see the way that, as prices go up, it becomes profitable to exploit unconventional oil deposits, such as Canada's huge oil sands reserves. And it becomes profitable to find substitutes for oil, such as ethanol or biodiesel. This postpones the day of peak oil, perhaps indefinitely.

Or, opponents also point out, consider the way that technology has indeed expanded supply. The percentage of wells drilled that actually go into production climbed in the 1990s to 45 percent from 25 percent. New enhanced production technology has increased the amount of oil that is actually recovered from an oil field to as high as 60 percent in some cases from 20 percent just a decade or two ago. Opponents say that oil production will grow until 2040 or 2050 as new technology opens up new sources of production or gets more out of existing fields.

But I think the controversy—and it often hinges on niggling disputes over the exact definition of "conventional" oil—over an exact date is largely beside the point. Here's the key insight of peak oil theory: as the production peak approaches, the price of oil rises, even with the development of unconventional sources of oil and substitutions, because these new sources and substitutes are more expensive to produce than oil used to be. If they weren't, they would have already been in production during the days of cheap oil. In effect, the rise of oil prices in peak oil theory creates a price floor for these new sources. As the floor moves up—to $40 from $30 oil, for example, and then to $60 oil—new sources and substitutes become profitable. That slows the price rise predicted by peak oil. But it doesn't reverse it because it is the rising price of oil that brings these new sources into production.

You can see this trend all over the world. Production costs at new conventional fields are startlingly large. Brazil's new field, Carioca, announced in April 2008, may contain as much as 9 billion barrels of recoverable oil. (To put that in context, proven U.S. oil reserves total 20 billion barrels.) Last year Brazil announced the discovery of the Tupi field with a potential 5 to 8 billion recoverable barrels. Eventually Brazil could wind up producing 3 million barrels a day, as much as today's Venezuela or Mexico.

Eventually.

Getting oil out of Carioca will require oil companies to drill through 6,500 feet of water, and then through 9,800 feet of rock and sand, and then through another 6,500 feet of salt. That's possible with cutting-edge current technology, but it's mighty expensive. Estimates for fully developing the Tupi field, which involves similarly challenging geology, run to about $50 billion. Count on a decade before these fields reach full production.

Unconventional sources are even more expensive. Production costs at Canada's oil sands are creeping upward toward $65 a barrel.

The higher costs are even hitting the Saudis. Through most of the 1990s it cost Aramco, the Saudi national oil company, about $4,000 to add one barrel of daily oil production capacity. It now costs closer to $16,000 to add a barrel of daily production.

You can debate whether the world is running out of oil all you want. It is certain, however, that the world has run out of cheap oil.

The second part of the bigger oil picture is politics. As the Cantarell story shows so clearly, geology can't be clearly separated from politics. Pemex is a national oil company and it must make decisions about production, exploration, investment, partnerships, and technology purchases with an eye on the political agenda in Mexico City—exactly as the national oil companies in Algeria, Russia, Iran, Kuwait, Nigeria, Angola, Venezuela, Kazakhstan, and other oil-rich countries make decisions about those same issues with a finger to the political winds.

Which wouldn't matter so much except that national oil companies are going to be the dominant players in the global oil industry
over the next thirty years. The International Energy Agency estimates
that over the last thirty years, 40 percent of global oil production came
from publicly traded companies—ExxonMobil, Chevron, Royal
Dutch Shell, BP, and the like. Over the next thirty years, the organization estimates, 90 percent of global oil production will come from national oil companies.

We're used to thinking of ExxonMobil as the giant of the oil industry.
And indeed the company has a huge level of reserves, about 11.2 billion
barrels of proven reserves, according to Energy Intelligence Research.

But that makes the company only number twelve in the world. And
every company ahead of it in the rankings is an oil company controlled
by a national government, including Russia's Gazprom at number
nine with 19 billion barrels, Venezuela's PDVSA at number five with
77 billion barrels, and Iran's NOIC at number two with 133 billion
barrels. Saudi Arabia's Aramco is number one with 263 billion barrels
of proven reserves.

It is impossible, of course, to predict where the world's undiscovered reserves are—that's why they're undiscovered, after all—but the
oil industry's oddsmakers point to the border between Saudi Arabia
and Kuwait, areas around the Caspian Sea belonging to Iran,
Venezuela's Orinoco River Basin, and Russia's Siberian north.

Oil supply optimists such as Daniel Yergin's Cambridge Energy
Research Associates calculate that the world will be able to raise oil
production by as much as 15 million barrels a day by 2010. That
would be an increase of 18 percent from 2005 production of 82 million barrels a day. If the International Energy Agency's projection that
global oil demand will grow by 1.6 percent a year during this period is
accurate, then that increase in supply would be more than enough to
meet global oil demand.

But that increased production will have to come from the big
proven and unproven reserves on territories controlled by national oil
companies that increasingly exclude the big international oil companies. Iran, for example, hopes to increase production from roughly 4

million barrels a day in 2005 to 5.6 million barrels a day in 2010. Venezuela's Orinoco River Basin contains an estimated 235 billion barrels of heavy oil—unproven reserves equal to 90 percent of Saudi Arabia's proven reserves. And Russia effectively controls access to increased production from the nations of Central Asia.

The national oil companies want to find all those reserves, develop them, and sell oil and gas to the rest of the world. The economies of Russia, Iran, Indonesia, Venezuela, Saudi Arabia, and the rest of the world's oil producers are as hooked on oil production as the developed and developing world is on oil consumption.

But standing in the way of turning those underground reserves into actual oil production is what I'd call the Pemex problem. Remember that Pemex wants to find and pump new oil and gas to replace declining production from Cantarell, but the company doesn't have the cash or the technology to do the job. Well, Pemex isn't alone among the world's national oil companies. It's a problem not just for the Mexican oil industry but for national producers in Iran, Venezuela, Russia— anywhere that the easy oil has been pumped and where getting more oil out of aging reserves and new deposits requires new and expensive technology. And that is just about everywhere.

For example, the Pemex problem has shown up in Russia recently. Russia's older western Siberian fields are in decline, following the path of such older fields as the North Sea. Russia has promising fields in eastern Siberia, but developing those is expensive. The fields are hundreds of miles from anywhere, meaning that getting workers and equipment to the fields and then supporting them in one of the world's more hostile climates is expensive. And then there's the additional cost of getting the oil and natural gas from remote wellheads to market.

How expensive is expensive? The eastern Siberian Sakhalin 1 project, on an island off Russia's Pacific coast, started producing oil in 2007, and production has now ramped up to 250,000 barrels a day. ExxonMobil, its Russian partner Rosneft Oil, and the rest of the Sakhalin 1 consortium invested $12 billion in that project. The Russian government used the excuse of rising costs to pull the plug on

Royal Dutch Shell as the lead developer of Sakhalin 2 (in favor of Russian players) when Shell's cost estimates for developing that field climbed to $20 billion from an original $10 billion.

Leonid Fedun, vice president of Lukoil, Russia's largest independent oil company, recently estimated that Russia needs to invest $1 trillion over the next twenty years to keep production in the current range of 8.5 million to 9 million barrels a day.

It's never exactly easy to find $1 trillion in investment capital, but the Russian government has made it hard for the oil industry in that country to attract even a small part of that capital. The Kremlin has structured taxes so that most of the extraordinary rise in oil prices flows into government coffers and not into oil company profits. When oil rises above $27 a barrel, the government takes 80 percent of any additional revenue in taxes. That means at $67 a barrel an oil company gets just $8 more a barrel in revenue than at $27. If the price climbs to $107 a barrel, the oil company's extra revenue increases by just $16 a barrel from what it was at $27 a barrel.

Sound like a replay of the problems that Pemex is facing in Mexico? Exactly.

The International Energy Agency estimates that the world needs to invest $2.2 trillion in building oil infrastructure over the next thirty years. Nobody knows exactly how much the national oil companies are spending—as opposed to how much they announce that they're spending—but the fear is that it isn't enough by a long shot.

This about finishes the picture from the supply side. Pretty gloomy, huh? It does all add up to higher prices in the oil market even after the run-up that took oil from $15 a barrel in 1986 to more than $140 in early 2008 and then back down to $70—temporarily, I'm afraid.

And remember that this is just 75 percent of the story. Understanding Cantarell—and expanding the lessons of that example to the rest of the world—tells you just about everything you need to know about global oil supplies. The other 25 percent of the oil story concerns the demand side. And here the news isn't any better if you're a consumer hoping for lower oil prices in the future. But the gloomy news is potentially very profitable for investors. Demand from the developed and developing world's economies will keep driving up oil consumption even as oil prices rise.

THE PICTURE'S JUST AS GRIM ON THE DEMAND SIDE

On the demand end, higher oil prices have so far *not* led to lower consumption. As oil and gasoline get more expensive, people use less, economic theory says. But not this time. Or at least not by very much. The slowdown in the U.S. economy and higher prices have reduced U.S. oil and gasoline consumption, for example—the Energy Information Agency estimates that gasoline consumption in the United States will fall by just about 1 percent in 2008. (That's a bigger swing than it looks like because gasoline consumption in the United States has risen 1 percent to 2 percent annually in recent years.)

Why? Lot of reasons. Not everyone is convinced that high prices are here to stay, so changing behavior radically doesn't seem worth it. A lot of consumption is built into the infrastructure of how we live: if you've got to drive to work, you've got to drive to work. Reducing consumption can require a long lead time: the next car purchased will be more fuel-efficient. Some consumption is subsidized, so higher prices haven't yet fully hit the market in places such as Iran, Venezuela, and China. And in the United States, which accounts for 25 percent of global oil consumption, we still don't have a national program to reduce demand for oil. The United States today uses 15 percent more oil than in 2000.

But the biggest addition to global demand comes from the developing economies of the world. A lot of consumers in China and India and elsewhere are just now getting paid enough to join the global market for cars, electrical appliances, air travel, and . . . So, for example, oil consumption in China is growing between 5 percent and 6 percent a year. Between 2000 and 2006, when global oil demand grew by 8 million barrels a day, demand growth from China alone accounted for about 32 percent of the total increase, according to the International

Energy Agency. (The United States, in contrast, accounted for 12.5 percent of global demand growth during those years.)

But the increased demand for oil isn't limited to China and India. There's another group of countries that when it comes to global growth in oil demand has been more important than the United States and only slightly less important than China. From 2000 through 2006 OPEC countries themselves accounted for 22 percent of global growth in oil demand. OPEC countries' consumption has been growing at two and a half times the rate of global consumption.

From 2000 through 2006 oil consumption by the OPEC countries climbed by 1.8 million barrels a day, or 29 percent. Consumption is projected to climb by another 400,000 barrels a day in 2008. Oil consumption by OPEC countries will grow by 5 percent to 6 percent a year over the next five years, the International Energy Agency projects.

By the end of 2008, consumption growth in OPEC countries will just about wipe out all the 2.2 billion barrels a day in increased production that OPEC has added since 2000.

It's hard to see why this trend toward rising consumption should go into reverse. Consumers in some of the countries showing the fastest growth in oil consumption remain insolated from climbing oil prices by government subsidies. Gasoline costs just 50 cents a gallon in Saudi Arabia, for example.

And where the cost of gas and oil isn't subsidized, even prices near $140 a barrel in 2008 haven't made much of a dent in the global appetite for oil. For 2008, the International Energy Agency projects global consumption to average 87.2 million barrels a day. That would be an increase in consumption of 1.3 million barrels a day from 2007—despite a U.S. economic slowdown and soaring oil prices.

How the Trends Play Out for Investors

- As oil becomes harder to find and more expensive to produce, oil prices will continue to climb.

- Those rising prices put a floor of support under investment in unconventional sources of oil such as oil sands and in advanced enhanced recovery technologies.
- Higher oil prices aren't putting the usual damper on oil consumption.
- Control of national oil resources by national oil companies creates a shortfall of capital and technology likely to lead to higher oil prices.
- The trend to politicize oil puts a premium on oil from safe, stable, open economies.
- National oil companies need cutting-edge exploration and production technology. They just don't want to partner with Western oil companies to get it.

TREND MAKERS AND TREND BREAKERS RIPPED FROM THE HEADLINES

TREND BREAKERS

- *Signs that higher oil prices are finally starting to bite into global economic growth.* The wildest development in the energy world is not that oil hit $140 a barrel but that $140-a-barrel oil didn't make oil consumers stop buying or produce a recession anywhere in the world.
- *Signs that an economy big enough to count—the United States, Germany, or Japan, for example—has gotten serious enough about cutting oil use to* launch a crash problem to fund conservation and alternative production technologies. And watch out for signs that OPEC has panicked at the announcement and done something silly—such as preemptively cut oil production—that will tank the U.S. economy.
- *Watch each OPEC meeting carefully* to make sure that the Saudis don't lose control to the radical bloc of oil producers (including Iran and Venezuela) that want to raise production. In the short run, more production at lower prices per barrel would increase oil country revenues for countries with lots of oil to pump but hurt revenues at oil

companies that don't have the ability to increase production. In the long run, of course, it would just hasten the day when oil gets really, really scarce.

TREND MAKERS

• Stories about *rising prices for the things critical to oil exploration and production* such as drilling pipe and about true scarcities of essential "raw materials" such as engineers. The longer it takes to develop new oil and the more it costs, the higher oil prices will go.

• Stories about *cancelled projects as costs rise and delays stretch out.* The delays are the real killers, of course. If you can't get a project on line within a reasonable time, no matter what you spend, any sane CEO will pull the plug. There's too much risk that oil prices will fall even temporarily to justify open-ended exposure. You can see this principle at work in the oil sands of Alberta, where, after stretching out deadlines for projects, companies started to cancel projects in 2008 as oil prices dipped.

• Watch to see *what price Wall Street analysts are projecting for the price of oil* when they set their target prices for oil company stocks. So, for example, in February 2008, when oil had pushed above $100 a barrel, analysts at Morningstar calculated the fair value of Chevron at $98 a share assuming that oil would sell for an average of $80 a barrel in 2008 and $68 a barrel in 2009. As a rough rule of thumb, it's safe to buy oil stocks as long as Wall Street analysts trail the market price of oil by $20 a barrel or more.

STOCK PICKS THAT PUT THE WIND FROM THOSE TRENDS AT YOUR BACK

Apache (NYSE: APA). This exploration and production company is no slouch when it comes to finding new oil. Projects in Egypt, Australia, and Canada are projected to add 108,000 barrels of oil a day by 2011. In January 2008, Apache reported new finds in Australia and Egypt. Reserves climbed by 6 percent in 2007. The company estimated in March 2008 that it is exploring geologies that hold potential resources of 2 billion barrels of oil equivalent. But it's Apache's ability to get more oil out of old fields that makes this an oil stock that I want to own during the supply crunch of the next five years (or longer). For example, Apache bought the North Sea's Forties Field from BP in 2003 for $688 million. Production at the field had declined from a peak of 500,000 to less than 50,000 barrels a day. Apache invested $911 million in new cranes, pumps, and other equipment and cut operating costs in half. By the end of 2005, the company had increased production to 81,000 barrels a day and raised cash margins per barrel to $24 from $6. The two parts of the company's strategy fit together well: buying older fields and increasing production there provides a steady cash flow that Apache can then use to explore for new oil. Apache had a five-year average return on invested capital of 13.3 percent as of the end of 2007. That's above the industry average of 11.7 percent but low compared to the 21.6 percent return for a company such as ExxonMobil, whose reserves require less intensive and expensive technology. But what Apache doesn't have is any shortage of places to reinvest its capital. The Western majors may be shut out of the best new oil fields by national oil companies, but Apache has a growing supply of older fields where it can apply its skills at enhanced recovery. For example, over the last five years Apache has been busy acquiring "depleted" fields in the Gulf of Mexico. The Gulf of Mexico now accounts for 25 percent of Apache's production.

ExxonMobil (NYSE: XOM). This is the one Western oil major that has found a way out of the box created by national oil companies' hammerlock on so much of the world's new oil. You just about have to be the world's biggest oil company and awash in cash flow to pull this off, however. First, you decide to turn your cash flow into an advantage—rather than a worry—by investing in the big capital-heavy projects necessary to get natural gas from where it's produced to where it's consumed. That means building huge plants to cool the gas, turning it into a liquid ready to be pumped onto tankers, in places like Qatar, and then building the infrastructure at the other end in, say, Bayonne, New

Jersey, for converting the liquid back into gas and then sending it on into the pipeline system. Second, it means investing, through 70-percent-owned affiliate Imperial Oil, in Canada's oil sands. And third, it means running the world's most sophisticated refinery system so you can actually refine the heavy gunk that comes out of Alberta's tar sands into usable oil and so you can refine the increasing percentage of the world's oil supply that is made up of heavy, hard-to-refine oil from places such as Venezuela. All this gets you a five-year average annual return on invested capital of 21.6 percent, a huge return for a capital-intensive industry such as oil. Standard & Poor's counts twelve new major projects starting up in 2008, seven in 2009–10, and another forty in the years after that. Production will grow, S&P projects, by about 2 percent a year through 2012.

Schlumberger (NYSE: SLB). If Schlumberger did its work in clean rooms in Silicon Valley, everyone would understand that this is a world-class technology company and price the shares accordingly. Fortunately for us, most investors still don't get it, so you can buy Schlumberger at 24 times earnings per share for the last four quarters (certainly not cheap) at a time (April 2008) when Apple was selling for 36 times earnings. But look at what you get for your cash: Apple earns a magnificent 26 percent return on its invested capital while Schlumberger earns an even better 27 percent. That means that you can buy a dollar of Schlumberger earnings for 33 percent less than a dollar of Apple earnings and that every year Schlumberger will be able to reinvest its earnings in its own business at a higher rate of return than Apple can. Think of Schlumberger as a certificate of deposit that sells at a discount and offers a higher compound rate of interest. That return on invested capital is a result of years of company investment in cutting-edge seismic technology for finding oil before an oil company drills and in best-in-the-world technology for managing oil field development and production. You'll understand the big returns Schlumberger gets in its business if you realize that the company sells information and information technology and not pipes and pumps. Besides benefiting from the increasing difficulty and expense in finding and producing new oil,

Schlumberger has another big advantage: it's not an oil producer itself, and national oil companies can get the technology they want from Schlumberger without the unwanted partnership with a Western oil company. For example, while Mexico may be off-limits to Western oil producers, it's a fast-growing market for Schlumberger. The company has drilled a thousand wells in the Burgos basin, an area that provides 22 percent of Mexico's total output of natural gas. A new drilling program in the Chicontepec basin started up in 2007.

Tenaris (NYSE ADR: TS). Selling things such as pipes and pumps to the oil exploration and production industry has grown into a very nice $10 billion (in sales) business. And Tenaris would do quite well on volume alone since the company dominates some segments of the market. (The company has about a 50 percent market share in Saudi Arabia, for example.) But the company's big drive now is to increase the profit margins in that business. The company knows that as companies drill in ever more challenging geologies, they'll pay extra for pipe that can withstand extremely high temperatures and pressures, that can flex to accommodate new trends in horizontal and guided drilling, and that won't surrender to extremely corrosive conditions. That's increasingly what Tenaris delivers—sales of its new Tenaris Blue high-performance connection technology, for example, continue to push margins higher. Gross margins climbed to 45.8 percent in 2007 from a five-year average of 41.5 percent. A slowdown in drilling activity in the United States and Canada in 2007 and 2008 cut into sales growth just after Luxembourg-based Tenaris purchased Maverick Steel to grab more market share in the United States. But with drilling activity projected to turn up in the second half of 2009, the margin story should earn top place in investors' minds again. Sales of higher-end, high-technology products such as Tenaris Blue are projected to make up 50 percent of sales by the end of 2008 from 40 percent in 2007, according to Deutsche Bank. With the acquisition of Hydril, the leading supplier of premium connections for the oil and gas industry, Tenaris can now offer its existing customers new products that make its pipe even more valuable.

Ultra Petroleum (NYSE: UPL). What energy supply could be more secure than natural gas from Wyoming and Utah in the good ol' U.S. of A.? And Ultra Petroleum owns a lot of it. I mean *a lot*. The company's proven reserves total 2.4 trillion cubic feet of gas. That's far below the 9.4 trillion cubic feet of proven reserves at a competitor such as XTO Energy. But the real prize here is Ultra Petroleum's 4,800 undrilled locations that are projected to yield 5 billion cubic feet of gas each and the 150,000 acres Ultra Petroleum owns in the heart of the Green River Basin. Only about 15,000 of those acres have been developed, so this company has years and years of expanding production ahead of it. Standard & Poor's projects an increase in production of 17 percent in 2008 and 18 percent in 2009. That expanding production should be very profitable too since, according to Morningstar, Ultra Petroleum shows the lowest cost per unit of natural gas produced of all North American producers over the last five years. It took convincingly higher oil prices and improved technology to make it possible to pry this gas out of the region's tight rock formations. Even after development became feasible, production has been held back by a lack of pipeline capacity out of the Rocky Mountains. That problem will move a big stop closer to solution when the new Rocky Mountain Express pipeline connects the natural gas fields of the Rockies to consumers in Ohio and points East in early 2009. As of early 2008 four other pipelines have been proposed to transport natural gas out of the Rockies.

Stocks for Building an Overweight Position in This Sector

- **Canadian Natural Resources** (NYSE: CNQ) to add exposure to Alberta's huge reserves of oil sands. The oil has to be cooked out of these sands, but the potential reserves would rank Canada second only to Saudi Arabia among world oil producers.
- **CGG Veritas** (NYSE ADR: CGV) to add more exposure to the high-tech side of oil discovery. This French company is more narrowly focused on seismic equipment and services than Schlumberger.

- **Devon Energy** (NYSE: DVN) owns huge natural gas reserves in the Barnett Shale of Texas and a big hunk of some of the most promising recent deep-water finds in the Gulf of Mexico.
- **National Oilwell Varco** (NYSE: NOV) is a one-stop shop for drilling equipment and oil field services.
- **Transocean** (NYSE: RIG) owns a fleet of 139 (as of February 2008) mobile offshore drilling rigs, but it's the 39 deep-water rigs that are in the most demand by the industry and where the day rates Transocean can charge are climbing fastest.
- **XTO Energy** (NYSE: XTO) has proven reserves of 9.4 trillion cubic feet of natural gas in areas from Wyoming to Texas and, most recently, east in Appalachia. The company costs of operation are among the lowest in its industry.

Mutual Funds and ETFs (Exchange-Traded Funds)

I don't have anything to recommend if you'd like to own the shares of oil producers through a fund. The problem with most oil stock ETFs and mutual funds, such as Energy Select Sector SPDR (Amex: XLE), is that they tend to bulk up on the big-capitalization stocks that are facing the toughest go in expanding future production. So in buying one of these funds you get a lot of ExxonMobil, which is good, and a lot of BP, Royal Dutch Shell, and Chevron, which isn't so great, and very little Devon Energy, XTO Energy, or Ultra Petroleum, which is too bad.

But if you shift from oil producers to oil service companies, I think there is an ETF that will work hard for you.

Oil Service HOLDRS (AMEX: OIH) owns a big hunk of Schlumberger (about 10 percent), which is good, and then a well-diversified portfolio of deep-sea drillers, oil equipment producers, and the like. Holdings include Transocean, Smith International, and Diamond Offshore Drilling. I wish it didn't own quite so much of land-drilling specialists such as Baker Hughes, but the total package is a good way to participate in the themes of this chapter.

8

THE COMMODITIES CRUNCH

Natural Resources for a Demanding World

At the bottom of AngloGold Ashanti's Savuka mine, more than two miles below the surface of South Africa, the temperature is always well above 100 degrees Fahrenheit. The rock in this deepest of the world's deep mines is under so much pressure that it shatters like glass. The weight of rock above the tunnels squeezes them shut a little more each day, and miners have to bore away at the tunnel edges to keep them wide enough for work. In 2006 thirty-seven South African miners died in AngloGold's mines.

But in September 2006 another South African mining company, Gold Fields, announced that it would extend its Driefontein and Kloof mines to 2.5 and 2.4 miles below the surface, respectively. That would temporarily make these two mines the deepest in the world. These moves revive an expansion project that Gold Fields had canceled in 1998. Work on sinking the shaft started in October 2007 and is scheduled for completion in 2011. The work is budgeted to cost more than $400 million.

Across the Indian Ocean in Australia, a South African engineering company, TWP, is at work on the Perseverance Deeps project for BHP Billiton. At the mine 450 miles northeast of Perth, TWP is in charge of sinking a twenty-foot-diameter shaft to a depth of 4,200 feet. When the nickel mine is completed in 2013 at a cost now estimated at $470 million, it will be the deepest mine in Australia by 900 feet.

Not too far away in Western Australia, in order for Fortescue Metals Group to get its first shipment of iron ore from its 1.1 billion metric tons of proven reserves to market in May 2008, the company had to build not just a huge open pit mine but also a private railroad capable of carrying trains up to 1.5 miles long and weighing 30,000 metric tons and a new port at Anderson Point in Port Hedland capable of taking the ore from the company's fleet of 816 rail cars and loading it onto ships.

Isn't there an easier way to get at the world's supply of metals than digging two miles into the earth or building a mine, railroad, and port from scratch?

Nope.

If there were, Chile's Codelco, the world's largest copper miner, wouldn't be looking to build a $350 million liquid natural gas plant to supply electric power to the company's copper mines in the Atacama Desert of northern Chile. If there were, Freeport McMoRan Copper & Gold wouldn't be starting a new copper and cobalt mine in the Katanga province of the Democratic Republic of Congo in the middle of what seems to be a permanent state of civil war. And if there were, HudBay Minerals wouldn't be exploring the cold, remote, and logistically expensive Canadian Yukon looking for new deposits of lead and zinc.

But the truth is that while the world isn't running out of the raw materials it needs to build everything from cars to batteries to skyscrapers, it is running out of easily exploited supplies of everything from aluminum to zinc.

Commodities and commodity stocks were pummeled in the second half of 2008 as the bear market dug its claws in deeper. Part of this was because the U.S. dollar rallied on fears that, bad as things were in the United States, things were even worse in the euro-zone economies. Part was because of fears that the Chinese economy was slowing and global demand for everything from copper to iron to coal was going to fall off a cliff. The dollar's strength is a temporary trend that's likely to turn on a quarter (with inflation, no one can turn on a dime anymore) once the fear recedes and everyone starts to wonder how the United States is going to pay for bailing out its financial system. And in the weeks following the end of the Beijing Olympics, China had already started to rev up its economy again. The feared slowdown there was ending before it had even begun.

Which made commodities stocks an amazing bargain at the start of the last quarter of 2008. Wall Street analysts were doing their best to point out that at October prices, these stocks were discounting a fall of 50 percent in copper, coal, and other commodity prices and a belief that once prices were down, they'd stay depressed for five years or more.

Read this chapter and you'll understand why that's just not going to happen. Supply is going to have trouble keeping up with demand, no matter what the stock market said in the short run in October 2008.

IT'S WAY EASIER TO INCREASE DEMAND THAN SUPPLY

Which is a big problem because the demand side doesn't face any of these problems. Creating new demand for copper, for example, is as simple as a Chinese home builder in Shanghai ordering new copper pipe or wiring. Put together enough of that kind of purchasing decision and you get huge growth in aggregate demand. China, for example, imported about 1.4 million metric tons of copper in 2007—a huge 134 percent increase from the 600,000 tons it imported the year before. That'll drop to 1.2 million tons in 2008, predicts Desjardins Securities, a Canadian brokerage company. But China isn't the only developing economy hungry for copper, and total global consumption is projected to climb to 18.95 million metric tons in 2008 from 18.15 million in 2007.

In 2008 that will leave demand in balance with supply, but it won't leave much to buffer any disruption in supply. And that will lead to a spike in copper prices every time miners go on strike, pushing copper above $3 a pound (roughly where it was in 2006) despite 2008's economic slowdown in the United States (and to a lesser extent in China and India). How far above $3 a pound? For the first quarter of 2008 Freeport McMoRan Copper & Gold reported it received a price of $3.68 a pound for its copper. In April 2008 Lehman Brothers (remember them?) raised its 2009 target price for copper to $4.75 a pound.

Here's how Desjardins Securities summed up the supply demand status of some of the world's most necessary metals:

Copper: a shortage of 50,000 metric tons in 2009

Aluminum: a shortage of 140,000 tons in 2008 and 950,000 tons in 2009

Nickel: a shortage of 9,000 tons in 2008 and 13,000 tons in 2009

Zinc: surpluses in 2008 and 2009, and a gradual tightening through 2012

Iron ore: tight supply in 2008; supply and demand should level off through 2011

Uranium: a growing surplus from 2008 through 2010

What you're looking at is what I'd call peak metal. The situation isn't a perfect analogy with peak oil (see Chapter 7, pages 135–137), since the commodity markets for metals are much smaller and much more speculative than the market for oil, but applying this theory to metals argues that the boom in the prices of metals and metal stocks is a long, long way from over. Over the long term, the only thing likely to derail it, in fact, is a big slowdown in the global economy and therefore in global demand—and I'm talking about something much bigger than the 2008 slump in the U.S. economy.

Peak oil is a controversial theory that argues that sometime soon global oil production is due to hit a peak. As oil production moves toward the peak two things happen. First, oil becomes harder to find. And second, producing oil from discovered fields gets more expensive. The price of oil rises as the peak approaches for both reasons.

Now look at the three similarities between peak oil and peak metal. It is becoming harder and harder to find significant new deposits of everything from gold to copper. For example, in South Africa, one of the world's traditional gold producers, gold production in tons is now less than one-third of its peak because the country's existing deep underground mines have to go deeper to find gold and South African mining companies haven't been able to find enough new gold deposits to make up the difference. You'd expect that higher gold prices would lead to more gold production since higher prices make the effort more profitable. But global gold production has actually tumbled as gold prices have spiked. After peaking in 2001 at 2,621 metric tons when gold sold for less than $260 a ounce, gold production fell in 2005 to 2,500 metric tons and then in 2007, when gold sold for more than $800 an ounce, to just 2,444 metric tons. China passed South Africa in 2007 to become the world's largest gold producer. (South Africa had held that title since 1905.) But before you get too excited about China's potential, take note of this: China's production of gold was up 12 percent in 2007 from 2006 but was still below 2005 levels. It isn't so much that China leapt ahead but that South Africa, which produced 1,000 tons of the yellow stuff in 1970, has fallen back faster. And estimates right now say China will exhaust current known gold deposits within the next fourteen years, so China will be running as fast as it can to stay even.

When new deposits are discovered, they are in politically riskier countries. In gold and copper that's meant replacing production from South Africa and the United States with production from Peru and Indonesia, for example.

Production costs are higher in newly discovered deposits wherever they are. Part of that's a result of location: it's more expensive to produce copper if you have to build roads, railroads, and ports from scratch in remote Indonesia than it is to produce copper from Arizona. And part of that is a result of the poorer quality of newly discovered deposits. Costs are rising at many gold mining companies because the grade of ore—the amount of gold per ton of rock—is lower in newly discovered deposits than in older mines. And part of that is a result of a global shortage and consequently higher prices for everything you need to find and then develop a deposit of gold or copper or iron, from mining engineers to the giant truck tires used by open pit mining operations.

To that I'd add these factors that could produce even sharper and more sustained price increases for peak metal than for peak oil.

Mining companies are even more conservative about adding new production than oil companies, largely because a mine eats more capital in a single chunk than an oil well. Oil companies that were initially hesitant to invest when oil hit $30 since they were worried that oil prices would fall back to $20 or less lagged behind the market by only a year or two before starting to factor prices of $30, $40, and then $60 a barrel into their long-term capital spending plans. Mining companies, scarred by the boom-and-bust cycle of an industry that is even more cyclical than oil, have shown far bigger reluctance to catch up with current market prices in their capital spending plans. Freeport McMoRan Copper & Gold, for example, reaffirmed its decision to use projected copper prices of 80 cents to 90 cents a pound in making its decisions on capital spending to increase production. "Metal prices, like all commodities, are cyclical," CEO Richard Adkerson told the *Financial Times*, "and I don't see any reason to change the long-term planning price because prices are higher." Copper had already traded at an average price of $1.26 in 2004 and $1.59 in 2005, and it was headed for $3.02 in 2006 when Adkerson made that remark. Copper sold for $3.80 a pound on May 2, 2008.

Oil producers have been able to exploit new technology to drill deeper, to force oil and gas out of stubborn geologic formations, and to bring vast new types of reserves into production. Nothing comparable has occurred in the metals sector. The last big technology shift—from deep underground shaft mining to vast open-air pit mining—is decades old. (The next big thing—genetically engineered bacteria and viruses that extract metals from even the lowest-grade deposits—is now just smears on laboratory petri dishes.)

All these peak metal factors make me want to rush out and add more metals stocks to my portfolio. Well, maybe not rush. But sometime in 2009 sounds about right.

Which specific stocks?

My peak metal approach gives me some clues there. First, because it's so hard to add new, high-quality proven resources right now, when picking stocks you should concentrate on those companies that are expanding production. One of the reasons that I like the shares of molybdenum producer Thompson Creek Metals, for example, is that the company expects to increase mining activity at existing mines and will be opening its new Davidson mine to production in late 2008. In late 2007 the company was projecting that molybdenum production would climb to 29 million pounds in 2009 from a projected 21 million pounds in 2007. That's the kind of trend you'd like to see.

Second, you want to see production costs rising as slowly as possible, certainly more slowly than the price of the metal that the company is producing. In the last quarter of 2007, for example, BHP Billiton reported that costs had climbed by 1.9 percent. That's equal to about 8 percent a year. Investors ought to think of that as a kind of baseline for how fast costs are rising at mining companies that, like BHP Billiton, aren't facing special circumstances.

What are "special circumstances"? One is distance. As miners go to the ends of the earth to find new deposits of valuable metals, their supply lines get longer and longer. That creates a logistical nightmare—and the rocketing costs associated with extended logistics—as companies try to get equipment and workers along extended and constricted supply lines to remote locations with inadequate local infrastructure. Costs in Alberta's oil sands projects were climbing at better than 15 percent a year in 2007, for example. Just getting workers to Fort McMurray, a city of 56,000 in the middle of the oil sands boom area but more than 400 miles from Calgary, for example, was expensive enough, but the surge in workers quickly gave Fort McMurray the highest rents in Canada, driving up what oil sands mining companies had to pay.

Another problem is declining ore grades. As metal prices go up, it pays to work lower-grade ores, which contain less metal per unit of rock. But moving all that extra rock to get at the metal in these lower-grade ores costs more. In the fourth quarter of 2007 Freeport McMoRan Gold & Copper missed Wall Street earnings estimates because of rising costs. One culprit, the company said, was lower ore grades. The problem wasn't about to end in 2007 either. Lower ore grades were one reason the company is projecting a 10 percent increase in operating costs in 2008.

So companies with higher-than-industry-average ore grades or with new mining projects that promise higher ore grades will have a big edge in costs. Higher industry-wide costs will drive up metal prices as companies pass them along to buyers. For companies with lower-than-industry-average costs those price increases will increase profit margins and bolster earnings.

My peak metal theory also suggests that I can find an important insurance policy by looking for metals where new technologies are creating new uses—and new demand—for the metal. In these cases, that technology-driven increase in demand gives me an insurance policy in case growth in demand created by global economic growth falters because of a global economic slowdown.

MINING THE MINOR METALS

I think this is an especially important factor for what are called the "minor metals." These don't normally cross an investor's radar screen because they don't have the production volume or the commodities market clout to generate headlines. But for molybdenum, cobalt, and platinum, supply is getting tighter because (1) the world economy is growing and (2) fast-growing new technologies rely on these metals.

Molybdenum demand is climbing, for example, because the metal increases the corrosion resistance of stainless steel in industrial processes and because adding small amounts to steel keeps oil and natural gas pipelines from fracturing in arctic temperatures. Potentially most important, molybdenum is used in catalysts that lower the sulfur levels of fuel. Such catalysts are in increasing demand as more and more of the world's oil supplies are high-sulfur heavy oils. In March 2008 Desjardins Securities was looking for a $4-a-pound increase in molybdenum prices in 2008 and another $5-a-pound jump in 2009.

New technologies are also driving higher demand for cobalt and platinum in the same way. Cobalt, for example, is used in rechargeable batteries for hybrid cars such as the Toyota Prius and General Motors'

Saturn Vue and in the lithium batteries used in electronic devices such as digital cameras. Cobalt is unfortunately tough to invest in—there are very few publicly traded pure plays with operating mines—and fast-changing battery technology that seems headed toward replacing cobalt in the next generation of lithium batteries makes the metal riskier than I'd like.

Projected increases in demand for platinum, the blindingly white jewelry metal, on the other hand, are based on much more reliable trends. Platinum demand soared in Europe, up 15 percent in 2006, because of the metal's use in the catalytic soot filters that have made Europe's clean diesels possible. In North America platinum catalytic soot filters were fitted to light diesel trucks for the first time in the 2007 model year. Platinum demand for use in catalytic exhaust filters climbed by 64,000 ounces in 2007. And the metal is easy to invest in through the shares of such South African platinum mining companies as Impala Platinum.

How the Trends Play Out for Investors

• Mining stocks aren't the cyclicals they once were when every jump in profit brought new mines into production and created a vicious crash in commodity prices. Thanks to rising demand from the fast-growing emerging economies of China, India, Brazil, and the rest of the gang, demand looks set to grow for decades.

• Mining companies are having difficulty in finding significant new high-grade deposits of iron, nickel, copper, and so on. That also stretches out the normal metals cycle by making it much harder for miners to quickly ramp up production.

• Many major metals are projected to be in supply deficit once the global recession is over for at least two or three years.

• Turning the new deposits that are found into producing mines is also increasingly difficult and expensive. New deposits are likely to be found in remote areas, so mines have to be developed at the end of long and fragile supply lines. The cost of everything mining companies need, from labor to oil to truck tires, is climbing at a general inflation rate of about 8 percent. Mining companies doing business at the end of long supply lines or trying to mine lower grades of ore are seeing expenses rise at even steeper rates. Those costs, of course, get passed along to the consumers of these metals.

- Investors should look for companies with a pipeline of new discoveries that will keep reserves climbing faster than the company depletes them by mining and for companies with lower-cost operations.
- In metals where technology is creating new uses and increased demand, investors have a demand insurance policy in case the global economy slows.

TREND BREAKERS AND TREND MAKERS RIPPED FROM THE HEADLINES

TREND BREAKERS

- *Big declines in growth in the two economies that count the most right now: China and India.* Moderate slowing—a 2-percentage-point drop when growth in 2007 was over 11 percent and over 9 percent, respectively—isn't a big deal. Keep your eyes peeled for projections from the World Bank, Asian Development Bank, or the Organisation for Economic Cooperation and Development that predict a bigger slowdown.
- *Russia is the 800-pound gorilla in many metals markets.* Russian companies such as Norilsk Nickel are huge forces in nickel and aluminum. Watch for news that the Russian budget is in trouble—from a drop in oil and gas revenue, for example. That could lead to increased sales of metals from Russian stockpiles at prices low enough to depress world markets.
- *Rising costs are manageable as long as they rise slowly enough so that companies can pass them along to customers.* But if costs go up too

fast, metals companies find themselves facing a lag during which they have to eat the higher costs. That can slam a stock in the short run (and create a buying opportunity in the long run).

• *Moderate turmoil in the financial markets* is good for natural resource stocks since it will send money fleeing from stocks and bonds into commodities markets and commodity stocks. Too much turmoil, on the other hand, isn't a good thing since it will disrupt the sources of leverage (Wall Street's jargon for "borrowing") that traders and speculators use to make bets in this market. If credit freezes up, there's less cash for everybody. This is exactly what hit stocks in this sector so hard in 2008.

Trend Makers

• Headlines showing *infrastructure problems in mining economies.* Hot spots in 2008 are energy supplies in China, South Africa, and Chile. When a specific mining company gets caught short by electricity shortages or a lack of workers and then has to curtail production, it's not good for that stock. But that kind of company-specific disruption can drive up the price of a commodity overnight as buyers in an already tight market decide to lay in extra supplies so they won't get caught short of essential raw materials.

• News *of creeping inflation and a sinking U.S. dollar.* Because natural resource companies own and produce real things and often run their business in some currency other than dollars, their stocks, like gold, oil, and real estate, are great hedges against rising prices and a falling dollar.

• *Political tensions between mining companies and national governments.* Royalty payments are on the rise all over the world as national governments seek to get a bigger piece of the pie for the exploitation of minerals found under their soil. Rising royalties are just a cost of doing business and get passed on to customers. Disputes over higher royalties that shut down production or result in the seizure of a mine are much more serious since they have the potential to disrupt a metal market and send prices soaring.

- *New technologies that create new demand for this or that metal.* Battery, lighting, car, and plane manufacturing are some of the areas most likely to produce these new uses.

STOCK PICKS THAT PUT THE WIND FROM THOSE TRENDS AT YOUR BACK

BHP Billiton (NYSE ADR: BHP) is as close as you can come to a one-stock portfolio of the entire global mining sector. The Australia-based company got 27 percent of its revenue in fiscal 2007 (BHP Billiton's fiscal year ends in June) from copper, silver, zinc, gold, and lead mining. What accounts for the rest of company revenues? Aluminum and iron ore each made up 12 percent of revenue, and metals used in stainless steel (nickel and chrome) accounted for another 15 percent. The company got 10 percent of its revenue from energy coal, where it is the world's second largest supplier. The remainder of company revenues comes from uranium, metallurgical coal, diamonds, natural gas, and oil. In 2007 BHP Billiton launched a bid to buy for $160 billion (in market cap) Rio Tinto, one of the big three in iron mining along with BHP Billiton and Brazil's Vale. Rio Tinto rejected the bid and, as of the press date for this book, Rio Tinto continued to keep BHP Billiton at arm's length.

Fortescue Metals Group (OTC: FSUMF). What a contrast to BHP Billiton, Vale, and Rio Tinto, the three giants that together control 75 percent of the world's seaborne iron trade. While BHP Billiton, Rio Tinto, and Vale bulk up through acquisitions, this Western Australian upstart is just starting production. But what potential. In December 2007 Fortescue announced that its Solomon holding contained 70 percent more iron ore than previously estimated. The company increased its estimate for the area to 1.7 billion metric tons from 1 billion and said it might upgrade estimates for the eastern part of the Solomon project by an additional 25 percent, or 175 million metric tons, during the first half of 2008. The company delivered its first ore to market in May 2008.

Freeport McMoRan Copper & Gold (NYSE: FCX) should think about changing its name to Copper & Gold & Molybdenum. Total proven and probable reserves of molybdenum totaled 2 billion pounds at the end of 2007 and gold reserves came to 41 million ounces. Copper does remain king—especially after the 2007 acquisition of Phelps Dodge. Proven and probable copper reserves totaled 93 billion pounds at the end of 2007. The company has announced plans to increase copper production by 25 percent and molybdenum production by 42 percent by 2010. The big upside and downside question is the company's huge Tenke Fungurume copper and cobalt mine in the Democratic Republic of the Congo. One of the largest undeveloped copper and cobalt concessions in the world today, the deposit is especially rich, with ore grading at 2 percent to 5 percent copper versus 0.5 percent to 1 percent at a typical mine. The company believes that production will begin in 2009, but in what looks like an effort to negotiate a bigger share of revenue for itself, the government has recently said it found irregularities in the company's contract. Unreasonable delays—a very flexible term when dealing with the government of the Democratic Republic of the Congo—would hurt the share price. During the first ten years of mining, the company expects to produce 250 million pounds of copper and 18 million pounds of cobalt.

Freeport McMoRan projects a forty-year life for the deposits that will be mined in the initial stage of operation.

Impala Platinum (OTC ADR: IMPUY). This hasn't been an easy period for South African mining companies. In early 2008 power shortages shut the country's deep mines, and the state-owned electric utility had been unable to guarantee reliable electricity supplies anytime soon. Without reliable power miners couldn't descend in electric lifts to work the face and the company couldn't get power to the equipment that carries ore out of the mines. The shutdowns just offered more evidence to those mining analysts who argue that

South Africa's mining industry is in long-term decline. Recent news that China passed South Africa to become the largest gold producer in the world just strengthened that impression. But nothing could be further from the truth in the case of the platinum metal group of platinum, rhodium, and palladium. South Africa was the source of 50 percent of the newly mined metal in the group in 2007, and that figure, Deutsche Bank projects, will climb to 55 percent in 2008. Impala Platinum, the second-largest of South Africa's three major platinum producers (the others are Lonmin and Anglo Platinum), was the only one to increase its output in 2007. Deutsche Bank projects a 214,000-ounce deficit for platinum in 2008 and estimates that prices will climb 7.5 percent in 2008 and 15 percent in 2009.

Thompson Creek Metals (NYSE: TC). Thompson Creek, the second-largest publicly traded producer of molybdenum (copper, gold, and molybdenum producer Freeport McMoRan is number one), projects that production will climb to 16.5 million to 17 million pounds in 2008, up from 15.9 million pounds in 2007, and then a big ramp-up to 34 million pounds in 2009 as the company starts to work richer grades of ore in its mines. In 2006 it cost the Toronto-headquartered company about $6 to produce a pound of molybdenum. That was down from more than $7 in 2005. You do the math.

STOCKS FOR BUILDING AN OVERWEIGHT POSITION IN THIS SECTOR

- **Anglo American** (NASDAQ ADR: AAUK). With the sale of its gold-mining interests, this is now a coal, iron, and platinum producer. The London-headquartered company continues to raise cash by selling businesses that aren't related to its core mining business, and that gives it lots of capital to use for buying and developing new resources.
- **HudBay Minerals** (OTC: HBMFF) looks like it's found a way to more than replace the declining production from its Chisel North

mine. Drilling studies by the Winnipeg-based company indicate that the new Lalor Lake deposit could contain 18 million to 20 million metric tons of zinc ores with 7.7 percent to 8 percent zinc and with copper- and gold-rich lenses at depths of 550 to 1,000 meters. Capital costs at Lalor Lake are projected at a reasonable $250 million since existing roads and mining ramps could be used to transport the ore to the company's nearby Snow Lake concentrator.

• **Vale** (NYSE ADR: RIO) is the third name in the global iron ore big three. The Brazilian company is further away from the big growth market of China than are Australian producers BHP Billiton and Rio Tinto, but Vale is the world's low-cost producer of iron ore. The company is in the midst of a huge $59 billion capital spending plan that will increase iron ore production by 43 percent and nickel production by 104 percent from 2007 to 2012.

Mutual Funds and ETFs (Exchange-Traded Funds)

Ah, what to choose. The basic distinction is between funds and ETFs that track commodity prices themselves and those that track mining company stocks.

• In the first group (those that track commodity prices) take a look at PowerShares DB Base Metals (DBB), PowerShares DB Commodity Index (DBC), which tracks metals, oil, and agricultural commodities, and iShares Goldman Sachs Commodity Index Trust (GSG).

• In the second group (those that track mining stocks), take a look at Metals and Mining Select SPDR (XME) for a mix heavy toward gold, coal, aluminum, and copper, and actively managed funds such as Vanguard Energy (VGENX) and T. Rowe Price New Era (PRNEX). The Vanguard offering tends toward the biggest of the big companies in the sector. Both actively managed funds held a portfolio heavy on oil and natural gas as of the end of 2007.

9

Food

The New Oil

You'd think drought, plagues of locusts, a rain of frogs—some disaster of biblical proportion—hit the world's grain-growing regions in 2007. Global wheat stocks ended 2007 with just a seventy-one-day supply. That was the smallest global margin standing between the world and a lack of bread in twenty-five years. The U.S. Department of Agriculture was projecting that global corn stocks would fall to just seven and a half weeks of supply, a thirty-three-year low.

And prices? Wow.

In mid-December 2007 wheat and rice prices for delivery in March 2008 hit what were then all-time records. That was enough to make soybeans, at a thirty-four-year high, and corn, at an eleven-year peak, seem cheap.

But 2007 wasn't a year filled with agricultural disaster. It was, in fact, exceptionally average. There's almost always drought somewhere, and in 2007 Australia's wheat-growing regions suffered through a second year of drought. On the other hand, China, the world's largest wheat grower, increased production to 100 million metric tons. India, the globe's number two wheat producer, did indeed see lower production as farmers took land out of cultivation, but the decline was just 1 percent.

Bad weather in Russia, the number four producer, took the winter wheat harvest down 6 percent. In the United States, the number three wheat grower, production dipped a seemingly insignificant 0.3 percent.

Overall, total world grain production in 2007–8 hit a record, according to the International Grains Council, of 1.66 billion metric tons. That's 89 million metric tons more than the 2006–7 harvest, which itself set a record. For example, U.S. corn production climbed 26 percent to a new record in 2007–8. Production in Brazil, the largest grower of corn in Latin America, climbed 25 percent from 2006–7.

World grain production in 2008–9 is forecast at 1.69 billion metric tons. That would be 32 million tons more than the 2007–8 record.

In early September 2007, wheat sold for $400 a metric ton, the highest price ever recorded and two times the average price over the last twenty-five years. Despite these bumper harvests, the price of a bushel of wheat climbed 23 percent in 2006 and 16 percent in 2007. Rice prices are at a record. Corn hit $175 a ton in 2007 to break its own record. Soybeans are selling at a nineteen-year high. Everything from barley to oats to lentils is in short supply and selling at higher prices.

But as high as prices got in 2007, it turned out that the world hadn't seen anything yet. By the end of April 2008 prices were even higher. Corn was up 68 percent over April 2007 corn. In the same period the price of soybeans for May climbed 76 percent, wheat 64 percent, and rice, the staple food for many of the world's poorest people, had climbed 134 percent from April 2007.

So why are prices so high? And why doesn't even a record harvest such as that of 2007 slow down their climb?

For thirty years, beginning in 1974, the real price of grain fell. During those three decades the price of corn, adjusted for inflation, fell by 75 percent. The real price of wheat fell by 69 percent.

No more. The trend has turned and is, in fact, just picking up momentum.

In 2007–8, from harvest to harvest, for the third year in a row the world consumed more grain than it harvested. In fact, 2007–8 was the seventh year out of the last eight when consumption outstripped production. The final figures aren't in, but in mid-2008 it looked as though global grain stockpiles would decline by another 17 percent in 2007–8, according to the International Grains Council. And the result is one of those huge, world-shaking shifts in economic trends that shakes the lives of food consumers to their core but which investors can ride to solid profits. I don't know if investors can count on this trend of tight supplies and higher prices lasting the thirty years of the previous trend. But it sure won't reverse itself overnight. According to my analysis, we've got at least a decade of tighter supplies and higher prices ahead of us.

As a consequence, we're on the verge of one of the longest, most sustained periods of growth in farm incomes since the late nineteenth century. Like that earlier period of farmer prosperity, this one isn't limited to the United States but includes Canada, Australia, Vietnam, Argentina, Brazil, and China to name just a few countries. And higher farm incomes mean more money spent on everything from fertilizer to high-yield seed to farm equipment to dry bulk cargo ships.

As an investor, this is one wind that you *must* put at your back. Food is the new oil.

If you want to understand why the thirty-year trend of lower farm prices is so decidedly over, compare global grain production in two periods ten years apart.

The world's farmers have done an amazing job at increasing global grain production over the last ten years. Average global grain production—actual and projected—for the harvest seasons of 2005–6, 2006–7, and 2007–8 agricultural fiscal years will be 2,029 million metric tons. That's a big increase—12 percent—above the average global grain production for the 1995–6, 1996–7, and 1997–8 agricultural years. Adding more fertilizer, using improved seed, and putting new land into cultivation have all resulted in a huge addition of more than 200 million tons a year to the average global grain harvest.

But it hasn't been enough because grain consumption was growing even faster. Average annual global consumption for the three years beginning in 1995–6 was 1,821 million metric tons. In those years the world ran a tiny supply deficit of about 9 million metric tons a year, or about 0.5 percent of global grain production.

Ten years later, though, global grain consumption was up to an average of 2,057 million metric tons a year for the three-year period that began in 2005–6. The supply deficit, despite that 12 percent increase in average annual production, had climbed to 28 million metric tons, or 1.4 percent of global grain production.

The world has been able to fill the gap between supply and demand by drawing down global grain stockpiles. But that's not something that can go on forever.

It's pretty easy to see why global demand is going up.

RISING INCOMES INCREASE THE DEMAND FOR GRAINS

The world's farmers would face a big enough problem if all they had to do was keep up with global population growth. By 2010 world population will reach 7 billion, up from just 2.5 billion people in 1950. That's an extra 4.5 billion people that need to eat something.

But it's not just more people demanding to be fed that's increasing the strain on global food production. As incomes go up, people who never had enough to eat are eating more. And people who have always had enough to eat are eating more. The average Indian, for example, consumed 2,400 calories a day in 2001–3, according to the Food and Agriculture Organization of the United Nations. In 1979–81, the average Indian consumed 2,080 calories a day.

But it's not just how much *more* people eat with rising incomes, it's *what* they eat. As incomes go up in the developing world, people there want to consume more protein—eggs and dairy products and meat. Especially meat: chicken, pork, and beef. For example, China's urban population, which lives where the country's economy is doing the best job of producing new wealth and higher incomes, consumes three times more meat per capita than the country's rural population. The country's urban population is growing by about 15 million to 20 million mouths a year.

In 1985 the average Chinese consumer ate forty-four pounds

of meat a year. Now that Chinese consumer eats fifty pounds of meat, a 14 percent increase.

But the drain on global food supplies is even greater than that per capita consumption figure suggests. It takes about three pounds of grain to produce one pound of pork. (It takes even more grain in countries such as the United States, which feed their hogs on high-grain diets.) Eight pounds of grain go into producing a pound of beef. Already 70 percent of China's corn and soybean crops and 50 percent of its sweet potato production go into feeding livestock. China's production of animal feeds has grown by an average of 18 percent a year since 1990.

No wonder China is on the verge of becoming a net importer of corn for the first time in a decade. China already accounts for 40 percent of global soybean imports. Half the world's hogs live in China.

This isn't a trend limited to China. The World Bank estimates that global grain production will have to climb by nearly 50 percent and meat output by 85 percent between 2000 and 2030 to meet projected global demand.

Biofuels Compete for Limited Supplies of Grain

That demand will be tough to meet. At the same time that we're looking to increase food and meat production, we're diverting a significant portion of our harvest to produce biofuels. In 2007, for example, U.S. farmers planted record acreage to corn, and reduced their planting of soybeans, to meet the demand for corn-based ethanol in the United States. As a consequence, there was less corn to go into either chicken and cattle feed or Fritos and Coca-Cola. (Corn syrup is far and away the sweetener of choice in the food industry.) And there were fewer soybeans to go into feed for pigs, tofu for people, and biodiesel for automobiles.

The U.S. Congress and president have called for increasing ethanol production to 35 billion gallons by 2022 from 5 billion gallons a year today. The Energy Independence and Security Act, signed by President Bush in December 2007, doesn't assume that all that ethanol would come from corn, but since the bill continues the high tariffs on Brazilian ethanol made from sugar and because the technology for producing ethanol from wood chips or switchgrass (cellulosic ethanol) at an industrial scale remains at a very rudimentary stage, the bulk of this ethanol would come from corn. I frankly doubt that corn-based ethanol will ever hit anything like the target of 35 billion gallons. It simply requires too much corn for too little fuel, but even a lower target would have a huge effect on grain demand. A May 2007 report from the Iowa State University Center for Agricultural and Rural Development estimated that producing just 14 billion gallons of ethanol from corn a year would consume about 5 billion bushels of corn, or about 40 percent of the 2007–8 U.S. corn harvest.

Within ten years, those raving environmentalists at investment bank Credit Suisse project, biofuels will take up 12 percent of the world's arable and permanent cropland.

So why don't farmers simply produce more corn, wheat, soybeans, et cetera? With prices for many grains near multidecade or historic highs, they've certainly got the incentive.

Well, it turns out that increasing food production is about as tricky as increasing oil production: You need lots of raw materials that are in short supply. In the case of the oil industry, those scarce inputs include oil engineers, drilling rigs, promising drilling sites, cutting-edge production technology—and money.

For a start, if you want to increase food production, there's one raw material that you can't do without—land.

LAND: GOD ISN'T MAKING ANY MORE OF IT, AND WE'RE MUCKING UP WHAT WE HAVE

Adding to the net total of the world's arable land is extremely hard. China feeds 22 percent of the world's population on just 7 percent of its farmland. And China has just about no chance of expanding the area devoted to agriculture. Instead the country is fighting a desperate battle just to keep the farmland it has. The rapid growth of China's cities, the loss of farmland to the country's growing deserts as a result of attempts to farm marginal land, and increasing levels of pollution are all reducing available farmland. China loses about 600,000 acres a year to desertification, for example. More than 24.7 million acres have been damaged by heavy metals, nitrates or other forms of pollution. The government has become so alarmed by the losses that it has scaled back its reforestation program, which would have converted 2.64 million acres of farmland to forests. The government estimates that the country needs a minimum of 120 million hectares (about 296.5 million acres) of farmland to maintain the country's food supply. After calculating the most recent losses of farmland to all causes except pollution, officials put the country's total farmland at just 122 million hectares (about 301.4 million acres).

The Chinese government estimates that it has lost 3.04 million acres of farmland each year between 2000 and 2005. The current goal is to reduce this loss to 1.07 million acres a year in the 2006–2010 period.

China isn't the only country facing a struggle to expand or merely preserve its acreage devoted to farming. In India, the amount of cultivable land per capita—not especially large to start with—has shrunk from 1.2 acres in 1950 to 0.38 acre in 2000, the last year for which reliable data are available. Since then, India, like China, has lost farmland to industrial uses, housing, and commercial projects. It certainly doesn't help that the *quality* of the land is collapsing as the *quantity* is shrinking. The states of Punjab and Haryana, which produce about 40 percent of India's wheat, are facing big declines in soil fertility and a sharply dropping water table, for example

No wonder, then, that the big economic powers of the developing world are scouting around to buy farmland outside their own borders. Indian producers of edible oils want to buy land in the U.S. Southwest. In 2007 China struck a deal to invest almost $4 billion to develop 2.5 million acres of farmland in the Philippines for the production of corn, rice, and sorghum. The favorite locations for agricultural investment include Brazil, Paraguay, Argentina, and Uruguay in South America, the Democratic Republic of the Congo and Sudan in Africa, and Kazakhstan and Russia in Eurasia.

Opening up land in those areas comes with its own set of problems, however. Cutting down rain forest in Brazil or the Congo to plant soybeans, for example, releases carbon dioxide into the air, thus adding to global warming. Destroying rain forest is also likely to alter rainfall patterns around the globe, turning some now productive farmland into deserts or near-deserts requiring massive irrigation. (Projections say that global warming *could* cut world farm output by as much as one-sixth by 2020.) Other areas where opening up farmland doesn't come with an immediate carbon cost—in the Sudan, Russia, Kazakhstan, Paraguay, and the drier areas of Brazil—require huge investments in infrastructure, ranging from water projects to roads and ports to produce and transport grain.

You Can't Grow Crops Without Water

You think we've got a global food problem? Wait until you look at the global supply of fresh water. Over the last century, water use has grown sixfold—that's twice the rate of population growth. By 2025 almost two-thirds of the world's population will live in countries where water is a scarce commodity.

The water we do have is increasingly polluted. In the Indian states of Punjab and Haryana, which produce about 40 percent of India's wheat, sharply dropping water tables are threatening wheat production. And the Punjab Water Pollution Control Board has found high levels of arsenic and mercury in tap water and mutated DNA in the blood samples of 65 percent of the people tested that are likely related to exposure to pesticides and irrigation runoff in the predominantly agricultural state. In China more than 24.7 million acres have been contaminated by heavy metals, nitrates, or other forms of pollution.

There are many ways to head off this impending water crisis, but one thing they have in common is that they're all expensive. China wants to siphon off water from the Tibetan plateau and send it through a massive new canal system to northern China. (Think how popular that will be with countries such as Vietnam and Cambodia, which rely on rivers that rise in the mountainous areas of China and Tibet.) Spain has built a generation of desalination plants to supply growing cities, vacation resorts, and farms. Almost 22 percent of Spanish agriculture depends on water from these plants. All that requires huge spending on concrete, pumps, water purification technology, and the like, which will add to the cost of farm produce. (All problems are, of course, investment opportunities, so the increasing scarcity of clean water is a major wind-at-your-back investment theme. You'll find more on this theme and my picks of stocks that have this wind at their backs in Chapter 10.

And let's not forget that modern industrialized agriculture—the kind that has enabled farmers to increase grain production by 12 percent in the last ten years—is heavily dependent on oil and natural gas. Tractors require oil; fertilizer requires natural gas; getting the food to storage and then to markets that may be halfway around the world requires more oil. In 1994 it took 400 gallons of oil equivalent per capita to feed the U.S. population. Here's how that use broke down for U.S. agriculture, the most oil-reliant of any in the world: 31 percent for the manufacture of inorganic fertilizer, 19 percent for the operation of field machinery, 16 percent for transportation, 13 percent for irrigation, 8 percent for raising livestock (but not including the energy needed to produce livestock feed), 5 percent for crop drying, 5 percent for pesticide production, and 8 percent miscellaneous.

In January 1994 oil sold for $12.37 a barrel, so those 400 barrels cost $4,958. In December 2007 oil sold for $90 a barrel, so the same 400 barrels cost $36,000. If oil and natural gas prices are headed up in the future, it's a good bet that the price of agricultural commodities will follow them.

What Happens to Prices When a Commodity Is in Short Supply?

Forget rationality and forget smooth moves in prices in response to changes in the balance of supply and demand, when consumers fear even the remote possibility that a market will run out of a commodity. The slightest whiff of scarcity produces irrational behaviors:

- Hoarding, where consumers afraid of empty shelves empty the shelves by buying more than they require to meet current needs
- Returns chasing, where producers flit from producing one good to another in search of the highest possible returns on their effort
- Speculation, where traders encouraged by the tight spread between demand and supply try to drive up prices by spreading rumors and creating the appearance of shortages

We've seen returns chasing by farmers in 2006 and 2007. For example, in 2007 U.S. farmers reduced the acreage planted to soybeans in order to grow more corn (in response to higher corn prices due to rising demand for ethanol) and more wheat (in response to higher wheat prices due to the Australian drought). That resulted in a surge in soybean prices in November 2007 to the highest level since 1973. The market knew that increased supply from Brazil—the world's second-largest producer—and the rest of South America could fill the gap, but prices rose on worries that counting so much on one area of the world for supply left the market vulnerable to regional bad weather. Adding to that worry: soybean stocks as a percentage of demand are at the lowest level in five years.

And now with soybean prices so high, more farmers are rushing back to plant soybeans.

Even crops that can't ever be substituted for each other see price moves as a result of this chase for the highest return. These are good times for cotton farmers, for example, because global cotton output was down 3 percent in 2007 as farmers reduced the acres they planted to cotton in order to increase their production of corn. Cotton prices are forecast to climb another 8 cents a pound in the 2007–8 agricultural year to 67 cents a pound. The peak is likely to be even higher—at 70 to 75 cents—as scarce supplies produce greater price volatility.

Food prices are starting to behave startlingly like oil. Short-term volatility is increasing, with bigger swings between tops and bottoms on ever smaller increments of news and near-news. This short-term volatility leads to extreme projections at both tops and bottoms. In the late summer and fall of 2007 oil fell from near $100 a barrel to near $80 a barrel. Wall Street analysts began talking about the return of $50-a-barrel oil. Earlier that year, when prices marched through $80 and then through $90, analysts had started to forecast $120-a-barrel oil.

These short-term fluctuations and the reactions to them disguise the long-term trend. As global supplies of food or oil struggle to keep up with rising demand from consumers, we're looking at decades of rising prices. In neither case does a big increase in supply seem in the cards; in fact, in both cases it's going to take trillions of dollars in new investment just to stay even.

INVESTORS SHOULD START THINKING ABOUT AGRICULTURE STOCKS

What does that mean? Here's how it worked in the oil sector.

First, rising prices increased only slowly, leading to surprisingly modest investments in new supply. In December 2004, Smith Barney's survey of oil producers on their planned exploration and production spending showed that spending outside North America would climb 3.9 percent in 2005 from 2004. This seems to make no sense. Oil prices had climbed 35 percent in a year, to $36.83 a barrel from $27.23 a barrel, but oil companies were going to invest a paltry 4 percent more to look for oil?

Except that oil companies weren't using $36-a-barrel oil when they looked at how much to invest in new production. They were still projecting oil prices of $25 a barrel or less. Some conservative oil giants were even using projected prices of $20 a barrel in their capital planning.

So what happened? Well, when Smith Barney updated its survey in June 2005, oil companies had upped their forecasted spending increase to 13.1 percent. Oil prices had by that time climbed another 27 percent to $46.65. That had convinced oil companies that prices weren't likely to drop back to $20 or $25 anytime soon. So by midyear they had started to use a price of $30 or $35 a barrel in their calculations.

At each stage oil company price forecasts have lagged well behind actual market trends. There's no reason to think that farmers, who like oil companies have been burned repeatedly and badly by investments in expanded production that come on line just in time to crash prices, will be any less cautious about taking risks.

Second, Wall Street analysts lagged almost as far behind in the forecasts of oil prices that they used to compute target prices or fair value prices for the stocks they cover. For example, at the end of 2007, as oil prices quickly recovered from a brief dip to move above $90 a barrel, the consensus forecast among thirty-five investment houses surveyed by Oppenheimer & Co. called for a decline in oil prices to $78 in the first quarter of 2008, to $75 in the second quarter of 2008, to $76 in the third quarter, and to $71 in the fourth quarter. Wall Street continued to believe that oil prices will fall to $55 to $65 a barrel in the long term.

Investors can decide for themselves whether or not they agree with Wall Street's price forecasts for oil in this time frame (I don't). But what investors should notice is that while Wall Street remains wedded to forecasting gradually declining oil prices, the forecasted decline constantly begins and ends at a higher price level. In Oppenheimer's survey, for example, the average price forecasted for oil in 2008 was, as of November 21, 2007, $75 a barrel. That's up 8.7 percent from the last time Oppenheimer conducted this survey and up 4 percent from $72 a barrel at the end of 2006. Wall Street may continue to believe in falling prices for oil—and other commodities including food—but the end point of the decline is itself in an uptrend.

Third, it takes Wall Street a long time to change its models for valuing a company. For example, the market has traditionally valued oil stocks—and agriculture and food commodity stocks as well—as cyclicals. That's kept multiples down since investors didn't want to pay as much for growth that would come to an end in three or four years as they did for a true growth stock. But if the cycle is now so long that it's hard to see its end, why shouldn't these stocks trade at true growth stock multiples?

To see what I mean, compare the way the stock market values a blue chip growth stock such as PepsiCo (PEP) and two "cyclical" oil stocks such as ExxonMobil (XOM) and Devon Energy (DVN). Over the last five years investors have bought PepsiCo shares at a price-to-earnings ratio of 20 (December 2007), 18.3 (December 2006), 23.30 (December 2005), 21.20 (2004), and 21.60 (2003). Investors have put a remarkably consistent value on PepsiCo's earnings, appropriately, since the company has a remarkably consistent record of delivering earnings growth. Earnings over the last five years are up an average of 12 percent annually. Earnings in 2008 will be up 10.3 percent and 11.1 percent in 2009, Wall Street projects. Analysts forecast an annual average earnings growth of 10.8 percent over the next five years. That's the kind of performance that defines blue chip.

Here are the equivalent numbers for ExxonMobil. The market values these shares at about half the multiple awarded PepsiCo. The December price-to-earnings ratio for the stock was 11.4 (December 2008), 9.9 (December 2006), 10.2 (2005), 11.7 (2004), and 11.5 (2003). That seems low if you look backward at ExxonMobil's earnings growth, but it makes sense if you look at Wall Street projections for ExxonMobil's earnings growth over the next five years. After growing earnings by an average annual 26.8 percent over the last five years, earnings growth, Wall Street says, will slip to 17.7 percent in 2008 and then, to 0.6 percent in 2009. Over the next five years, in fact, Wall Street says ExxonMobil's earnings growth will average just an annual 4.6 percent.

I think Wall Street's wrong. Oil prices aren't going to drop and stay low the way much of Wall Street expects, and besides, ExxonMobil, as a vertically diversified oil company, has a lot of ways to grow earnings even when oil prices fall. The company is among the world's most efficient refiners, for example, owns a huge retail gasoline network, and sees profits rise in its chemicals business when crude oil prices fall. But you can make a case, as I do in Chapter 14 on stock fundamentals, that ExxonMobil has a long-term reinvestment problem that should depress the multiple that an investor is willing to pay for the stock. Simply put, the company can't find ways to invest the huge amounts of cash that its existing business throws off that earn anything like the returns that its existing business earns.

In 2007 ExxonMobil generated $52 billion in cash from operations. It could find a way to reinvest only $15 billion of that in its own business. Why so little? Because the company's past investments are so unbelievably profitable. Return on invested capital was 22.4 percent in 2007 and averaged 19.1 percent over the last five years. (By contrast, General Electric shows an average return on invested capital of just 3.7 percent over the last five years and IBM just 11.2 percent.) Any investment of its capital that ExxonMobil makes that earns a return of less than 20 percent or so actually reduces the company's return on investors' money. With oil harder to find and more expensive to produce, with other oil companies bidding up the price of new reserves and oil exploration equipment, and with national governments raising royalties and taxes, there just aren't enough big projects around with that kind of return for ExxonMobil to invest all the cash it generates each year in its own business. So in 2006 it paid out $7.6 billion to investors as dividends and spent another $28.4 billion to buy back its own stock.

To an investor, that lack of reinvestment opportunities makes the stock less valuable. Most of the people who got cash from Exxon-Mobil in the form of a dividend check or in exchange for selling shares don't have any way to earn 22.4 percent on any investment. So the compounding effect that helps make equities so valuable is diminished at ExxonMobil. But I think this reasoning is way too subtle to explain why most Wall Street analysts slap such a paltry price-to-earnings ratio on ExxonMobil. ExxonMobil gets a multiple of 10 or so because that's the kind of multiple Wall Street has always given oil stocks. Evidence that oil is in a long cycle that will drive prices up and up again fights an uphill battle against Wall Street tradition.

For evidence, look at an oil stock that has none of ExxonMobil's problem of figuring out where to put its cash. Devon Energy is sitting on top of promising new field after promising new field that give it the opportunity to invest huge amounts of cash now to earn huge future returns. Devon Energy produced cash from operations of $6.7 billion in 2007, but the company invested almost all of it as capital spending came to $6.2 billion. Because the company is investing so heavily in fields that haven't yet hit peak production, its return on invested capital was 8.4 percent in 2007, relatively modest by ExxonMobil standards but quite handsome compared to General Electric's 3.7 percent return on invested capital. That means any current investment by Devon Energy doesn't have a very high hurdle—just 8.7 percent—to jump. So Devon Energy can invest lots of cash and count on increasing rates of return on that investment and on reinvested cash as its projects mature.

And what multiple does Wall Street give Devon Energy? The stock's 2006 price-to-earnings ratio was just 10, almost exactly the price-to-earnings ratio of ExxonMobil. Do you think Wall Street is valuing these companies based on their very different prospects and stage of development? Or do they both get a multiple of 10 because that's what oil companies always get?

I think the same logic still rules Wall Street about agricultural and food commodity stocks. These have always been cyclical companies awarded relatively modest price-to-earnings multiples. And despite evidence that the cycle is so much longer that it really doesn't look like a cycle anymore, the traditional valuations still rule.

For investors who believe that these are now, for all intents and purposes, growth stocks since the upward-trending part of the cycle still has ten or more years to run, it means these stocks are still remarkably cheap and remarkably attractive since the price-to-earnings multiple will gradually expand as Wall Street slowly revalues these equities.

Look at it this way: if farm equipment maker Deere & Co. really will grow earnings by 15.4 percent annually over the next five years—and the food cycle isn't anywhere near a turn for the worse—then why should this stock trade at 15.8 times projected 2008 earnings per share when Cisco Systems, with an estimated annual earnings growth rate of 13.8 percent over the next five years, trades at 17.9 times projected 2008 earnings per share? Just because Cisco Systems is a growth stock and Deere is a cyclical? I don't think so—not in any world that I see.

How the Trends Play Out for Investors

- We're at the end of a thirty-year period of falling food costs that began in 1974. The cycle of rising food costs may not be as long, but there's no reason to think it can't stretch for a decade or two.
- It's not just how much but also what people want to eat. Rising incomes increase the demand for meat, and it takes anywhere from three to five pounds of grain to produce a pound of meat.
- Cheap fixes for the supply/demand imbalance are a thing of the past. It's hard to find new farmland, and we're losing farmland so quickly that we'll be lucky to break even globally.
- Everything from fertilizer to water to tractor fuel is in short supply and is climbing in price. That pushes the price of food higher as well.
- The current global food system relies on cheap fuel and transport to move vast quantities of food around the world.
- The effects of higher food prices will fall disproportionately on those least able to pay. To the degree that national governments can't meet the food needs of their people, expect a rise in violence and terrorism. If you're going to starve to death anyway, what do you have to lose? Violence, of course, makes it even harder to produce food.
- Increasing food supply will depend in the short term on winning battles against desertification, water pollution and waste, a lack of fertilizer in the hands of individual farmers, and inefficient storage and transportation networks that in India in some years cause 40 percent

of a crop to rot. In the long term it will require breakthroughs in seed and farming technologies that increase yields.

Trend Breakers and Trend Makers Ripped from the Headlines

Trend Breakers

- Watch for the *massive destruction of agricultural resources that limit supply*. China's aquaculture industry is on the verge of collapse as water gets so polluted that farmers can't grow fish without using such high levels of antibiotics and other chemicals that the fish are unfit for market.
- *Natural and political disasters that so reduce demand that they overwhelm any possible drop in supply.* Famines and endless civil strife disrupt demand and can actually lead to gluts of supply since they effectively remove millions of consumers from the global market.

Trend Makers

- *Beggar-your-neighbor agricultural export policies* that clamp quotas on food exports set off hoarding and drive up prices. In 2007 a headline watch would have turned up stories about Argentina and Russia restricting exports. That list expanded to include the Ukraine, Vietnam, and Cambodia in 2008.
- *Temporary shortages* are likely to result as farmers bounce from one crop to another. Those are a sign that supply remains only an inch ahead of demand
- *Stories about promising new farm techniques, crops, farm equipment, or new types of farming* (such as aquaculture) are a sign that farming remains sufficiently profitable to attract new investment into research and commercialization of new ideas.
- *Prominence of headlines and stories about all-time commodity price peaks.* When these types of news stories make their way from the

back of the financial section to feature stories on the local TV news, it's often an indicator that Wall Street analysts will raise the price-to-earnings multiples they award a sector. They follow the news too.

STOCK PICKS THAT PUT THE WIND FROM THOSE TRENDS AT YOUR BACK

Bunge (NYSE: BG) is the world's leading oilseed (including soybeans) processing company and one of the top global sellers of vegetable oil. Not a bad place for the White Plains, N.Y.-headquartered company to be, since soybean consumption has increased by 5 percent a year over the last fifteen years and growth shows no signs of slowing down. But what I really like about the stock is the company's position as the largest producer and supplier of fertilizer to South American farmers, with about 25 percent to 30 percent market share. At the base of that business is control of four of the five major phosphate mines in Brazil. That gives the company control over the cost of one of the major components of fertilizer. South America is increasingly important as a source of wheat, soybeans (Brazil is the world's second-largest producer), vegetable oils, and sugar-cane-based ethanol. The continent is one of the few areas of the globe where it is still possible to open up new farm acreage without overwhelmingly large infrastructure investments and (outside the Amazon rain forest) without creating severe negative environmental effects. Bunge's joint venture with E. I. du Pont (DD) has produced a low-linolenic-acid soybean oil suitable for used in reduced- and zero-trans-fat products.

Burlington Northern Santa Fe (NYSE: BNI). God isn't making any more land, and in the United States, at least, nobody is building any more transcontinental railroads. That gives the existing four transcontinental railroads control of the exceedingly lucrative and fast-growing business of shipping bulk freight—coal, timber, and grain—from the U.S. heartland to ports on the West Coast that serve the growing markets of China and the rest of Asia. How good is business for Fort Worth–headquartered Burlington Northern, the best managed, in my estimation, of the transcontinental roads? Operating margins are on track to hit 24 percent in 2008, Standard & Poor's projects. That's up from a recent low of 15.4 percent in 2004. Even more significant, the railroad is now earning a return on invested capital that exceeds its 8.7 percent cost of capital for the first time in a generation. That means the railroad can actually reinvest in its own business and make more money in the future. That's been a huge problem for the railroad industry and has led to a generation of underinvestment in track and rolling stock. After all, who wants to invest if you can't earn a profit that at least covers what it costs to raise the capital that you're investing? That turnaround in return on invested capital marks a huge shift for Burlington Northern from a cyclical company to a growth company. Revenue from 2007–2012 is forecast by Standard & Poor's to grow by a compound annual average of 7 percent. Free cash flow is expected to grow by 10 percent annually.

Deere & Company (NYSE: DE). Earnings as high as an elephant's eye. Yes, I'm being corny, but corn is the big story for Deere. Illinois-headquartered Deere gets about 55 percent of its sales from farm equipment, and the company controls about 50 percent of the North American market for agricultural equipment. So you can see why Deere is the nearest thing there is to a pure play on farm incomes. When farm incomes go up, Deere sells more equipment. It's as simple as that—at least it is if you ignore the history of hard work and innovation that put Deere in command of this market. The brand is probably the best-known label in farm equipment because it's backed by a relentless commitment to producing a constant stream of new products while removing costs from the company's manufacturing operation. From a low of 5.6 percent in 2001, Deere had increased operating margins to 15.4 percent at the end of 2007. Return on equity, negative in 2001, climbed to 20.8 percent by the end of 2007. Deere is a classic example of a Wall Street cyclical stock that is surprising Wall Street by constantly pushing out the peak in the cycle. In 2007 the stock soared. Analysts had thought the company had peaked in 2006, when earnings growth climbed by 22 percent, but as

Deere beat Wall Street expectations in each quarter and then told Wall Street to expect even better performance in the next quarter Wall Street had to scramble to keep up. Wall Street has now pushed the peak out beyond 2009, but I think there's still a lot of surprise and upside left in this stock. As of May 2008 Wall Street was looking for earnings growth to decline in the fiscal year that ends in October 2009.

Monsanto (NYSE: MON) created and now dominates the global seed market—for better (if you've been a shareholder) or worse (if you're a subsistence farmer in Africa who can't afford to buy Monsanto seeds every year). The key here is a research and development budget that spends 10 percent of sales as it turns out a steady stream of new products: modified seeds, disease-resistant seeds, and herbicide-resistant seeds. St. Louis–headquartered Monsanto has gradually strengthened its hold on the market by buying up the best of the smaller seed companies. Its DeKalb brand now controls 23 percent of the North American corn seed market, for example, up from 10 percent in 2001. By acquiring Agroeste Sementes in 2007, Monsanto expanded its share of the Brazilian corn seed market to 40 percent from 30 percent. The 2007 acquisition of Delta and Pine Land gave Monsanto a bigger share of the market for cotton seed, and the 2008 acquisition of De Ruiter Seeds upped Monsanto's share of the global vegetable seed market. Wall Street analysts expect earnings growth of 67 percent for the fiscal year that ends in August 2008 and 20 percent for fiscal 2009. Analysts expect earnings growth at Monsanto over the next five years to average an annual 19 percent.

Potash Corporation of Saskatchewan (NYSE: POT). They may not be making any more real estate or railroads, but they sure are making a lot more fertilizer—just not enough of it to meet increased demand from a world that needs more food and more plant-based fuel at the same time. Potash Corporation is the world's largest producer of— what else?—potash, a key ingredient in agricultural fertilizers. The company has managed to line up the majority of the world's excess capacity of potash, which makes it (1) the low-cost producer in this market and (2) the swing producer in the industry. When demand is high and supply tight, Potash can bring new supply to market in a fraction of the five years—and $2 billion—it takes to develop a potash mine de novo. The developing world and its need/desire to feed as many people as it can from its own farms but with limited land is the driver for growth in potash demand. The developed world applies about twice as much potash fertilizer to its fields as do Brazil, China, and India. Bringing application rates in those countries up to developed-world standards offers the best hope in the short term for increasing farm productivity in those countries. Outside of its potash business, the Saskatoon-headquartered company also has a major cost advantage over many other nitrogen fertilizer makers thanks to its low-cost nitrogen production from natural gas fields in Trinidad.

Stocks for Building an Overweight Position in This Sector

- **Canadian National Railway** (NYSE: CNI) earns the highest profit margins of any of the four transcontinental North American railroads.
- **Canadian Pacific** (NYSE: CP) hauls mostly bulk commodities such as grain, fertilizer, and coal. Less than 13 percent of its traffic is composed of cyclical goods such as timber products and cars.
- **E. I. du Pont** (NYSE: DD) owns Pioneer Hi-Bred, the world's largest seed company.
- **Mosaic** (NYSE: MOS) is the world's largest producer of phosphate fertilizers, with about a 15 percent market share.
- **Syngenta** (NYSE ADR: SYT) is a leader in seed treatments applied to seeds before planting that protect crops in their earliest stages of growth. The Swiss company grew seed protection revenue by 22 percent in the first quarter of 2008.
- **Yara International** (OTC ADR: YARIY) sees fertilizer demand in its key markets in Latin America and India growing at double-digit

rates for at least the next three years. The Norwegian company thinks growth in those markets will give it 10 percent of the global market, up from 7 percent in 2007.

Mutual Funds and ETFs
(Exchange-Traded Funds)

I don't have a lot to recommend. The problem is that agricultural stocks tend to fall between the cracks. You can find some stocks from the sector in natural resource funds or in a materials ETF such as Materials Select SPDR (XLB), but not many. Materials Select SPDR, for example, owns both Monsanto and E. I. du Pont among its top twenty-five holdings, but as chemical and not agricultural companies. You can find a few more in industrial funds or transportation funds, but again, not many. Your best bets here are:

- **PowerShares DB Agriculture** (AMEX: DBA), an ETF that owns commodities futures. As of May 2008 the fund had 16 percent of its assets in corn and 15 percent in soybeans.
- **Goldman Sachs Commodity Strategy A** (GSCAX), a mutual fund that invests in derivatives that track various commodity indexes.

10

The Environment, at Last

Save the World, Make a Buck

You don't need a degree in environmental science or to travel to the remote ends of the earth to see signs that the globe is facing profound environmental challenges. In fact, you can see a good cross section of the problem just driving around your hometown or while you're on your next family vacation.

We, as much as the polar bear in the Artic or the poison dart frog in the Costa Rican rain forest, are living the environmental trends of our time.

Take my Christmas visit to San Diego, for example.

I first visited San Diego close to thirty years ago at the end of a cross-country drive from Washington, D.C. As we drove into the city from the desert hills and canyons to the east, my friend, who was returning to where she'd grown up, told me that her grandparents had once owned a dairy farm east of the city. "It was right about there," she said, waving her hand at a wide swath of houses, condominiums, and shopping malls.

I next saw the city about ten years later when research on a book took me to U.C. San Diego and the Salk Institute in the bluffs above La Jolla. Lifelong East Coasters, my wife and I luxuriated in the easy, lightly trafficked drive on Interstate 5 between La Jolla and downtown. We also noticed the office buildings, condos, and the spectacular Mormon Church going up on what had been farm or scrub land along the highway.

I've visited frequently in the last few years. My brother-in-law, his wife, and their new baby live north of the city in Encinitas. I've taken my own two kids to Legoland, a little farther north in the middle of the last strawberry fields near Carlsbad. I've fought my way through what is now constant traffic at any time of day to drive my kids to the zoo in Balboa Park. I took my son to his first professional football game— Chargers 23, Broncos 3—and marveled at the sea of RVs parked around Qualcomm Stadium for pregame tailgate parties. I've walked the sand in Solana Beach looking at houses now hanging over the cliffs thanks to the erosion from winter waves.

San Diego and North County is still a great place to live and I love to visit, but the problems are increasingly hard to ignore. The traffic has become discouragingly terrible—even with improved commuter rail service—and the round-trip to downtown downright expensive when gas costs $4 a gallon. The produce in grocery stores is still California-glorious, but there are fewer farm stands in San Diego County than in my home borough of Manhattan and the produce at the Encinitas Trader Joe's is no more local than that in the Trader Joe's on Fourteenth Street in New York City. Talk of brownouts and possible blackouts have become a regular part of summer telephone conversations as families on each coast laughingly wondered who was going to be without power next. Over the 2007 Christmas vacation, the local paper carried a story about the need to declare a water emergency in San Diego County because the city might lose up to 30 percent of the water it imports from northern California's Sacramento River Delta.

I could come up with a similar list for my hometown. Each year New Yorkers wonder whether this will finally be the year when the Environmental Protection Agency rules that our once pristine water supply from upstate reservoirs needs chemical treatment. The mayor, Michael Bloomberg, recently proposed (although the state legislature opposed) charging drivers to take their cars into the core of Manhattan as a way to cut our nearly constant gridlock. My utility wants to raise my electric bill 17 percent this year—for service that threatens to go down every time the temperature spikes during the summer. I'm constantly on alert for the next electronic recycling day so I can dispose of the broken digital whatnots that accumulate in my house because I know the city now produces 25,000 tons of discarded TVs, computers, and other electronics containing toxic mercury, lead, and cadmium every year.

I'm sure you can put together a similar list for wherever you live just from what you observe as you walk and drive the streets.

That kind of a list is a good guide to what you can do to make the world a better place for this generation, and the next and the next, of human beings and the plants and animals that travel through space with us. And it's also a good place to start your efforts to put together a portfolio of stocks of companies solving our very real environmental problems.

Save the world, make a buck. That's my motto.

To go from a list of environmental problems awaiting solution to a profitable strategy for investing in environmental solutions, you need to keep two principles in mind. First, that the existing infrastructure—and by that I mean all the human investment in cities, homes, streets, power plants, power lines, cars, gas stations and more—that was built at so much cost will shape any future solutions. Second, that when procrastinators finally spring into action, the ensuing panicked activity doesn't produce the best decisions or result in the cheapest solutions.

EXISTING INFRASTRUCTURE

If you were starting with a clean slate, you wouldn't put a major metropolitan area with 3 million people such as San Diego in a near-desert. With an average annual rainfall of just 12 inches—a true desert gets 10 inches or less—San Diego imports 90 percent of its water from the Sacramento River delta and the Colorado River.

For that matter, you wouldn't set your capital in Beijing no matter what Kublai Kahn did in the thirteenth century. The city of 17 million suffers huge seasonal storms fed by the erosion of deserts in northern and northwestern China. Added to man-made pollution, that dust gives Beijing some of the unhealthiest air on the planet.

And you certainly wouldn't put 1.5 million people into Perth and then make them compete for a limited supply of groundwater with the wheat farmers of Western Australia. You wouldn't put 140 million of the world's poorest people into the land where the Ganges and Brahmaputra rivers flow into the Bay of Bengal so that even a three-foot rise in sea level would put 15 percent of their country underwater and make the survivors even poorer when the rice crop failed. And . . .

Well, you get my point. If we knew then what we know now, we would have done things differently—I like to think. But we didn't. And it's now naive to think that people are going to walk away from the money, time, and emotion invested in existing landscapes without fighting tooth and nail to save them—without much thought for the cost of preserving that investment either.

So we'll build floodgates to protect Venice, London, and someday New York. We'll construct massive desalination plants to turn seawater into freshwater in San Diego, Perth, and Tampa Bay, Florida. We'll dig huge canals to ship water from the wetter south of China to the drier and more polluted north, and we'll lay plans to plant millions of trees to control dust storms—and then reverse course on worries that the trees are taking up too much potential farmland.

Projects like that are on such a gigantic scale that they'll be readily visible. But the same kind of efforts—at a much lower magnitude and with far fewer press headlines—will go on with the infrastructure of daily life. We don't think of the desirability of preserving the investment that went into building the 117,000 gas stations in the United States—with 85,000 attached convenience stores—but you can bet the oil industry does. The cost of writing off the existing network for refueling cars and investing in some alternative network for refueling hydrogen-based or electric cars profoundly influences the economics for and against specific alternative transportation fuels. The same is true with existing investments in roads, pipelines, and power lines. Anything that can hook up to the existing infrastructure, preserving the economic value of that infrastructure and minimizing the amount of alternative infrastructure that must be built and paid for, has a profound edge. That's why the question of whether either biodiesel or ethanol can be shipped through existing pipeline networks is so important to the future of those two fuels.

Enough on my first principle.

WHEN PROCRASTINATORS FINALLY SPRING INTO ACTION, THEY ACT IN A PANIC

Most of the world has been procrastinating rather than seeking solutions for the environmental problems that have come marching gradually above the horizon in the last few decades. Much of the world is still committed to delay for the next five years or so, I'd say. The United States may be the most high-profile of those committed to further procrastination.

Want some evidence? Look at the "breakthrough" bill—that's House Speaker Nancy Pelosi's word, not mine—passed by Congress and signed by President Bush on December 19, 2007. The Energy Independence and Security Act requires cars and light trucks sold in the United States to deliver a fleet-wide average of 35 miles per gallon, up from the current 27.5 miles per gallon, by 2020. It sets new energy efficiency standards that would phase out incandescent lightbulbs in favor of compact fluorescents and other energy efficient bulbs by 2014. It mandates an increase in the production of biofuels, such as corn-based ethanol, to 36 billion gallons by 2020. It throws a small barrel of subsidies, mostly for research, at energy technologies: $90 million a year for advanced battery research, for example, and requires the Department of Energy to study a grand range of topics, from durability to biodiesel engines and greater use of biogas.

In other words, aside from the rather timid increase in miles per gallon by 2020—I call it timid because current European clean diesel cars can easily get 40 miles to the gallon—this is a recipe for doing nothing meaningful in the next five years.

Everybody, even the ethanol fanatics, knows we aren't going to get to 36 billion gallons of corn-based ethanol by 2020. Between demand for food and demand for fuel, competition for corn supplies has already pushed corn prices up to the point where making ethanol is barely profitable, and that's with production running at 6.4 billion gallons of corn-based ethanol and consuming just 20 percent of the corn harvest in 2007. Most estimates show corn-based ethanol production peaking at somewhere near 15 billion gallons a year.

And where's the rest of that 36 billion gallons of biofuels going to come from? From technology that would turn switchgrass, wood chips, or other sources of cellulose into ethanol or some other fuel. Problem is, this technology isn't quite ready for prime time. Range Fuels, a company with funding from venture capitalists and $76 million from the U.S. Department of Energy, has begun work in Georgia on what it calls the country's first commercial-scale cellulose (from wood chips and forest residue) to ethanol plant. Plans are to begin production in 2009. Other government grants awarded on January 3, 2008—a total of $385 million—went to Iogen Biorefinery Partners, Abengoa Bioenergy Biomass of Kansas, Alico, BlueFire Ethanol, and Broin Companies.

But getting from these plants to a cellulose-based biofuels industry that can provide billions of gallons in competitively priced fuel to the transportation market is at least five years away, most in the field agree. Others say the schedule is more like ten years. The technology needs to be improved to bring costs down to something like the $1.50 a gallon that corn-based ethanol costs to produce. And the industry will have to solve the problem of how to collect enough bulky biomass from sources like forests and grasslands to feed a plant.

If you need any final convincing that delay is the official U.S. energy policy, look at the December 15, 2007, "breakthrough" agreement out of the Bali conference on climate change. The United States agreed to international talks on replacing the Kyoto pact by 2009. But the United States only signed on after the rest of the world agreed to drop all specific guidelines for reducing carbon emissions from the compromise. More talk. No action.

If you accept that the United States faces real problems—whether you see those as global climate change, a threat to U.S. national security from a dependence on imported oil, or simply painfully high prices of heating oil and gasoline—then a national energy policy of delay undoubtedly strikes you as insane. Nonetheless, that's exactly what we have.

But I think this next five years is the last stand for the procrastinators. The damage is just too great and the threat too imminent for much of the world to sit on its hands any longer.

Now that more than 370 miles of the 3,860-mile-long Yangtze River and 30 percent of its tributaries are so polluted that drinking the water is the cause of a wave of sickness and death, China is finally doing something about the rampant pollution in its longest river (and source of 35 percent of China's freshwater), caused by inefficient irrigation, uncontrolled industrial and residential waste discharges, and unregulated dumping from boats.

Now that Al Gore and the United Nations environmental team working on climate change have won the Nobel prize, now that Greenland's farmers are looking to move from raising a few sheep to growing vegetables, and now that Antarctica's glaciers are calving at a rate that threatens to set loose an entire ice field, most of the world—well, the European Union and Japan, at least—has made a real commitment to reduce carbon emissions below the levels of 1990.

Now that the U.S. Southeast is in the grip of a drought that has given residents of Atlanta a view of the bottom of their reservoirs, that city is ramping up water conservation measures, from tax incentives for water-saving plumbing fixtures to a mandatory 10 percent reduction in industrial water consumption.

It was easy enough to see many of these problems coming, but just like Sarah Palin, when she was just Alaska's governor—who argued in the *New York Times* in January 2008 that it was too early to call the polar bear threatened, because while we can see the species hitting the wall as earlier and earlier melting of the polar ice pack causes more and more bears to starve to death, the bear population is currently high—when anticipation battles procrastination, procrastination wins.

Of course when things get bad enough, even procrastinators spring into action. And as all good procrastinators know, the last-minute flurry of panicked activity under deadline pressure doesn't always produce the best decisions.

Years ago, we had a chance for relatively inexpensive and gradual fixes to a wide range of environmental problems. But instead, we procrastinated until the problems seem so pressing that we suddenly have to do something. Now, of course, like the high school student who has wasted the days away and has to do a term paper overnight, we're desperate for a solution. The quick fixes that seem most available at this late stage will be very expensive. And, since decisions made under pressure often turn out to be bad decisions, they may not even work.

So what do these two framing principles tell us about where to put the investment dollars that we're allocating to the environmental trend?

BEWARE FALSE OPPORTUNITIES

The most prominent of these is corn-based ethanol. President Bush's call in his January 23, 2007, State of the Union address for the country to produce 35 billion gallons of alternative fuel by 2017 set off an ethanol boom. But that boom has already hit the wall, as increased ethanol production helped drive corn prices to above $6 a bushel in the spring of 2008. At the same time, demand for ethanol hasn't kept up with the growth in supply. Supply is likely to hit 13–15 million gallons in 2008 and demand is projected at around 12 million gallons. Together those two trends have driven profits for ethanol makers to the edge of vanishing. Costs for corn-based ethanol production are up to around $2.45 a gallon with corn at $6 a bushel. Ethanol makers were getting from $2.30 a gallon in the Midwest to $2.40 a gallon on either coast in the spot market as of March 2008. No wonder that ConAgra, NRG Energy, Agassiz Energy, Alchem Limited, Heartland

Energy Group, and Alternative Energy Sources all suspended construction or cancelled plants in the first three months of 2008. Alternative Energy Sources in fact ceased operations in June 2008.

SEARCH OUT THE REAL WINNERS

Delay means the United States will continue to consume an increasing amount of oil every year. Oil consumption in the United States is projected to fall by about 2.3 percent in 2008 from 2007 levels, according to the Energy Information Administration, thanks to slower economic growth. That will leave U.S. oil consumption at about 20.7 million barrels a day. Consumption is projected to pick up again in 2009 with an economic recovery, growing by about 2 percent, and then settle into a steady 1 percent annual growth. That doesn't seem like much, but since the United States accounts for roughly 20 percent of global oil consumption, even a 1 percent increase in U.S. consumption adds about 200,000 barrels a day to global consumption. That will help keep global supply extremely tight once the U.S. economy recovers. If oil producers deliver on all their promised increases in production, and they never do, global supply will climb by 2.2 million barrels a day in 2008 and global demand will grow by 1.3 million barrels a day, according to Energy Information Administration projections. That should leave the market tight enough so that fear of supply disruptions will keep oil prices above $100 a barrel on average for 2008. Oil prices averaged around $74 a barrel in 2007.

With oil at $100 or even $80 a barrel on average in 2008, the year will see big hikes in capital budgets from the international oil majors and from the state-owned oil companies that now control about 80 percent of global oil reserves. In March 2008 Lehman Brothers projected that global oil industry capital spending would climb by 14 percent in 2008, with the bulk of the increase coming outside North America. That extends the boom times for drillers and oil service companies for at least another year and makes them a major winner from a U.S. energy policy of delay.

Procrastination on doing anything meaningful to slow global warming on the part of the United States and the big developing economies of China and India has also created a huge short-term opening for coal. The high price of oil makes replacing oil with coal an economic no-brainer—coal prices would have to climb four- or five-fold to make the fuel as expensive as oil. Environmentally, coal is a big problem since producing a ton of oil from coal requires the use of five to eighteen tons of water and releases seven to ten times as much carbon dioxide as does refining oil. But the U.S. energy policy of delay and China's and India's refusal to cap their carbon emissions short of developed-world levels have left a big window open. The possibility that a future global agreement on climate change would restrict building of new coal-fired power plants or new coal-to-oil facilities has unleashed a rush to build, especially in Asia. Shenhua Group will start China's first large-scale coal-to-oil plant in 2008 with an initial output of 20,000 barrels a day. By 2030, the International Energy Agency projects, China will be producing 750,000 barrels a day from coal. India is getting in on the act too, with talks under way about setting up the country's first plant in 2008.

Procrastination has made those parts of the existing energy and water supply infrastructure that can be quickly turned to solving environmental crises extremely valuable. Adding significant new quantities of electricity from wind power, solar power, and nuclear power to the national energy supply will require a massive juggling of energy supply and demand across the national electrical supply grid to keep nuclear plants running at their most efficient peak rates when electricity supply rises when the sun shines in Arizona or falls when the wind stops blowing in Kansas.

THREE INFRASTRUCTURE WINNERS FROM PROCRASTINATION

The existing national electricity supply grid, which connects 3,000 electric utilities and 2,000 independent power producers with 120 million residential, 16 million commercial, and 700,000 industrial customers along 700,000 miles of high transmission lines owned by 200 different entities, isn't up to that task. The system is riddled with bottlenecks that make moving power from one region to another difficult and in times of crisis impossible. Parts of the country aren't fully connected to the national grid, so electricity rates in Texas are the highest in the lower forty-eight states because the state's customers can't take full advantage of lower wholesale power prices in other regions. The grid is woefully stupid—it's slow at catching shifts in customer behavior, and balancing the load relies on a series of ad hoc local or at best regional responses. And there's no mechanism for sending real-time information on demand and supply to customers so that users can modify their consumption to take advantage of lower hourly or seasonal prices for electricity.

Despite all those shortcomings, the national grid has a value of about $130 billion, the Center for Smart Energy estimates.

So think what a grid that could do all those things would be worth to a world that is desperate to reduce its consumption of electricity in order to cut back on the production of greenhouses gases such as carbon dioxide. And where holding the line on the company electricity bill in a world of rising prices for virtually all forms of energy will mean the difference between corporate life and death. And where an ever larger part of the global civilization of computers connected by the Internet is dependent on uninterrupted and unvarying supplies of electricity.

Think too what such a grid, which has been dubbed the "smart grid," would be worth to the companies that own it. For example, the increasing need for uninterrupted, guaranteed high-quality (that is, unvarying) electrical supply has led some utilities to begin to fantasize about charging a premium price to customers who need this quality of service. Getting that premium would require making the grid smart enough so it could prioritize service to premium customers and constantly monitor power demands at those customers, and adding flow buffers—high-temperature superconductivity storage is one possibility—that would flatten voltage spikes. A smart grid would also let a utility fend off competition from other power providers to sell electricity to low-price-first consumers by offering packages of load-shifting deals that would let a consumer pay less for using electricity at times when demand was low.

These possibilities are leading to a long-delayed resurgence in investment in the gird. The North American power industry spent $20 billion on grid infrastructure equipment in 2005. That investment is projected to grow to $45 billion in 2008. Sales of advanced metering equipment, which allows real-time tracking of customer energy use, time-of-day or demand-based pricing, and two-way communication between the power supplier and the power consumer (including the possibility of agreed-upon supply reductions to consumers at times of high demand in exchange for lower electricity prices) are currently climbing at 20 percent a year.

I see the same dynamic at work when I look at the 100,000 miles of pipeline used for shipping refined petroleum products in the United States. We're seeing a resurgence of investor interest and capital investment in the entire sector as it becomes clear that the environmental crisis is going to make this network more valuable than ever.

That's quite a shift from four to five years ago. Back in 2002 and 2003, the online Jubak's Picks portfolio that I run on MSN Money actually included shares of Kinder Morgan Energy Partners, a master limited partnership that owned about 26,000 miles of pipeline in the United States. But I sold in June 2003 because I bought into the prevailing Wall Street wisdom at the time: growth in the pipeline business was just about played out because there really wasn't much remaining need to build new pipelines. (The portfolio earned about 22 percent on its low-risk investment in Kinder Morgan, by the way.)

Was that ever the wrong thing to do! As of the end of 2007, the shares had gained another 40 percent in price. Not bad for a low-risk investment that paid a 5 percent to 6 percent dividend for all that time as well.

What changed? The sources of oil and gas flowing to U.S. refineries and consumers changed. New links have had to be built—will be built—to connect new sources of natural gas in the Rocky Mountains to consumers in the East. New pipelines are needed for the north-to-south flow of oil that is just beginning from Canada's oil sands in Alberta to refineries in the United States and that reverses the traditional south-to-north flow from refineries along the Gulf Coast. New natural gas pipelines are on the books to carry Alaskan natural gas southward. These pipelines and others will carry natural gas for export to Asia to liquefied natural gas terminals along Canada's Pacific coast.

Just look at the projects one pipeline company has on its schedule. In the next two to three years Enbridge, a Canadian pipeline company headquartered in Calgary, will finish the Alberta Clipper Project, which is projected to deliver up to 800,000 barrels a day of heavy crude from Alberta's oil sands to Wisconsin by mid-2010; the Southern Access Expansion, which will deliver 400,000 barrels a day of heavy crude to Chicago and southern Illinois from Wisconsin by 2009; and the Clarity pipeline, which will transport natural gas from the Barnett Shale and Anadarko Basin in Texas.

That's just the beginning of the pipeline story too. There's the potential flow of new fuels such as ethanol and biodiesel. Both fuels are now carried by truck, rail, and barge because of the relatively low volumes being shipped and because both fuels present challenges to existing pipelines. Ethanol, for example, leads to corrosion and cracking of the pipeline. But blending and changes in pipeline technology are likely to conquer those problems at about the time that the shipped volume of these fuels grows large enough to economically interest pipeline owners. A presentation to a 2007 conference of the Association of Oil Pipe Lines put that number for biodiesel blend at a 30 percent market share and noted that the fuel now has about 6 percent to 8 percent of the entire diesel market.

And there's the as yet vague role that pipeline operators might play in getting wood chips or switchgrass, the raw materials for ethanol made from cellulose, to production plants. One suggestion: grind up the plant matter, mix it with water, and pipe it to the ethanol plant.

But as much as I like the electric grid and energy pipelines, I like the makers of water pumps even more.

WATER IS AT THE CENTER OF THE CURRENT CRISIS

The water crisis has two parts. First, there's the global shortage of water that's clean enough to drink and use in industrial processes. The World Bank reports that eighty countries now have water shortages that threaten health and economies. The dimensions of the problem get even larger when you include water-short regions of otherwise water-wealthy countries. For example, the United States has, on average, enough water, but the cities of the Southwest, California, and Florida all face severe water shortages.

A growing population—especially a population that insists on moving to water-short areas such as Florida—is part of the problem. More people equals a demand for more water. But that's only part of the problem. Since 1900, water use has grown sixfold while global population has increased only twofold. As economies grow and as living standards go up, the per capita demand for water climbs. We also insist on fouling the planet's limited supplies of freshwater. According to the World Bank, about 95 percent of the world's cities still dump raw sewage into their waters.

And second, many solutions to the global energy crisis consume vast quantities of water. For example, China is putting a big bet on solving its energy crisis by building plants to turn coal into liquids that can be used to replace oil.

Water—or more precisely the lack of it—could stop this plan dead in its tracks. A November 2007 report for the State of Montana's Energy and Telecommunications Interim Committee estimated that a coal-to-oil plant would use anywhere from 1 to 1.5 barrels to 5 to 7 barrels of water per barrel of liquid oil, depending on the technology of the plant and the specifications of the coal used in the process. (I've cited figures from the Montana study since the state government is a big proponent of coal to liquid technology and can't be dismissed as an environmental extremist.)

So producing 750,000 barrels of liquid a day by 2030, as China plans, would require somewhere between 750,000 and 5.2 million barrels of water a day. At 42 gallons to the barrel, that's 32 million to 220 million gallons of water a day.

That's not exactly a drop in the bucket for a country on the edge of a water crisis. China will face an official water crisis by 2030, according to the Ministry of Water Resources, when water resources per hectare of arable land will fall to just 80 percent of the world average. Half of China's 617 largest cities face water deficits. The problem is even worse when you realize that only 15 percent of the country's water resources are north of the Yangtze, where much of the country's coal lies.

So where will the water come from? China will build desalination plants. Why am I so sure? Because we're building them around the world from Perth to Tampa Bay. Once upon a time cities and industries could have afforded to take the slow, more efficient, and less expensive road of water conservation, water pipe repair, and increases in industrial efficiency. Cities and regions could have spent time getting farmers to reduce the fertilizer runoff into rivers. They could have installed new metering systems that would have helped reduce use. (Even in the developed world most residential water use isn't metered.) But now it's a crisis: with the water table dropping in Florida, with Perth about to run out of water, with San Diego at the end of its ability to tap the Colorado, mayors and governors don't think they have a choice.

Nobody's going to build just one plant either. In China just the needs of its coal-to-oil industry will require (using the upper figure for the industry's water use) ten times the output of the Tampa Bay seawater desalination plant, the largest ever built in the United States. The Tampa plant went on line in late 2007, more than eight years after the original contract was awarded in July 1999. China has announced a goal of producing the water equivalent of thirty Tampa Bay desalination plants by 2020. And China isn't alone: the Saudis recently offered a contract for twenty new desalination plants.

All those desalination plants, in China and elsewhere, mean big business for companies such as General Electric and Shaw Group, which supply the guts of the water purification system and the big project engineering expertise.

But it's the opportunity in water pumps that really excites me. The number of pumps per project can be huge. Although a desalination plant has to be built near a big source of water, it has to be hooked into the existing water infrastructure, often miles away. In Tampa Bay, for example, the water has to be pumped through fifteen miles of water transmission mains (after crossing two navigable rivers). Moving all that water all that way will require a lot of pumps—added to the huge 800-horsepower vertical pump and the 2,250 horizontal pumps in each of the plant's seven supply trains.

Also, with the pump makers you get exposure to the other big crash solution to the water crisis: moving huge amounts of water over long distances. San Diego and other California cities such as Los Angeles already rely on water moved from the north of the state to the south, from rural areas with water supplies fed by the snows of the Sierra Nevada, and from rivers that spend the bulk of their life in other states. But China's plan to move massive quantities of water from the south to the much drier north dwarfs the California system. Planned for completion in 2050, it will eventually divert 11.8 trillion gallons a year to the drier north. It will link China's four main rivers—the Yangtze, Yellow River, Huaihe, and Haihe—and requires the construction of three diversion routes. That's a lot of pumping.

Finally, with the pump makers you get to participate in the growth of the global oil and gas industry too, since that industry moves oil like it was, well, water.

Is It Time for Nuclear Energy?

We might as well call nuclear a new technology—the world hasn't completed a nuclear power plant in fifteen years, and in many ways the industry is beginning all over again from scratch.

But because nuclear power fits so well into the existing infrastructure—the end product is just electricity—and because a crash program of building nuclear power plants to begin an immediate reduction in global carbon emissions to fight global warming seems possible, the world is building nuclear power plants again. In August 2005, Finland began construction on the first nuclear power plant to be built in Europe since 1991. China has started construction on 4, begun planning on 23 others, and announced proposals for 54 more. Globally, as of May 2007, 30 new nuclear power plants are under construction, another 70 are planned, and 150 more are proposed. Even the United States is edging into the game: the Nuclear Regulatory Agency has granted two early site permits to U.S. utilities, and it looks like the Tennessee Valley Authority will complete its Watts Bar Unit 2, 80 percent finished when construction was halted in 1985, and become the first utility to bring new nuclear generating capacity on line in the United States.

The ramp up hasn't been going so smoothly, however. The industry is having trouble rebuilding the skills that atrophied during the long layoff. Areva and Siemens, the French and German companies building Finland's Olkiluoto reactor, have had to reforge legs of the reactor and pieces of the pressure vessel. Substandard concrete has had to be ripped out and replaced. It's turned out to be harder to manufacture the structural steel plates for the reactor than expected. Areva has had trouble finding companies anywhere in the world capable of specialized work such as forging for the steam generator tubes. There are currently only two companies in the world, one in France and one in Japan, that can produce forged reactor vessels.

Those problems are going to get worse as the pace of building increases: if building one reactor challenges industry resources, think of the bottlenecks that building a dozen at the same time, and then two dozen, will create. The lack of experienced contractors and subcontractors will stretch out delivery times and drive up costs. The projected expansion of global nuclear construction capacity is staggering—from a recent five reactors a year to a projected fifty a year. This is at a time when the oil industry, the mining industry, and projects for airlines, railroads and shipping companies are all drawing upon the same pool of construction engineers and limited supplies of the same raw materials. In 2007 Areva revised the cost of its new reactor at Flamanville in France by 10 percent due to rising costs of raw materials.

As if this weren't tough enough, the nuclear industry is trying to introduce a new generation of designs at the same time as it ramps up construction. Some of these, such as the Westinghouse reactor with its passive gravity-controlled safety systems, do seem to mark a huge advance in reactor safety. But no one has ever built one of those reactors or one based on General Electric's new-generation design. And even the relatively conventional Areva design incorporates enough new features that Finnish regulators say that they didn't have a detailed design of the project when Finnish utility Teollisuuden Voima Oy signed the contract.

As a result, the Olkiluoto-3 reactor, originally scheduled to start producing power in May 2009, is now projected to come on line eighteen months late, in December 2010. It's also going to be significantly more expensive to build than the $4.1 billion originally budgeted.

Delays such as this play havoc with one of the hot investment ideas of 2006 and early 2007: the stocks of uranium mining companies. The world's current total of 437 nuclear power reactors uses about 67,000 metric tons of uranium each year. Uranium mines produced only 42,000 metric tons of uranium in 2005 with the rest of global demand being met from utility stockpiles or the use of uranium and plutonium from decommissioned nuclear weapons. Add the 30 plants under construction and then another 220 not too far down the road, for a 57 percent increase in the total number of nuclear reactors in operation, and even with the increased fuel efficiency of new reactors, you're looking at a huge shortfall in uranium production. And the shortfall gets even bigger when you take into account the projected decline in the amount of uranium available from decommissioned nuclear weapons over the next twenty years.

That math drove the price of uranium for immediate delivery (the spot price) to double in the twelve months that ended in July 2006 and then to double again to $136 a pound in late June 2007. The price of uranium then headed pretty much downhill for the rest of 2007. On January 11, 2008, it hit $90 a pound. What happened?

The case for higher uranium prices isn't nearly as straightforward as it seems. Higher prices will bring more uranium exploration, more uranium mining, and more uranium supply. The effect of this new supply means that higher uranium prices depend on timing. If the addition of new supply lags the addition of new demand from new reactors, then the price of uranium will climb. If, however, the new supply comes on line before the new reactors do, then the price will tumble.

Cameco, the Canadian company that produces 20 percent of the world's uranium, projects a net increase of seventy-seven nuclear reactors globally from 2006 to 2016. That's a more conservative total than the bulls who bid up uranium prices in the first half of 2007 project. That, in the company's opinion, will result in an increase in uranium demand of about 2 percent to 3 percent a year.

All this means that while the nuclear future will arrive—we've procrastinated ourselves into a fix on global climate change that will require a contribution from nuclear—it will arrive later than the governments betting on a nuclear solution to rising oil prices and rising carbon emissions now project. Look at the proposed government schedule in the United Kingdom, a country on the edge of giving the green light to a new generation of nuclear power plants. A 2009 study would identify sites for new nuclear plants. Construction won't begin until 2012. And if it takes about as long to build these reactors as it's taking to build Olkiluoto-3 (assuming a trade-off between gains in experience and newly created bottlenecks), then these plants won't start producing electricity until 2017. As crash solutions go, that timetable leaves a lot to be desired.

With the returns to investors so clearly hinging on the details of that timetable, the nuclear trend is more difficult to profit from than it seems to be on first glance.

SOLAR ENERGY WINS FROM PROCRASTINATION

The long-term prospects for the solar industry are bright *because* the energy bill that President Bush sighed into law on December 19, 2007, didn't launch a crash program to expand the use of solar energy in the United States or even extend solar tax credits that were set to expire in October 2008.

I know that seems illogical. After all, how can a fledging industry struggling to create demand so it can scale up and bring down costs benefit from anything that delays growth in demand? So let me explain why government neglect in 2007 and into 2008 could make 2009 the best year ever for solar companies—and investors in them.

The solar industry had a problem in 2007, and it wasn't a lack of demand. Global solar production, measured by the megawatts of power that solar cells and modules would produce once hooked up to the grid, climbed by 57 percent in 2004, according to Jefferies International, and then by 30 percent in 2005, 35 percent in 2006, and a projected 13 percent in 2007.

See a problem there? Young growth industries facing a virtually untapped market—solar provides just 0.02 percent of energy generation in the United States in 2005, for example—shouldn't show slowing growth rates. If solar has the potential that its supporters say it does—and I agree that it does—the industry's growth rate should be accelerating at this point, not dropping. (Global solar installations, which always lag production and which are growing from a smaller base because of that lag, climbed 60 percent in 2007.)

So what happened? Beginning in 2005, demand from solar wafer, solar cell, and solar module makers for silicon completely overwhelmed supply from the companies that provide silicon to the solar and semiconductor industries. Companies that turn silicon ingots, the first stage in producing either solar cells or computer chips, into solar wafers couldn't get enough crystalline silicon to meet orders from solar cell makers. That forced solar cell and module makers to idle capacity. Utilization rates—the amount of its maximum production capacity that a company is actually using—among solar cell makers fell to 70 percent in 2005 from 86 percent in 2004. And the problem kept getting worse in 2006 and 2007. German solar wafer and cell maker ErSol Solar Energy, for example, cut its forecast for 2007 production to 55 megawatts from 70 megawatts, a 27 percent drop, due to the wafer shortfall.

That shortfall in supply had a predictable effect on silicon prices: they went up, way up. Companies able to arrange long-term contracts with suppliers saw the silicon raw material required by wafer and solar cell manufacturers jump in price to $45 a pound by the middle of

2007 from $20 in 2003. On the spot market, cell manufacturers who didn't have a stable long-term supply were paying $95 a pound.

Those higher prices have had the salutary effect of bringing more companies into the business of making silicon for solar wafers and encouraging existing suppliers to expand. After climbing by just 14 percent in 2007 from 2006, silicon production is projected by Jefferies International to climb 43 percent in 2008, 50 percent in 2009, and another 50 percent in 2010. The industry bottleneck that restricted production and produced higher prices for raw materials was broken in 2008.

That's critical, since the big barrier to growth in the solar industry isn't a lack of subsidies from the U.S. government but the cost of electricity produced from solar cells. Right now it costs about 30 cents to produce a kilowatt of solar electricity versus the 15 to 18 cents a kilowatt hour retail customers pay in the United States. So, at the moment, solar isn't competitive with other technologies for generating electricity.

But solar is gradually closing the gap. Solar wafer makers are getting more wafers out of a kilogram of silicon by making wafers thinner. The industry is on track to get 35 wafers out of a kilogram of silicon by 2010, up from 29 wafers per kilogram currently. That 20 percent increase in wafers produced per kilogram of silicon is a huge cost savings since silicon accounts for about 30 percent of the final cost of a solar module. At the same time, solar cell makers are getting more energy out of their cells. Solar cell efficiency is projected to go up to 17 percent from the current 15 percent by 2010. Combine the cost savings from more efficient manufacturing with the improved electricity production and the cost of electricity produced from solar cells will fall almost 30 percent by 2010 to about 21 cents a kilowatt hour.

I think you can see the punch line coming. As electricity from solar gets cheaper and as electricity generated from conventional sources gets more expensive with the rising cost of carbon-based fuels, at some point the cost of solar-generated electricity reaches parity with the retail cost of electricity from all sources. Hemlock Semiconductor, the world's largest producer of silicon, projects parity around 2012. (Hemlock is owned by Dow Corning, Mitsubishi Materials, and Shin-Etsu Chemical.) Jefferies

International is a bit more conservative: the investment company sees parity in the sunshine-rich U.S. Southwest in 2013.

Government support either in the form of rebates to buyers of solar equipment (the U.S. approach) or in the form of guaranteed above-market prices for the purchase of solar electricity from solar power generators (the European approach) is crucial to getting to that inflection point. Without the economies of scale created by the demand growth generated by these subsidies, solar costs won't fall fast enough to hit parity on that schedule.

So why, then, do I say that the U.S. government's delay, which put the existing U.S. subsidies due to expire in October 2008 in jeopardy and postponed plans to increase subsidies, is a good thing for the solar industry? Earlier versions of the energy bill included provisions to extend U.S. solar subsidies through 2016 and to eliminate the current $2,000 cap on tax credits for the installation of residential solar systems. Those provisions were stripped out of the bill that President Bush signed in December.

First, existing subsidies in Germany, Spain, Korea, Greece, and individual U.S. states such as California will generate enough demand to keep solar efficiencies climbing and solar costs dropping in 2008. And it's likely that by later in 2008, a Congress facing increasing political pressure to do more about the high cost of energy and the increasing threat of global climate change will produce an energy bill with increased subsidies for solar.

Second, the delay in increasing U.S. subsidies avoided creating more demand than the industry could meet during the silicon supply crunch that peaked in 2007. A big surge in demand would have produced runaway silicon price increases, generated an excruciating profit margin contraction at wafer, cell, and module manufacturers who didn't have long-term reasonably priced contracts for silicon, and led to shutdowns at some wafer, cell, and module manufacturers who couldn't get supplies of silicon at all. In short, a surge in demand while the silicon bottleneck throttled supply would have produced exactly the kinds of price distortions and industry disruption that can set back an industry for years.

With the bottleneck breaking up in 2008, the industry looks like it's ready to ramp up to meet a surge in demand that will result from an extension in U.S. subsidies passed as part of the $7 billion plan to bail out Wall Street and new directives in China to increase the use of solar power. The Beijing government has decreed that utilities generate 5 percent of their electricity from renewable sources by 2010 and 10 percent by 2020 (and hydro electricity doesn't count). That could result in 6 gigawatts of annual demand—roughly 50 percent more than total global installed solar power systems in 2007—if even 25 percent of those renewables were solar. Granted that since the Beijing government hasn't yet provided any money to back up its decree, the real rate of adoption will be slower than now projected on paper, I still think the global solar industry can expect to see demand from China gradually kick in over the next few years.

And then there's the potential boost from nuclear power. I know, I know. Nuclear and solar are normally placed on opposite ends of the power supply spectrum. But from the point of view of a world increasingly likely to need a crash solution for reducing carbon emissions to combat global climate change, solar and nuclear are both privileged front-runners. They both easily tie into the existing electric grid, so nobody needs to build a new distribution network. The end product, electricity, can be adapted to power the existing car-based transportation system while reducing emissions in this carbon-intensive sector. And that end product works equally well with proposed solutions such as electric or hydrogen-powered cars (where carbon-free electricity is essential so that the production of hydrogen reduces net carbon).

At the moment I'd say that nuclear and solar are dual-tracked. They're both seen as possible solutions by different constituencies favoring each. Nuclear currently has an edge in many government circles because it seems best suited to generating a lot of carbon-free electricity quickly. That's why efforts to expand nuclear power in the United Kingdom and in the United States are currently getting more government attention than solar.

But if nuclear doesn't deliver on schedule, there's a good chance that solar could move up in the list of government rankings for crash solutions to throw cash at.

How the Trends Play Out for Investors

• We've procrastinated and procrastinated some more, but now we've run out of time and we'll have to face up to some of the world's environmental problems.

• A partial to-do list includes more clean water, more water in the right places, less carbon entering the atmosphere, less pollution of water and air, less reliance on fossil fuels, less sprawl, and more sustainable agriculture.

• We won't attack all of these problems—just those that seem near crisis.

• Because we're in crisis mode, the solutions we pick will be expensive, brutish, quick-acting, and compatible with existing infrastructure.

• Solutions that force the write-off of sizable portions of the existing infrastructure will be nonstarters; solutions that protect the existing infrastructure or make it more valuable will have an edge.

• Pipelines, the electrical grid, and the water infrastructure, especially water pumps, will be key zones of value creation in solving the environmental crisis.

• Nuclear will be a major crisis solution, but timing issues make it tough for investors to capitalize on the trend

• The solar industry may be gaining efficiencies of size at exactly the right time.

Trend Makers and Trend Breakers Ripped from the Headlines

Trend Breakers

• The big trend destroyer for this sector and indeed for the global economy as a whole would be *a fall in demand for oil and a slump in oil prices.* How big a slump would we need to undermine the fundamentals of everything from oil sands to ethanol to solar? Anything below $60 a barrel would do the trick.

• Watch out for *a furthur retreat in solar subsidies in Germany and Spain.* Spain, now the fourth-biggest solar market in the world, is growing faster than the number one market, Germany, thanks to a government-guaranteed purchase price for solar-generated electricity that has sent the Spanish national budget into sticker shock. The next round is less generous but still enough to keep the sunshine-rich Spanish market chugging in 2009.

• Congress is working on a second energy bill that would include all the subsidies and greenhouse gas reduction plans that Congress couldn't agree on for the December 2007 bill. The market doesn't have to worry about solar and wind subsidies. They were extended in September. *But a failure to extend government support for alternative energy technologies under a new president in 2009 would be a major setback to stocks in this sector in the short run.*

• Look for stories about *truly disruptive new technologies that would decrease the value of existing energy infrastructure.* A disruptive technology would have to offer savings that would justify scrapping some part of the current electrical grid, pipeline network, or water-delivery infrastructure. The grid is the most vulnerable of these because it relies on decades-old transmission technology in many areas. So far technologies such as superconductors (supercooled materials that increase the efficiency of electricity transmission) look to be complementary to the existing grid. But technology has a way of sneaking up on the world as it exists and sending it in new directions. One area I'd watch: wireless transmission of electricity.

TREND MAKERS

• Watch for stories about *a shift after the 2008 election in Washington's take on global climate change and alternative energy technologies.* Almost any conceivable incoming administration will be more committed than the Bush administration to doing something beyond throwing subsidies at ethanol. Legislation with real money behind it would signal an end to the current gridlock on energy.

• With $60-a-barrel oil being sufficient to support a variety of alternative energy technologies, *oil prices averaging more than $100 a barrel in 2009 would accelerate the trends in this chapter.*

• *China could put real money behind Beijing's decrees about renewable energy.* The central government is notorious for putting ambitious rules on paper and then not following through with money or enforcement. On paper, for example, China has some of the best environmental laws in the world. On the ground, though, it's another story entirely, as enforcement is so lax as to be nonexistent. If China puts some cash behind the rules requiring utilities to get 5 percent of their power from renewable sources, that would be a huge boon for solar.

• Wall Street is learning to expect shortages of engineers and components as any energy technology goes on a building spree, and investors won't be surprised at delays as the nuclear industry gears up to build all the plants now in the planning stage. *Delays of the sort I've outlined in this chapter would push more money toward other power technologies that reduce carbon emissions. If those delays don't materialize, that would be great for stocks of nuclear suppliers and uranium miners.*

STOCK PICKS THAT PUT THE WIND FROM THOSE TRENDS AT YOUR BACK

Enbridge (NYSE: ENB) just keeps adding more pipeline projects to its, well, pipeline. Besides the three that I mention in this chapter— the Alberta Clipper Expansion from Alberta's oil sands to Wisconsin, the Southern Access Expansion from Wisconsin to Chicago, and the Clarity natural gas pipeline in Texas—in March 2008 the company announced a joint venture, the Rockies Alliance Pipeline, that would run north from natural-gas-rich Wyoming to Canada, where it would connect with existing pipelines that distribute natural gas in the United States. That's why I think Calgary-based Enbridge will be able to at least match the 11.5 percent annual earnings growth that the company has turned in over the last five years. The stock paid a dividend of 3.2 percent as of April 30, 2008. (Investors can trade some of the growth potential of these shares for more income by buying Enbridge Energy Partners, a master limited partnership paying 7.6 percent as of April 30, 2008.)

First Solar (NASDAQ: FSLR). The holy grail for the solar industry is finding something cheaper than semiconductor-grade (99.99 percent pure) crystalline silicon that will deliver the same or better energy efficiency. That would let solar power deliver electricity at a cost that's competitive with electricity from coal or natural gas—without subsidies. One of the most promising technologies is called "thin film." One direction in thin film research has concentrated on using cheaper amorphous silicon to replace crystalline silicon. Another direction is to replace silicon completely with materials that offer lower costs but improved efficiency at converting sunlight into electricity. First Solar has used cadmium and tellurium to achieve 10.6 percent efficiencies as of March 2008. (That compares to 8 percent efficiencies with thin film technologies using amorphous silicon.) At its December 2007 Wall Street analyst day, the company repeated its target of selling solar modules at a cost of $1.00 to $1.25 a watt by 2012 and at less than $0.70 a watt by 2012. At that price the company believes it will be able to sell solar cells to utilities for commercial power production. In 2008 First Solar acquired DT Solar to give it a sales channel in that market. To ramp up production to meet the potential demands of that market, the company is building new factories in Malaysia that are scheduled to go into production in the second half of 2008. Revenue grew by 194 percent in the first quarter of 2008. Wall Street pegs the average earnings growth rate over the next five years at 48 percent annually.

Flowserve (NYSE: FLS). Global capital spending in the water/wastewater sector is projected to grow by 10 percent a year in 2008–10. Nothing to sneeze at. But growth in the sector segments of filtration, desalination, and exports of water equipment to China are projected to grow by 15 percent. Looking out beyond the next few years, I think growth rates are more likely to head up than down as growing populations in developing economies with more income use and demand more clean water. Flowserve makes pumps, valves, and seals, and sells to customers in the industrial, nuclear, oil and gas, and water supply markets. Wall Street projects annual earnings growth of 11.3 percent a year over the next five years; I think that target is low considering the revenue growth in the company's water and energy markets and Flowserve's success in raising operating margins by 3.5 percentage points from the first quarter of 2007 to the first quarter of 2008. The company has set a target of growing operating margins to 15 percent by 2010 from 11.8 percent in the third quarter of 2007.

General Cable (NYSE: BGC) will be one of the biggest beneficiaries of investment in the electrical grid in the United States and globally. In the United States, electric companies are projected to spend $14 billion a year over the next ten years to make up for years of underinvestment. General Cable, which once sold only in the U.S. market, has expanded internationally until in 2007 only 45 percent of sales came from North America. In 2007 the company's market broke down like this: 25 percent of sales are in Europe, the Middle East and India, 15 percent in Africa and the Asia-Pacific region, and 15 percent in Central and South America. You can see the benefits of that move overseas in recent rates of revenue growth. Revenue grew by 42 percent in the first quarter of 2008, even though sales dropped by 1 percent in the company's North American markets. Revenue in Europe and North Africa grew by 30 percent in the quarter, but the biggest contributor to the quarter's growth was the rest of the world, where revenue grew by 71 percent. The company's global footprint grew in October 2007 when it acquired the global wire and cable business of Phelps Dodge International from Freeport McMoRan Copper & Gold. General Cable's acquisition gives it equity stakes in two companies selling to China's energy market, and it's a market leader in South and Central America. Not everything is rosy in General Cable's markets, however. Demand for lower-power residential electrical cable is down along with U.S. housing starts, and the telecommunications business has been soft for most of 2007. But that's been balanced by continued huge demand from the global build-out of electrical distribution systems, and I'd use any weakness from the U.S. housing slump as an opportunity to buy General Cable shares.

Q-Cells (OTC: QCLSF). This German company is the largest producer of solar cells in the world. Q-Cells will be one of the major beneficiaries of the end of the silicon supply bottleneck in 2008 as new supply lowers the price of the silicon wafers and removes the uncertainties that have hobbled production. Q-Cells' cost for silicon wafers will fall 10 percent by 2010, Jefferies International estimates. That will drive its EBIT (earnings before interest and taxes) profit margin to 18 percent from 16.6 percent and the profit growth rate in the company's solar cell business to 43 percent from 39 percent in 2007. Q-Cells also has a promising thin film business.

STOCKS FOR BUILDING AN OVERWEIGHT POSITION IN THIS SECTOR

- **Exelon** (NYSE: EXC). This utility's eleven nuclear power plants generate 18 percent of all U.S. nuclear power. With the price of carbon-based fuels rising along with the prospects for some kind of carbon tax or cap, those nuclear plants get more valuable every day.
- **General Electric** (NYSE: GE) has stakes in solar, wind, nuclear, water purification, and electrical power generation, making this a one-stock portfolio of energy technologies.
- **Gorman-Rupp** (NYSE: GRC) is a small-cap that's big in water pumps. A company subsidiary recently received a big order for water pumps to handle flood control in New Orleans. In the fourth quarter of 2007 revenue climbed 18 percent and, more significant to my mind, gross profit margins climbed by 25 percent. Wall Street projects 16 percent average annual earnings growth over the next five years.
- **Itron** (NASDAQ: ITRI). Momentum is building at this maker of smart utility meters. New order backlog grew to $484 million in the first quarter of 2008, up from $118 million in the first quarter of 2007.

That doesn't include the big contract win at Southern California Edison in December 2007, worth about $470 million. The California Edison deal is a sign that the logjam is breaking, and I think we'll see a lot more orders with Itron and its competitors as utilities buy new meters that cut costs and increase their ability to manage power peaks.

• **Pentair** (NYSE: PNR). A decline in the company's residential pool and spa business with the crash of the U.S. home-building sector makes this a value-priced water play. The company's pump and filtration business makes up about 70 percent of sales. About 32 percent of those sales come from overseas, but the Minnesota-headquartered company wants to raise that to 40 percent by 2010. In 2006 Pentair inked a joint venture in China.

• **SunTech Power Holdings** (NYSE ADR: STP). There's a risk that the Chinese government's renewable-energy initiatives will turn out to be just window dressing, but I think it's a risk worth taking for the size of the potential domestic Chinese market alone. Suntech Power has recently signed a contract with Asia Silicon that will lower the company's raw material costs in the second half of 2008. Standard & Poor's projects that sales will climb 49 percent in 2008.

Mutual Funds and ETFs
(Exchange-Traded Funds)

It's hard to find an exact match to the way I've picked the winners in this sector in an exchange-traded fund, but you can come close—especially if you put together an alternative-energy ETF with an infrastructure ETF.

• PowerShares Progressive Energy Portfolio (PUW) invests in technologies that improve the environmental performance of old energy sources such as coal, oil, and nuclear power.
• PowerShares WilderHill Alternative Energy (PBW) will give you good exposure to a portfolio of solar stocks.
• PowerShares Global Clean Energy Portfolio (PBD) and Van Eck

Global Alternative Energy (GEX) provide a more global approach to the sector.

- For a dose of the infrastructure theme that I've emphasized in this chapter, look at iShares S&P Global Infrastructure (IGF) or SPDR FTSE/Macquarie Global Infrastructure 100 (GII). I think the iShares Global Infrastructure is a better fit with my view of where infrastructure profits will come from. This ETF is made up of 40 percent utilities, 22 percent highways and railroads, 20 percent oil and gas storage and transportation, and 8 percent marine ports. The SPDR FTSE/Macquarie ETF is 88 percent utilities, 5 percent energy, 3 percent industrials, and 2 percent telecommunications.

- In the traditional mutual fund world you can get good alternative energy exposure with New Alternatives (NALFX) or Guinness Atkinson Alternative Energy (GAAEX).

11

HIDDEN TECHNOLOGY

Tech Stocks Are Dead; Long Live Technology Investing

BE PATIENT, PLEASE, AS I TELL YOU WHY TECHNOLOGY IS STILL one of the ten long-term macro trends that you should build your portfolio around. To be successful, any long-term investor has to own this sector. But first I've got to clear away a lot of the rubble that remains from the 2000–3 bear market in technology stocks, then redefine the sector in light of what's happening now in the global economy, and finally lay out the trends that you can profit from.

The technology sector has changed radically since the good ol' days before the bear market that began in March 2000. Way back then, the sector was very clearly defined: the stars of technology, the stocks you wanted to own, were somehow connected with the Internet. They were either the companies building out the network, such as Cisco Systems and Global Crossing. Or they were companies building onramps so we could all get on the information superhighway, such as AOL and Yahoo. Or they were companies that had found a way to use the Internet to revolutionize an existing business, such as Amazon and RealNetworks.

Many of those stars of that era didn't survive the crash. Remember Metromedia Fiber? How about Cascade Communications and Stratus Computer, both acquired by Ascend Communications before it was acquired by Lucent Technologies?

Others are still with us, but these days they're hardly a blip on most investors' radar screens. Names like JDS Uniphase, Extreme Networks, and Inktomi used to keep the Internet stock tip boards buzzing. Today, who cares?

And the big names that were once reliable landmarks in the sector? They've either merged to irrelevance, like AOL (now the slow-growth orphan at Time Warner) or Lucent, or like Yahoo and Microsoft they turned into perennial disappointments to even patient shareholders.

Even the names of yesteryear that are doing well aren't doing so well that we feel that the future value of our portfolio will be significantly lower if we don't own them. Cisco Systems hasn't done badly in the years after the technology crash, and the stock was up an average of 11.9 percent a year over the three years that ended in December 2007. But wouldn't you rather have owned ExxonMobil, up 24.5 percent annually during that period? How the mighty have fallen when a plodding oil company with its roots in the nineteenth century outperforms a former technology superstar by 100 percent a year.

All this has left investors groping to make sense of the sector. In 2000 the themes and trends were clear: Internet use was growing to the sky and beyond, and you wanted to own a piece of it, whether that piece was shares of a gear maker such as Cisco Systems, a service provider such as AOL, or a merchant such as Amazon.

What's the theme today? Some Internet companies are doing fine—Google is an example—and others are struggling, as Yahoo is. Some of the stocks that have done best are just awfully hard to pigeonhole. What is Apple, for example? A computer company? A phone company? A consumer electronics company? A music retailer that sells more music than Wal-Mart?

The sector is so hard to define right now because the hottest markets for technology are in applying technology to big challenges in energy production, environmental protection, and materials science. We often label these stocks "energy stocks," "environmental stocks," or "chemical stocks" and give them the relatively modest price-to-earnings ratios the market traditionally assigns to those sectors. But alongside the commodity producers and the traditional cyclical industrial companies in sectors such as these stand companies that are in the technology business as the stock market has always defined it: they're in the business of making money from producing things that have never been made before.

You might call them hidden technology companies.

Fortunately, I think the three great rules for finding a highly profitable technology stock still work as well as they did back in the days when Microsoft, Intel, Dell, and Cisco Systems were the kind of stocks that set an investor's blood racing and produced lip-smacking profits for portfolios. I just don't think they work very well for traditional technology stocks like these because these companies have matured into something like traditional growth companies. Investors are better off thinking about Microsoft or Dell in the same way they think of ExxonMobil or PepsiCo, respectively, than they are analyzing them by the three great rules of technology investing.

THE THREE GREAT RULES
OF TECHNOLOGY INVESTING

The three great rules of technology investing still fit what I've called hidden technology companies to a T—or maybe that should be a J. What are these rules?

• **Look for the "hockey stick,"** the J-shaped growth curve that describes how sales grow at technology companies. The hockey stick has nothing to do with sports. Instead it describes a highly desirable pattern in a company's sales growth. Initially sales start off at a low level as the company and its new product scratch for initial customers daring enough to take a chance on an unfamiliar and untried product. Sales grow over time, but slowly, and that sketches in the blade of the hockey stick. Then, if all goes well, at some point sales start to increase more rapidly. Customers who use the product, rather than the company's sales force, become the best source of new business. That creates the upward curve that is the stick's neck. And then, if this technology company is really on to something, sales take off and growth becomes almost vertical. That's the handle of the stick. Do I need to say that you'd like to own a stock when the company's sales—and earnings—growth goes vertical?

- **Look for the killer app.** The killer application—the software program, piece of hardware, product improvement, or whatever—that everyone has to have is what powers hockey stick growth. It took everyone a while to figure out what an Internet browser was and what it was good for, but once that period of slowly growing use was past, everybody had to have one because being browserless was just inconceivable. Same with digital cameras and wireless phones and before that with routers and personal computers themselves.
- **Look for a company with high and growing margins.** In the technology markets of the 1990s a company could ride a sustainable proprietary edge to years and years of outsized profit margins. As the company's sales climbed up that hockey stick, fixed costs would be spread over a larger and larger volume of sales and profit margins would grow. As advantages of scale kicked in, successful technology companies would wipe out competitors who were unable to spread costs over a big enough sales volume, and that would allow the victor to increase profit margins again. Think of Cisco Systems in the 1990s. Or even earlier, Intel or Microsoft.

These rules don't actually fit those companies and other mature technology companies very well anymore. Instead of hockey-stick growth, these stars of the traditional technology sector now exemplify mature blue chip growth. I think Cisco Systems is a great company—but I think it now has more in common with a company such as PepsiCo or Kellogg than with itself or its competitors in the 1980s and 1990s.

Instead of killer apps, think killer fashion sense. Why has Nokia taken over from Motorola at the top of the wireless phone market and why has Korea's Samsung become such a dangerous competitor?

Because Nokia does a much better job, year in and year out, at matching its phones to the fast-changing trends in the consumer market, and because Samsung is now using what it learns in Korea's cutting-edge wireless phone market to design ever more fashionable phones. (Well, Nokia's and Samsung's abilities to actually manufacture phones efficiently so that they can supply a fashion-driven market at a healthy profit do have something to do with it.)

Instead of growing profit margins, think shrinking margins. There's so much capital in the world right now, even with the financial market meltdown that began in 2007, that a high profit margin for any product becomes a red flag drawing a horde of well-funded competitors from everywhere around the globe—and at least a few of those are always willing to run at a loss for years because the government that has arranged the financing has goals other than profitability. So if flash memory chips, the chips that store still pictures and video in digital cameras and recorders, start to increase profit margins at SanDisk and Intel, you can count on a plethora of new competitors springing into the market from Korea, Taiwan, and China. Of course, the above-average profit margins that attracted these competitors vanish as new capacity floods the market and everyone from first movers to newcomers cuts prices in an effort to sell into a glutted market.

But the three traditional rules of technology investing are still a great fit in fields where applying new technology to solve seemingly intractable problems results in big profits.

WHERE THE TECHNOLOGY RULES STILL APPLY

The hockey stick lives in the energy sector where truly innovative—and therefore extremely risky but potentially very profitable—technologies are just now moving from proof of concept to the early stages of the hockey stick. Take a company like Color Kinetics, for example. Sales grew by 28 percent in the first quarter of 2007, but sales were still tiny, $65 million in 2006. The company had just started to penetrate the market for intelligent white LED lighting. In 2007, the company estimated that white lighting would make up just about 5 percent of sales.

But this is where the future lies in a quintessential hockey stick fashion: as white LED sales grow, the company (and its competitors) can bring down the prices so that this technology, which is much more energy-efficient than either incandescent or fluorescent lighting, can pick up market share. As LED prices drop and energy prices (and carbon offset costs) rise, white light sales grow—and so on. The logic was compelling to Philips, which bought Color Kinetics in the summer of 2007. The price of Color Kinetics shares went from $24 to $34 in about a month.

The killer app lives. Here's a startling figure that should guide your investing strategies for the next decade: all together, the giant multinational oil companies of the world, the Chevrons and the BPs, own or have access to less than 10 percent of world oil resources. The rest belongs to state-controlled national oil companies. Think that puts the multinational oil companies in a bind? They've got the cash flow now to invest just about anywhere, but they can invest just about nowhere. Sitting back and doing nothing isn't a viable strategy for any oil company CEO since it amounts to presiding over the liquidation of the company. So any company selling a "product"—and I'm using the term very loosely here—that promises to solve this problem can charge just about anything.

In the case of the energy sector, any product that can help these oil companies tap the deep-water oil deposits of the continental shelf fits the bill. In many cases, these areas belong to countries—such as the United States—still willing to grant production rights to the multinationals. And in all cases, drilling for this oil requires expensive technology that only the multinationals can afford, so they have more negotiating clout. Drilling in deeper and deeper water is pushing the envelope for current drilling technology. It requires the invention of new ways of "seeing" under miles of water and challenging rock and salt formations and the development of new pipes and valves that can withstand tremendous pressure and often corrosive environments.

And it will require the outfitting of new deeper-water drill ships or drill platforms that can explore ever more challenging environments, including the icy seas that cover the continental shelf bordering the Arctic Circle. Sure, those new solutions will be expensive, but when it's pay up or go belly up, Big Oil will pay.

Growing profit margins live. For a company such as Tenaris, for example, adding more and more technology to its steel pipes for oil and gas wells ups the profit margins on the pipe, which in turn gives Tenaris the cash to buy competitors such as Maverick and to acquire Hydril and its pressure control technology. That in turn gives Tenaris a bigger share of the North American market—a plus in the long run but not a great move in the short run since pipe demand in that market slowed in 2007—and the ability to add more technology to its products and increase margins even more. Tenaris estimates that in 2008 sales of its high-technology products will amount to 50 percent of all company sales, up from 45 percent in 2007, as global oil companies drill in tougher and tougher environments and torture their drilling rigs in the process.

Even some traditional technology companies have found a way to be reborn as, well, technology companies with growing margins. Applied Materials grew into the 800-pound gorilla of the chip equipment industry in the 1980s and 1990s by constantly reinventing its chip-making equipment in order to cut costs for its consumers. That gave the company big profit margins, which it plowed back into increasing the scope of its product line so that chip makers could buy more and more of what they needed for an entire chip fab from Applied Materials. But the technology bust of the early part of this decade hit Applied Materials hard. Net profit margin fell from 21.6 percent in 2000 to 10.6 percent in 2001, 5.3 percent in 2002, and finally to −3.3 percent in 2003.

Looking around at what was now a mature chip-making industry, Applied Materials determined to break into new markets. What new growth products, products at the early stage of their hockey sticks, needed the company's skills at depositing thin films of materials onto large wafers of silicon or glass or at etching tiny circuits onto wafers of silicon or glass?

Well, how about flat-panel displays for LCD television screens? From nothing, equipment sales to makers of flat-panel displays climbed to about $500 million a quarter in the first two quarters of fiscal 2008. (Applied Materials uses an October fiscal year.) Flat-panel equipment sales were equal to about 50 percent of traditional silicon sales in those quarters. And with LCD TVs projected to take over the TV market from both traditional cathode-ray sets and from competing plasma technologies, high growth rates in this market seem assured for another five to ten years.

Or what about adapting its equipment and sales force to sell to the companies making solar cells? The technology isn't that different from what's found in the traditional computer chip industry. Both involve depositing films onto a substrate or handling silicon wafers in conditions of extreme cleanliness. At Applied Materials new orders for equipment from companies that make solar cells to generate electricity have climbed from a big fat goose egg in fiscal 2006 to $260 million in the second quarter of fiscal 2008. In March 2008, company executives told those attending the Morgan Stanley Technology Conference that it sees $2.5 billion in solar equipment revenue by 2010 with—and this is the best part—operating margins of 25 percent to 30 percent in that business. Applied Materials saw an operating margin of 20.4 percent in the second quarter of fiscal 2008.

So how do we look for hidden technology stocks that show the hockey stick growth, the killer apps, and the growing profit margins of classic technology stocks? I think you start by looking for companies that are providing technology solutions to the problems and opportunities posed by the other nine trends of this book, using the kind of top-down, macro trend approach that I've followed in this book. So, for example, you look for companies with

- Technologies that help increase oil discoveries and oil production from newly discovered as well as older fields

- Technologies that can produce more energy while reducing greenhouse gases or for companies that sell products to the companies that make solar cells or wind turbines

- Technologies that are bringing financial services at a low cost to the hundreds of millions of people in the developing world who for the first time in centuries have enough income to save and maybe invest some of it—and enough security to think beyond the end of next month

- Technologies that are carving out crucial roles in feeding a world that is demanding more and better-quality food every day

Finding profitable technology stocks, then, is just a specialized version of the strategies that I've used in the rest of this book. You're still looking for ways to swing the odds in your favor and to increase the percentage of times that you'll pick the right (meaning the profitable) stock and minimize the percentage of times that you'll be wrong.

There's one other characteristic that you ought to be looking for in technology companies, one that is uniquely important in this part of the stock market and that will tilt the odds even more in your favor.

There's real value to investors in this sector in finding companies that understand that the business of a technology company is technology. That is to say, understanding that what's really important isn't today's technology product but the ability to manage a company so that it successfully invests in research and development to produce tomorrow's technology products, and tomorrow's and tomorrow's and tomorrow's. Such companies also know how to bring a new technology product to market and successfully build sales from a trickle to a gusher.

Some of the companies that know how to do that are the obvious stars of the sector. Apple, for example, is riding an incredible winning streak that includes the iPod, the iPhone, and iTunes and that has spilled over to revive its computer business as well. Apple's share of the personal computer market climbed to 5 percent from a low of 3 percent before the winning streak started. It certainly didn't hurt either that the company has done a superb job of getting a steady stream of ever more user-friendly, powerful, and relatively glitch-free operating systems out to users on a rapid and predictable schedule. Right now nobody in the technology business does a better job at designing and selling "cool" technology.

Google is the other example that probably comes to mind of a technology company that gets it. Google has built a huge core competitive advantage—the company's technology matches what a user has searched on to advertising more effectively than competing algorithms from Yahoo or Microsoft. That means an ad on Google is likely to generate more clicks from what are really potential customers than an ad on Yahoo or Microsoft. That lets Google charge more for its ad space. Given the company's huge share of the search market—around 75 percent in recent quarters—that results in revenue for Google outstripping that at Yahoo by $16.6 billion to $7 billion for the last twelve months as of March 2008. It gives Google an even bigger edge in income: on its $16.6 billion in revenue Google earns income of $4.2 billion (or 25.3 percent), while on its $7 billion in revenue Yahoo earns income of $660 million (or 9.4 percent).

Google isn't inclined to let Yahoo or Microsoft catch up either. In January 2008 Google decided to sacrifice short-term click growth to long-term revenue growth and profitability. It put in place a new set of policies and technologies designed to reduce random and erroneous clicks on ads. That reduced the number of advertising clicks recorded by advertising market researchers. The stock took a big hit as Wall Street analysts worried that the reduction in clicks meant that Google's growth was slowing. But by reducing the number of valueless clicks that an advertiser pays for, Google is bidding to get a bigger share of the higher-quality advertising placed by big ad agencies such as Interpublic Group. Google knows, even if no one else is paying attention, that Internet advertising still captures just 6 percent of advertising spending. Google wants a bigger part of that market tomorrow. This is exactly the kind of thinking that an investor wants from a technology company.

But this kind of thinking isn't limited to just the obvious suspects. You can find it among a few older industrial producers who have realized that technology is one way to avoid becoming just another maker of commodity products at the mercy of the next low-cost manufacturer. The drilling pipe company Tenaris has discovered that it can use technology to differentiate its pipes from those of commodity pipe makers and then use the extra profits earned by that high-technology pipe to keep pushing up the technology value ladder.

You can see the same thinking at a company such as Japan's Toray Industries. Founded in 1926, this chemical company is still Japan's largest producer of synthetic fibers such as nylon, polyester, and acrylic. But it's also the world's largest producer of carbon fiber, the lighter-than-steel but stronger-than-steel material that's at the heart of Boeing's new 787 Dreamliner. The extensive use of carbon fiber has allowed Boeing to cut the weight of the plane so much that it is projected to use 15 percent less fuel than current jetliners.

And that's just the beginning for Toray and carbon fiber. In the summer of 2007 Toray and Nissan Motor announced that they had developed a technology to use carbon fiber to replace steel in car body platforms. Steel car body platforms now weigh about 480 pounds, but a carbon-reinforced body could weigh just 240 pounds. That would be enough to cut the total weight of a car by 10 percent, which would reduce fuel consumption by about 5 percent.

Deutsche Bank has done a back-of-the-envelope calculation that using carbon fiber in 1 percent of global auto production would create a new market worth $1 billion. At 5 percent the market would be $4.5 billion and at 10 percent about $9 billion. That's huge considering that the total carbon fiber market in 2007 was just $1.5 billion. Toray has a 40 percent share of today's market.

Another company in the old-dogs-learn-new-technology-tricks category is Johnson Controls. The fastest-growing business at this 123-year-old maker of interiors for cars and lead-acid car batteries is what was once called its controls business. This part of Johnson Controls makes heating and cooling control systems for nonresidential buildings. Johnson Controls took a big step to expand this business with the December 2005 purchase of heating and cooling equipment maker York. And it took another big step when it decided to go into the outsourcing of energy-efficiency business. A corporate customer can now hire Johnson Controls to run its heating and cooling systems on a contract that guarantees savings to the customer even after it pays Johnson Controls for managing its energy systems. Now called the building efficiency business, this unit contributed 37 percent of revenues at Johnson Controls in 2007 and grew income at 33 percent in the first quarter of fiscal 2008.

At other companies the change is more incremental, a result of a continuing focus on innovation that gradually transforms the company even if no one notices until—wham—some big transforming event brings the change into focus. For E. I. du Pont, that event was the 2004 sale of its textiles and interiors unit—the old-line chemical company's core business in nylon, polyester, and Lycra, with about $6.3 billion in sales. The remaining company looks anything but old-line. About 23 percent of sales come from its agriculture and seed business. If you don't think the seed business is high-tech these days, you should take a look at du Pont's AcreMax program to use biotechnology to produce a 40 percent gain in soybean yields over ten years. Another 13 percent of sales come from the electronic and communications segment, which produces photoresins, films, and laminants used in the latest display technologies. An additional 19 percent of sales in the safety and protection division comes from high-strength fibers such as Kevlar. Of course, many investors only see the continuing auto paint business (du Pont is one of the largest suppliers of automobile paint in the world). But that's why a stock with so much growth potential was trading at just 14.5 times projected 2008 earnings in February 2008.

Technology innovation is a corporate asset, just like land or factories or a highly trained workforce. Companies with a history of innovation—and successful development of innovation into best-selling products—have a kind of technological momentum. They may stumble and lose their way for a while, but for these companies it's like riding a bicycle—they never forget.

Corning is an example of a company where technological innovation has long been central to its culture. In 1912 Corning, primarily a manufacturer of lightbulbs, developed heat-resistant glass for railroad-signal lanterns. That material grew up to be Pyrex, the heat-resistant glass used in lab and kitchenware. In 1952 an accidental overheating of a batch of glass resulted in CorningWare. (Corning has since sold the Pyrex and CorningWare businesses.) In 1947, at the dawn of television, Corning developed spin-casting, which makes the mass production of cathode-ray tubes possible. It then dominated that business for two decades.

The core of Corning's current businesses go back to the 1970s and 1980s. In 1972 the company developed ceramics used in automobile and truck catalytic converters to remove pollutants from exhaust—about 13 percent of sales in 2007. In 1983 the company became an early pioneer in optical fiber—about 30 percent of sales in 2007. (The company is the only remaining U.S. maker of optical fiber.) And in 1984 Corning commercialized the glass used to make LCD screens for computers and televisions—about 45 percent of sales in 2007.

Those technologies are growing extremely rapidly at present. For 2008, the company is projecting LCD glass production to climb by 25 percent and 30 percent in 2009 as LCD televisions grow to 50 percent of the market in 2008 and 60 percent in 2009 from 38 percent in 2005. In the fiber-optic market, Corning is expecting a steady 15 percent growth, with growth resuming in North America in 2008.

But no technology grows forever, as Corning's history amply shows. The key is to have new products ready to pick up the slack in growth as today's core technology ages. And you can already see those emerging next-generation technology products in Corning's portfolio today. For example, sales of ceramic filters to clean diesel emissions, Corning's newest filtration product, are projected to grow by 25 percent in 2008 even with the slowdown in the U.S. economy. The company has just started to deliver samples of a green laser, the elusive third laser color that, with existing red and blue lasers, will make possible a new generation of displays for uses such as projecting images from a handheld device or in nighttime displays in cars. And at its 2008 investor day Corning announced that a new silicon-on-glass technology for displays in mobile consumer devices such as cell phones and personal navigation devices is now in testing at four manufacturers who are considering using this technology in their products.

The neat thing about a technology company such as Corning, one with tomorrow's products in the pipeline, is that you almost never pay anything extra for the pipeline. In March 2008, for example, Corning was quite a bargain just on the value of its fiber-optic and LCD glass business. Those two units alone were worth $30 a share in my estimation at a time when the stock was trading for $23.50. At that price you got the diesel filter business, the potential silicon-on-glass business, and the potential green laser business for free.

Technology stocks can be wonderful that way, especially the hidden ones that haven't been hyped sky-high in price. The stock market almost never pays full price for the future. (The exceptions are the overly hyped darlings of the moment. Buy those and you'll pay full price and more for a future that may never arrive.) That's why technology stocks, the shares of companies in the future business, are *potentially* so profitable.

Let's say that a company such as Corning has started to sample what is likely to be the world's first green laser. Combine this new laser with existing red and blue lasers and you've got a new technology that could revolutionize displays for everything from handheld phones to wall-size projections. The future revenue from this market for Corning? As much as $2 billion by 2015.

But what would you pay *today* for that $2 billion of revenue in *2015*?

If that future revenue were already in hand, it would be worth about $12 billion to shareholders, or about $7.50 a share, since the market values Corning at about six times trailing twelve-month revenues. Add that to the March price of $22.91 and you get a stock worth about 33 percent more than its March 7 market price.

But investors aren't going to value the future revenue from a green laser just now being tested by customers as if it were in hand today. Maybe customers won't adopt the green laser in their displays. Maybe another technology will work better and cost less. Maybe Corning won't be able to produce the laser in volume for a reasonable cost.

Popeye's friend J. Wellington Wimpy grasped the point. Money in hand today is always worth more than money that might be in hand tomorrow. That's why Wimpy always announced, "I'll gladly pay you tomorrow for a hamburger today."

So investors are going to give the value of Corning's future revenue a haircut that reflects the uncertainty of this future revenue. Working backward from my calculations of the value of Corning's other businesses, I think there's no more than 50 cents a share—out of that possible future $7.50—in Corning's price for the potential of that green laser technology. The market is discounting about 93 percent of the future potential of that technology now because investors are so uncertain that the full $2 billion in revenue will actually hit Corning's books in 2015. That's a huge spread—50 cents versus $7.50 a share.

Time will narrow that gap. As the years tick by, investors will gradually be able to see if the laser business is growing into a $2-billion-a-year business. The longer you wait, the more certain that revenue will be, but the less money you'll make on the stock from the development of this technology. By the time the success of that business is certain, the stock market will have already priced the value of the green laser business into Corning's shares.

If you can get ahead of the market's uncertainty—if you can become certain that Corning's $2 billion in revenue will appear before the market does—you stand to make more money buying the shares of Corning or any other technology stock. In this chapter I've given you two ways to do that. First, you can look for macro trends, like those in the other chapters of this book, that take some of the "if" out of that future by making it more likely to happen as projected. Second, you can look for companies that are, historically, better than average at finding commercially valuable new technology products and taking them successfully from lab to market.

Either way, you'll be able to buy the future at a discount and make a bigger profit on your technology shares because you'll be more certain of the future than the market is on average.

Which is why, despite all the current difficulty in defining and understanding the sector, you want to own a good dose of technology stocks in any long-term portfolio.

How the Trends Play Out for Investors

- The three traditional rules of what to look for in a great technology company still hold even if they don't fit the aging superstars that still dominate thinking about the sector very well. Look for the hockey stick, for the killer app, and for growing and high margins.
- Picking companies in areas of the economy where technology has a big payoff for customers will help your odds. Concentrate on technology companies working in energy, the environment, and food.
- Find companies that understand that the business of a technology company is technology, and that have a history of successfully developing new technologies and taking new technology products from lab to market.
- Don't forget the old dogs that are learning new tricks. Wonderful—and potentially profitable—technology companies are often embedded in more traditional businesses these days. Watch out for those growing fast enough to lead to a gradual overhaul of the entire business.

Trend Breakers and Trend Makers Ripped from the Headlines

Trend Breakers

- *Disruptive technologies* that can break a company's hockey stick before a new product has reached market maturity.
- *Products that don't scale.* A product that's successful with 100,000 customers is not a guaranteed success in the mass market. Service or manufacturing quality might go into decline as the company moves from sales to early adopters to the larger market. The cost

of manufacturing, which with most technology products falls as production ramps, might start to climb instead. The new product can turn out to be a novelty or fad and start to fade once too many people own it. (I learned that Motorola's RAZR phone was in danger of shifting from a hot everyone-has-to-have-one product to a fading everybody's-got-one item when the other twelve-year-olds in my son's car pool began to name the "uncool" kids who had one.)

- *Signs of bottlenecks.* The solar energy boom of 2006 and 2007 wasn't nearly as profitable as it could have been for the manufacturers of solar cells because a shortage of silicon prevented factories from running at full capacity.

- *Quarterly earnings reports showing that selling prices are falling faster than unit sales are climbing.* Only the most efficient, low-cost manufacturers can make money in this kind of environment.

- Signs that *competitors are jumping into a market faster than the first mover expected.* Everybody realizes that competitors will attack any market with high profit margins as fast as they can these days. But the first company into a market almost always plans for some time to elapse before the onset of full-out competitive war. It's a big danger sign if a first mover gets less lead time than initially expected.

- *One-trick ponies.* In today's technology markets, especially in today's consumer technology markets, a company has to follow a hit product quickly with another hit. Look at Motorola to see the bad things that happen when a company can't follow up on the success of a hot product, its RAZR phone. (The company is now planning to spin off its wireless phone business.) Look at Apple to see what happens when a company can. (Apple's iPod was followed by the iPhone, and that has dragged computer sales higher as well.)

TREND MAKERS

- Watch the style and fashion pages for signs that *a consumer technology product has become a pop culture hit.* These days I find the fashion pages a better guide to this phenomenon than the technology magazines and columnists.

- Read the stories about *major technology events such as the Consumer Electronics Show to see which of the companies exhibiting there are getting the most positive ink.* Editors will lead with stories on companies that they think readers most want to hear about.

- Headlines about *breakthroughs at suppliers of raw materials and subassemblers* that will lead to increases in supply of raw materials and components at lower costs.

- *Check prices.* Falling prices with rising volume are a key reason that the hockey stick goes vertical. (As long as selling price doesn't fall faster than manufacturing cost.)

- Read product reviews to see if *low-cost competitors are closing the perceived quality or coolness gap* with the first mover in the market.

STOCK PICKS THAT PUT THE WIND FROM THOSE TRENDS AT YOUR BACK

Corning (NYSE: GLW). I like what its incredibly strong and orderly pipeline says about this Corning, New York–headquartered, company's ability to produce a steady stream of new technology products. Corning's mature but still growing fiber-optics business makes up about 30 percent of revenue. The segment showed 10 percent sales growth in 2007 and a jump of 75 percent in net income. This part of Corning's business continues to bounce back from the depression created by the overcapacity generated in the dot-com boom. Corning projects that the total market grew by 15 percent in 2007 and is positioned for 10 percent to 15 percent annual growth for the next five years. The display unit, the part of Corning's business that produces glass for LCD screens, accounts for the bulk of revenue growth from post-fiber-optics products. Corning estimates that unit LCD television sales will grow by an annual rate of 31 percent between 2007 and 2009. Corning's environmental technologies unit—filters for autos and diesels—represents one part of the company's future. The diesel market, for example, will show sales growth of 17 percent in 2008, Corning projects. And finally, there are new technologies such as green lasers and silicon-on-glass that are just now about to make the transition from the lab to the commercial marketplace.

Google (NASDAQ: GOOG), the Internet's dominant search company, had about 70 percent of the global market for search in January 2008 compared to a 17 percent share for second-place Yahoo. But Google's big technology lead right now is in software that matches the ads that users see on their search page to their queries. The better the match, the more users will actually click on the ad, and the more conversions—clicks that generate sales or requests for more information, for example—will occur. And since advertisers increasingly pay for conversions, the company with the best matching software will earn the highest ad rates. Which is exactly what Google has done. Starting in late 2007, Google has steadily worked to improve its already industry-leading Ad Sense program to match ads to search pages even more accurately. The goal at this point is to improve the conversion rate so that Google can pull in more of the high-quality ad agency accounts that have so far been hesitant to commit ad dollars to the Internet because the conversion rate wasn't high enough. It's not exactly a coincidence that Google's new acquisition, DoubleClick, specializes in exactly those ad agency accounts. Investors need to remember that while ad growth at Google, Yahoo, Microsoft, and other competitors has been extremely rapid (ad revenue from Google-owned sites climbed 68 percent in 2007), the Internet advertising market is still in its infancy. Internet ad dollars accounted for only 6 percent of advertising spending in 2007.

Johnson Controls (NYSE: JCI). In 2005 the company's automotive business making door and dashboard systems made up 69 percent of sales at Johnson Controls. By the end of 2007 that had dropped to 51 percent. In that short period the Milwaukee-headquartered company has transformed itself from just another auto industry supplier into a technology growth company. In 2007 its building energy efficiency systems made up 37 percent of sales, up from 21 percent in 2005. In this business size counts because customers are increasingly looking for complete solutions to their heating and cooling problems that will cut costs. Johnson Controls has recently expanded into the energy management side of this business: the company will now undertake to manage a corporate customer's energy use for a fixed fee. Johnson Controls then passes on part of the energy savings it produces to the customer but pockets the rest. The company's most interesting future technology growth potential lies in one of its oldest businesses, automotive batteries. Johnson Controls gets about 13 percent of sales from its battery business now. Almost all of that comes from traditional lead-based car batteries. But the company has recently signed joint venture agreements to develop the next generation of lithium ion batteries for hybrid and electric cars.

Nokia (NYSE ADR: NOK) owns huge market shares in the markets that are the future of wireless phone technology, with about two-thirds of the handset market in India and a 40 percent share in China. That's turned the Finnish company into a huge annuity on phone sales in the world's developing markets since users tend to upgrade with brands they own as incomes rise. But Nokia's technology edge comes in the way the company has married this huge base of users of its handsets to the build-out of software that will enable local wireless operators to turn phones into Internet portals, branchless banks, e-mail desktops, music players, and mapping servers. The bulk of potential wireless customers in the developing world is likely to skip right past the PC-as-Internet-access-device history of the developed world and go straight to a wireless phone delivery model. And Nokia intends to be there with the phone handset and the software package when wireless service providers decide to build out the services on their network.

Schlumberger (NYSE: SLB) increased spending on research and engineering by 18 percent in 2007. Why is that important for a company that provides services to the oil and gas industry? Because the oil and gas industry has developed an insatiable appetite for new technology such as 3-D seismic imaging and innovative services such as real-time data management from drills thousands of feet under the surface.

Companies exploring or drilling for oil in increasingly difficult geologies need to find ways to increase the odds that increasingly expensive test wells will produce significant volumes of oil and gas. And that's where Schlumberger steps in. For example, in 2007 Schlumberger introduced a family of stage fracturing services that fracture underground rock formations to free trapped oil and natural gas so that it will flow to a well and eventually to the surface. Schlumberger's new technology increases the amount of oil and natural gas production after fracturing and—here's the big kicker—lowers the cost of fracturing. Win/win. No wonder revenue grew by 21 percent in 2007. It helps that Houston-headquartered Schlumberger has an international footprint that matches up well with the areas of the world seeing the most drilling and underemphasizes the slower-growing North American markets. In 2007 revenue grew by 31 percent in the Middle East and Asia, by 30 percent in Europe/Russia/Africa, and by 30 percent in Latin America. In May 2008 Wall Street projected that earnings per share at Schlumberger would grow by 15.4 percent in 2008, rise by 23.1 percent in 2009, and average 19.1 percent growth annually over the next five years.

STOCKS FOR BUILDING AN OVERWEIGHT POSITION IN THIS SECTOR

• **American Superconductor** (NYSE: AMSC) because superconductor technology is a key to reducing strain on the world's electrical power grids. Using superconductors from the Massachusetts-headquartered company to transmit electricity increases the amount of electricity the grid can carry, reduces electricity lost to transmission leakage, and improves the reliability of the system.

• **Apple** (NASDAQ: AAPL) has mastered a lesson that few other technology companies have begun to understand: design counts. In the increasingly fashion-driven consumer technology market, Apple knows that creating the hot product is as important as creating the best product. No one is better at this than Apple.

• **Applied Materials** (NYSE: AMAT) is about one-third of the way through a transformation from the 800-pound gorilla in the market for equipment for the manufacture of computer chips to the 800-pound gorilla that dominates the market for equipment that puts a thin film on any wafer, whether it's a computer chip, an LCD flat screen, or a solar cell.

- **Ceradyne** (NYSE: CRDN) is busy turning the expertise it gained building high-strength ceramics for such military uses as body armor into products for the civilian markets. Because of their high strength and resistance to intense temperature, ceramics promise to reduce costs and increase efficiency in industrial uses ranging from the production of aluminum to nuclear power plants.

- **First Solar** (NASDAQ: FSLR) is ahead of the pack in developing the thin film technologies that will cut the cost of producing electricity from sunlight. The company's technology seems especially well suited to large-scale solar energy production by corporations and utilities.

- **Intel** (NASDAQ: INTC) is the global leader in putting more and more computing power on smaller and smaller chips. The company's newest product lines show that Intel has finally turned its full attention to making sure that those smaller and more powerful chips consume less energy as well.

- **Maxwell Technologies** (NASDAQ: MXWL) is a small company with a tiny technology. Its ultracapacitors can quickly store and then release relatively huge amounts of energy in a package the size of a D-cell battery. The technology is a big improvement on batteries in fast-store, fast-discharge uses such as electric and hybrid cars.

- **Tenaris** (NYSE ADR: TS) is getting higher profit margins out of its pipe for oil and gas wells by making the pipe do more. Oil and gas drillers will pay more for pipe that's resistant to highly corrosive and hot environments.

- **Toray Industries** (OTC ADR: TRYIY) is the world's biggest producer of high-strength, low-weight carbon fiber. Carbon fiber is a big winner in an energy hungry world where lighter is better.

- **Verenium** (NASDAQ: VRNM) produces enzymes and other catalysts that can turn things such as wood chips and switchgrass into ethanol. The future of ethanol is in making this biofuel from cellulose rather than corn.

Mutual Funds and ETFs
(Exchange-Traded Funds)

Investing in the technology sector using an ETF has the same problems as investing in the energy sector: the indexes that ETFs are based on are weighted by market cap so most ETFs give you exposure to the usual suspects.

- If the usual suspects are what you want, then these ETFs will deliver the goods: **Technology Select Sector SPDR (XLK)** or **iShares Dow Jones U.S. Technology (ITW)**. For example, the top five holdings for the Technology SPDR were Microsoft, AT&T, Cisco Systems, IBM, and Intel as of the end of 2007. Substitute Google for AT&T and you've got the top five holdings for iShares Dow Jones Technology.

- If you want more exposure to the smaller technology stocks that are likely to deliver bigger returns over time—with more volatility, I warn you—you'll have to look at an actively managed fund: **Allianz RCM Technology (DRGTX)** or **Matthews Asian Technology (MATFX)**. The Allianz fund owns stocks such as Activision and McAfee along with the Microsofts and the Googles. Co-managers Walter Price and Huachen Chen have run this fund together since it started in 1995. The ten-year annualized return is 12.08 percent. The Matthews fund doesn't go back quite so far, but its five-year annualized return was 25.19 percent as of the end of 2007. As you'd expect from the name, the fund owns Asian technology stocks such as Nintendo and Baidu.com.

12

THE STABILITY PREMIUM

Safe Investing Havens in an Unsafe World

Y OU'RE NOT ALONE IF YOU THINK THE FINANCIAL GODS ARE OUT to get you. Just when you—and the rest of an aging global population—need a long period of steady financial growth so that your savings can multiply into something like enough to retire on, the financial markets deliver nothing but one boom and crash after another. Dotcom boom and then bear market bust. Housing boom and then mortgage market meltdown, followed by a full-scale financial crisis and yet another bear market.

Remember the old joke about paranoia—"You're not paranoid if they really are out to get you"? Right now your fears of financial paranoia are totally justified. This really is a terrible time for folks who need to find stable investments to underpin a retirement plan.

And I've got some even worse news. The financial market meltdown that started in the subprime mortgage market in 2007 and then quickly spread to global financial markets in all types of assets isn't a onetime aberration. It's part of a long-term trend toward less stability in global financial markets in general, along with a decline in the relative stability of some of the world's most traditionally stable financial markets and economies.

But I do have *some* good news. Some traditional safe havens are hanging tough. The U.S. financial markets, even though it doesn't look like it now, will come out of this crisis with relatively light damage—mostly because European markets and especially London, New York's big competitor, are suffering damage that's perhaps even more severe. And the global economy is throwing up a few newcomers that can give investors shelter in our turbulent times. Because the stability of these newcomers isn't recognized by the average investor, any money you put into these still relatively unappreciated stable markets won't be just safe but could also show a handsome profit. The more investors value stability and the more the stability in these markets is recognized, the bigger your gains will be.

There seem to be three reasons for the decline in global financial market stability: the difficulty in controlling the huge amounts of money now slopping around the global economy, the relative declines of the credit quality of the world's developed economies, and the fact that the financial markets in the developing-world economies that are improving in credit quality are smaller than those in developed economies that are showing a decline in credit quality.

1. *It's extremely difficult to control the huge amounts of money now slopping around the global economy.* When global financial markets don't control these cash flows, the result is a runaway boom that sooner or later turns into a bust.

The amounts of money involved are truly staggering. China had built up foreign exchange reserves of $1.53 trillion by February 2008. The U.S. deficit in the trade of goods and services ran at $712 billion in 2007—and that was good news compared to the 2006 deficit of $759 billion. The oil producers of OPEC represent only about 40 percent of global oil production, but these countries took in $675 billion in oil revenue in 2007.

Recycling all that money—moving it out of a vault in China and into U.S. Treasuries or out of a vault in Russia and into the purchase of energy resources in Western Europe—without temporarily sending too much to one place or asset class or another has turned out to be just about impossible. So in the last ten years we've had an Asian currency crisis, the Russian financial crisis, the Long-Term Capital Management hedge fund crisis, the dot-com boom and bust of 2000, the real estate boom (in the United Kingdom, Spain, China, and the United States) and bust of 2007 and counting. And I think we can already see the next boom/bust on the horizon. In February 2008 the Chinese were currently struggling with the highest inflation in eleven years as a result of trying to keep their currency cheap while they accumulated a flood of dollars. I say the odds that they'll be able to keep these huge floods of cash from crashing their economy are no better than fifty-fifty over the next five years.

2. *The relative declines of the credit quality of the world's developed economies.* Debt is growing at the same time as economic growth is slowing, and the political will to tackle today's problems before they spiral completely out of control is distressingly absent. Net public debt in the United States—all the money that the government owes to public investors in its debt—equaled 37 percent of our total economy (gross domestic product) in 2007. That's positively rock solid compared to Italy, where net public debt equaled 106 percent of the country's GDP in 2007, according to the *CIA's World Fact Book,* or Japan, where net public debt equaled 194 percent of GDP in 2007. And this is before the big wave of spending on pensions and health care for retirees really reaches its peak.

And what are the developed economies of the world doing about their problems?

In Italy the pension reforms that would cut benefits and raise the retirement age from fifty-seven to sixty starting in January 2008 and passed with so much fanfare in 2004 have been pushed back to 2010. Only 30 percent of Italians from fifty-five to sixty-four have jobs in the official economy. Italy's economy is projected to grow by just 0.8 percent in 2008.

In Japan, the lower house of parliament passed a budget for the fiscal year that began in April 2008 with expenditures of 83.6 trillion yen (about $800 billion) on tax revenues of only 53.6 trillion yen. About 20 trillion yen of that budget will go for interest payments on the government's debt. Social security payments will climb by 3 percent in a budget that will increase overall by just 0.2 percent. The International Monetary Fund projects that Japan's economy will grow by 1.5 percent in 2008.

And in the United States? We're still unwinding a massive Ponzi scheme that promised institutions such as pension funds that Wall Street could turn risky subprime, no-income-verification, no-money-down mortgages into AAA-rated securities. The risk that those investments might not be all that they claimed to be was dismissed on Wall Street's theory that if everybody owned a small piece of it, no one would get hurt very badly. Instead it looks like there was plenty of risk to go around and everybody is taking a big hit. According to the Federal Reserve, household wealth fell by $553 billion in the fourth quarter of 2007 as lower housing prices and a declining stock market delivered a double whammy. The drop in wealth amounts to a little less than 1 percent and leaves total household wealth in the country at $57.7 trillion. That doesn't sound like much of a decline until you remember that the home-owning generation is counting on real estate appreciation to fund its retirement. That bit of retirement planning works only if housing prices are climbing, not falling.

The Fed data also showed that homeowner equity fell to 47.9 percent in the fourth quarter. That's the first time home equity has dropped below 50 percent since 1945. Moody's Economy.com estimated that as of March 2008, 8.8 million homeowners—about 10 percent—have zero or negative equity in their homes.

A drop in home equity has a direct effect on retirement savings since many in the United States, as I've noted, count on their homes as the major source of retirement cash. But it also has a second, indirect effect. Falling home values limit the amount of cash that home owners can draw out of their houses to spend on day-to-day expenses and on big-ticket items such as vacations. So a drop in home values takes a bite out of economic activity, which in turn means more people lose jobs, even if only temporarily, and work for lower or stagnant wages. That in turn decreases their access to pension plans of any sort and inhibits their ability to save for retirement. The Federal Reserve projects that economic growth in the United States for 2008 will run at just 1.3 percent to 2 percent.

3. *The financial markets in the developing-world economies that are improving in credit quality are much smaller than the financial markets in the developed economies that are showing a decline in credit quality.* Yes, the relatively small amount of debt and equity bought and sold in the financial markets of these developing economies is improving in quality. But for the bulk of the world's investors, who buy and sell in New York, Tokyo, Paris, and London, that improvement is irrelevant. All they experience is the decline in stability in the big markets and economies of the globe.

It's Not All Doom and Gloom

The stability of *some* markets and economies is improving. For example, Brazil, a former debtor nation that needed a $30 billion bailout from the International Monetary Fund in 2002 to escape a currency crisis, is now one of the world's biggest creditor countries, with foreign reserves climbing to $190 billion in January 2008. This marks the first time in its financial history Brazil has turned into a creditor nation. The domestic benchmark interest rate, at 11.25 percent, is the lowest in the nation's history, and the country's currency, the real, is at a nine-year high against the U.S. dollar. In May 2008 Standard & Poor's raised Brazil's credit rating to "investment-grade" from "speculative."

Russia, a country that required its own bailout in the financial crisis of 1997–98, has now run a budget surplus every year from 2001 through 2007. Foreign reserves, now the third-largest in the world, climbed to $470 billion by the end of 2007 from $12 billion in 1999.

But the stock markets in the countries showing an improvement in credit quality are tiny in comparison to the stock markets of the

United States or Japan. All the shares listed on Brazil's stock market, the Bovespa, had a market value of $1.3 trillion in January 2008. The stocks on the Shanghai stock market had a value of $3.1 trillion. Compare that to the $14.6 trillion value of the stocks listed on the New York Stock Exchange and the $3.7 trillion listed on the U.S. NASDAQ stock exchange.

The difference gets even bigger when you subtract shares that can't be bought or sold by foreigners. On that basis the Bovespa, at just $500 billion, is the largest developing-economy stock market in the world, because so many shares on the Shanghai stock market can't be bought or sold by foreign investors.

And these numbers include just the markets that trade stocks. The global markets for debt of all kinds—government and cooperate bonds—are much bigger than the global markets for equity. It stands to reason if you know that a company such as General Motors has $12 billion in stock and $38 billion in long-term bonds outstanding. New York, London, and Tokyo dominate this much larger global market for debt to an even greater extent than the markets in these cities dominate the global market for shares.

The financial crisis beginning in 2007 that shook the global economy and the global financial markets has largely played out in the debt markets of London and New York.

WHERE'S THE STABILITY?

First, you can't count on the developed world financial markets to deliver the stability premium anymore. The world has had better than fifty years of steady delivery in rain and snow and dark of night, but you can no longer take the stability premium for granted.

The stability premium? You've probably never given it a moment's thought or even heard of it. That's because, like the air we breathe, you don't miss it until it's gone.

You've heard of risk premium, of course. After the financial market meltdown of 2007–8, who doesn't understand by now what the bankers and the mortgage lenders didn't: that you're supposed to get paid more in interest, not less, when you take on an investment with higher risk?

The stability premium is the other side of that picture. It's the premium that companies in developed and stable economies reaped for the stability of those economies in the form of lower interest rates. It's the premium that anybody who lived in those economies reaped because the rest of the world was so willing to send its money to the stable developed economies that it was content with a lower yield and a lower return in exchange for safety and stability. It's the premium that investors in developed economies received in bigger gains on their stocks and bonds because investors in the rest of the world didn't keep their money at home—that was too risky—but instead shipped it overseas for investing in developed-country financial markets.

The United States was the only economic power left standing in the years after World War II. Ever since it has reaped the benefits of that stability premium. Because our economy was the biggest in the world, our financial markets were the most trustworthy in the world, and our politicians (as bad as they sometimes were) never staged a coup or seized private property en masse, investors were willing to lend the U.S. government money at low interest rates. They were willing to collect heaps of dollars and then collect some more. They were willing to buy U.S. equities at high price-to-earnings multiples and then buy some more when prices climbed.

As a result, for sixty years or so, the United States investor has reaped a sizable gain from the willingness of non-U.S. investors to pay for the stability that the U.S. financial markets offered. In August 2007, Richard Clarida of asset management firm PIMCO estimated the gain in 2006 alone from U.S. control over the U.S. dollar, the global currency of trade, at more than $800 billion.

But, Clarida pointed out, the advantages of being able to run up deficits to your foreign trading partners and then cover the deficits simply by printing more dollars don't last forever. I'd go further than that and say I think we're witnessing the beginnings of a decline in the stability premium the United States and the other developed economies of the world are awarded by the world's investors. Financial stability has declined in the United States, Japan, and Europe in the last ten years—and not just as a result of financial debacles such as the global debt market bust that began in 2007. (Although the fact that so many "safe" bonds and derivatives in the U.S. markets went bad certainly has raised questions about the regulation, transparency, and safety of U.S. financial markets.)

No one knows for certain where U.S. interest rates or U.S. stock prices would have been if overseas investors hadn't been willing to pay up for that stability. But the financial market crisis of 2008 gives us some unpleasant hints. A falling dollar has pushed up the prices of commodities, taking a bite out of share prices in industries such as airlines, and sent equity prices in general tumbling. Interest rates on even safe (and tax-exempt) municipal bonds have climbed, rising above yields on Treasury bonds for the first time in decades. Despite cuts of 1.25 percentage points in the first two months of 2008 by the U.S. Federal Reserve, interest rates on long-term Treasury bonds and the home mortgages tied to them have either held steady or actually climbed higher. Overseas investors continue to buy U.S. bonds and stocks, but in 2007 the pace of buying slowed to $596 billion, down from $722 billion in 2006, according to the U.S. Treasury.

The result is not an absolute end to the stability premium awarded to the developed economies over the last sixty years. The United States, for example, still maintains a sizable stability premium not only over a developing economy such as Egypt, where net public debt is 105 percent of GDP, but also over Russia, where private ownership struggles in the absence of a legal system that protects property rights, and even over some of its developed-world peers, such as Japan, where a rapidly aging population will present a creaky political system with a challenge unprecedented in world history.

But we are seeing the beginnings of a redistribution of stability premiums around the world. The redistribution so far has had a huge but largely unappreciated impact on investors. It's not clear which is the cart and which the horse, but rising stock prices in some developing economies have been accompanied by a shrinking gap between the stability premium for those economies and those of the developed world.

For example, when in the late 1980s Cemex started its drive to expand outside of its home market, the Mexican cement maker faced a huge handicap. To raise money to finance its international expansion, the company had to pay investors in its bonds about 12 percent interest. That was two times what companies from the developed economies of the United States, Europe, and Japan paid for their capital. That put expansion projects out of the Mexican company's reach that were slam dunks for a European competitor such as Lafarge.

By 2007, however, Cemex was paying just 4 percent to raise capital. That's about the same—and in some cases maybe a little better—than the rate its developed-market competitors pay. That means the stability premium that used to put Cemex at a disadvantage has been eliminated. You can see the result in the change in the kind of acquisitions Cemex has been making recently. Up until, say, 2005, the typical Cemex target was a cement maker in a relatively small national market, often in the developing world. In March 2005, however, Cemex bought the London-based RMC group to become the worldwide leader in ready-mix concrete. After a tough battle in 2007 Cemex bought the Australian-headquartered multinational Rinker Group for $14.2 billion.

This trend—first to narrow traditional stability premiums and second to eventually reverse them—plays out at individual companies such as Cemex and on a larger scale across national economies. Brazil's bonds, for example, carried an interest rate in mid-2008 just 2 percentage points above that on U.S. Treasuries.

This Trend Will Get Stronger over the Next Decade or So

Not in any uniform and simpleminded way. As an investor, you shouldn't just bet that the stability premium will be completely eliminated for all developed economies and will start to work in favor of all developing economies. That's just not going to happen. There's too much difference, even in this global economy, between national economies, cultures, and political systems for that to happen.

As an investor, what you need to do is to try to reap as much of any continued stability premium that will remain with specific developed economies and companies, and also to collect as much as you can of any increase in stability premium that is headed toward specific developing economies and companies.

I think this is especially important if you're putting together a portfolio for a retirement that isn't too terribly far down the road. That's when you want to put more rather than less of your own money into stable assets because you don't have unlimited time to ride out market volatility. And if those stable assets should increase in value because the world as a whole is getting older and more and more people are willing to pay up a bit for a stable asset, then more power to your portfolio.

So where, then, do you look for these gems, those stable assets that will both protect your retirement portfolio and at the same time keep going up in value precisely because they offer stability in an unstable world?

I'd target four economies, and then look for specific stocks in each market that offer the potential for an especially large stability premium.

1. *The United States.* Surprised? Well you shouldn't be if you can look beyond the financial meltdown that began in 2007. Yes, it does indeed look like every banker in the United States suddenly was taken over by aliens from a galactic civilization that had never heard of the idea of getting paid more, not less, to take on risk. And yes, it does indeed look like huge parts of the U.S. financial industry thought that they were in the running for a prize that would go to the company that borrowed the most on the smallest possible amount of real capital. But the U.S. financial markets are still the deepest and—in most years anyway—the most liquid in the world. The U.S. economy is still the world's largest. The U.S. consumer is still the world's richest, even when you look at debt and net assets. And the U.S. population is aging

less rapidly than any other in the developed world. Certainly the last round of financial monkeyshines will cost the United States a good bit of its traditional stability premium, but what remains is substantial.

The debacle that has destroyed the AAA or AA rating of so many U.S. companies or asset classes actually works to increase the value of the stocks and bonds of those companies savvy (or lucky) enough to escape with reputations intact. In the financial sector, for example, the debacle at Citigroup, Wachovia, and Washington Mutual sure makes the strategy and execution of U.S. Bancorp more valuable to investors. The same is true with companies such as PepsiCo, E. I. du Pont, and Cisco Systems, which have managed to keep earnings growth chugging along at double-digit rates even as a slowing U.S. economy meant lower earnings growth for most U.S. companies. In a booming economy, performance like that can get lost in the crowd, but in a down economy, it sure stands out.

2. *Canada.* Stashing part of a long-term retirement nest egg in Canadian stocks is likely to pay off big. The biggest potential for profiting from the stability premium results from the nature of the Canadian economy. Canada is an export-driven economy. In 2007, Canada's exports added up to 33 percent of the country's $1.4 trillion economy, the eighth-largest in the world. In the United States, by comparison, exports accounted for just 10 percent of a $14 trillion economy in 2007. Canada isn't just an exporter of commodities such as wheat and nickel. Its auto industry contributed 11 percent of total exports in 2006, for example. But commodities do dominate Canada's export economy. Mining, energy, agriculture, and forest products added up to 61 percent of total exports in 2006. That makes Canada one of the leading beneficiaries of soaring global commodity prices. It's among the top ten global producers of copper, lead, zinc, nickel, gold, oil, natural gas, and wheat—all commodities trading at near-term or all-time record prices in 2007 and 2008. Canada was also the only country among the old Group of Seven developed economies—France, Germany, Italy, Japan, the United States, United Kingdom, and Canada—to record a budget surplus in all years from 2003 to 2007. (The G7 became the G8 with the addition of Russia in 1997.) All this is enough to make the country one giant hedge

against a falling dollar and rising global inflation. That hedge grows in value the more global financial conditions deteriorate.

3. *Australia.* Think of Canada with fewer people (33 million in Canada and 20 million in Australia in 2007) and with kangaroos instead of moose. This is another fast-growing commodity-based economy that's an ideal hedge against a falling dollar and rising global inflation. The farming and mining sectors account for 30 percent of GDP but 65 percent of the country's exports. Australia's economy was growing so fast (a projected 3.5 percent for 2008), even as those in most of the rest of the world showed signs of slowing in 2008, that its central bank continued to raise interest rates in 2007 and 2008. That gave the bank a lot of room—Federal Reserve, eat your heart out—to cut interest rates at the first sign of the slowdown that arrived in late 2008. Domestic inflation is projected at 3.2 percent in 2008, according to the Organisation for Economic Cooperation and Development, the developed economies' think tank. Budget estimates show a surplus in 2008 and 2009.

4. *Brazil.* What's the poster child for fiscal irresponsibility and hyperinflation doing on this list? Well, if any country in the developing world has the potential for stability over the next decade or two, it's Brazil. Brazil is often linked with Russia, India, and China, the four economic giants of the developing world, under the acronym BRIC. But Brazil has its own strengths that set it apart from the other giants of the developing world. Unlike China and India, for example, Brazil is a commodities superpower. Fears that the populist government of Luiz Inácio Lula da Silva would return the country to the bad old days of fiscal irresponsibility have proven baseless. In fact, fiscal prudence is more ingrained now than it was when introduced by Lula's predecessor Fernando Henrique Cardoso, who defined a policy of a government budget surplus (before interest payments) high enough to reduce debt as a percentage of GDP, a floating exchange rate for the real, and inflation targets with real meaning. The economy is forecast to grow by 4 percent annually on average from 2008 to 2012, a big improvement from its long-term postwar average of just 2.2 percent. Inflation in 2006 came in at just 3 percent, below the 4.5 percent limit set by the central bank. Thanks to moderating inflation and substantial government pay-

ments to the poor, inequality in Brazil, one of the most unequal societies in the world, has improved. Exports have soared thanks to booming agriculture (soybeans) and mining (iron ore) sectors. And due to the combination of a booming sugar-cane-based ethanol industry and new oil discoveries, Brazil has become a net oil exporter and the national oil company Petrobras is on the path to becoming the dominant source of oil industry technology in Latin America. The country's new stability got a stamp of approval in April 2008 when Standard & Poor's upgraded the country's credit rating to investment-grade.

In the future, stability isn't going to be something an investor in the world's developed economies can just assume a portfolio will acquire as a matter of course. It will increasingly be something that you have to search for and buy—like earnings growth—in sectors of the global economy and corners of national stock markets. But stability is out there to be found by the diligent, and the fact that it will take work to find it will make it even more valuable to the portfolio that owns some.

How the Trends Play Out for Investors

- No, you're not paranoid—global financial markets are getting more volatile as the global economy generates huge waves of cash that can slosh from one market to another, generating extremely rapid boom-bust-boom-bust cycles. Existing national regulatory schemes, designed to deal with a simpler financial world, are proving inadequate to the task of preventing even the worst excesses of the cycle. The best they can do is mop up afterward.
- The general increase in volatility and the general decline in stability across the global financial markets are accompanied by relative shifts in stability between what is still called the developed and developing markets and economies.
- As a general rule, the economies of the developed world are showing less stability as they come under stress from aging populations, slowing growth rates, and rising fiscal deficits.

• As a general rule, the economies of the developing world are far more stable than they were a decade ago. Many now show sizable foreign exchange reserves and run consistent balance-of-trade surpluses. They are, again in general, less dependent on flows of overseas hot cash to support fiscal and trade deficits.

• The differences among countries in the developed and developing groups remain huge and of immense significance to investors. In the developed group, despite the recent financial debacle set off by a collapse of lending standards in the subprime mortgage market, the United States retains a substantial portion of its postwar stability premium—if only because its demographic challenges are far less daunting than those facing Europe and Japan. The smaller natural-resource-based economies of Canada and Australia, however, have the best stability potential in the coming decade among developed economies. In the developing group, huge political uncertainty dogs China, Russia, and India—all otherwise promising on economic grounds. Brazil, with its huge advantage in the farm and natural resource sectors, has reversed decades of instability and continues to close the gap on developed economies by this measure.

• In an aging world full of retirement portfolios longing for stable returns, companies and economies that can provide that safety combined with a decent return should earn a substantial and rising premium.

TREND BREAKERS AND TREND MAKERS RIPPED FROM THE HEADLINES

TREND BREAKERS

• *A flight from the U.S. dollar by central banks and other overseas investors who hold huge piles of greenbacks would be bad news for the United States.* I expect a gradual shift over the next decade away from the dollar and toward a basket of currencies that includes the euro. But since a big move out of the dollar would send the currency tumbling and hurt the very folks who own so much of it, I'm not looking for anything worse than a slow slide. But, hey, investors and bankers have done irrational things in the past, so even self-interest isn't a total guarantee.

• *Regulatory inaction that decreases transparency in the United States and other financial markets.* The relatively unregulated market for derivatives—securities that are based on other securities—has been a big source of risk in the mortgage-securities-led bust of 2007 and counting. I hope that we'll add some regulation; even requiring that derivative-contract buy and sells be recorded and settled promptly would be a big step forward. If we don't get meaningful changes, stability in global financial markets will continue to decline.

• Headlines that show *national governments giving in to political pressure from retirees and running the printing presses rather than biting the bullet and cutting benefits or raising the retirement age.* Of the four countries I've mentioned as potential investments in stability, I'd keep the closest eye on the United States and Brazil as potential backsliders on fiscal responsibility.

• Headlines that indicate *a currency—and here the one to watch is the dollar—is headed down the path of the yen.* The dollar is in danger of becoming a low-interest-rate, falling-value currency, like the yen, at the mercy of traders who borrow in that currency to buy assets denominated in other currencies. The government of Japan for all intents and purposes has lost control of its own currency. The United States could suffer the same loss of control and as a consequence become much less able to set its own monetary policy.

• *Budget crises in Italy, Greece, Spain, or Eastern Europe that would weaken the growing reputation of the euro as a stable global currency.* Signs that the European Central Bank is listening to national politicians clamoring to fix local economies would be bad for the euro.

Trend Makers

• It takes years and years for a national central bank to build up its capital as an inflation fighter. But once that reputation is in place, *the stability effect can last for decades.* The U.S. Federal Reserve is currently living off a reputation as an inflation fighter put in place in the

1980s and confirmed in the earlier years of the Greenspan Fed. The Bank of Canada has solid credentials. Brazil's central bank is building a reputation on inflation that can lead to future stability. Australia's central bank is helping its credentials with a current round of interest rate increases. Bank to watch: the Reserve Bank of India, which has been shown more spirit in fighting off political meddling recently than I would have expected.

• *A continued decline in the U.S. trade deficit,* as a falling dollar makes U.S. exports cheaper to consumers in the rest of the world and U.S. imports more expensive, would lend support to the U.S. dollar.

• Any signs that *the U.S. government elected in 2008 understands that you can't spend money you don't have* would add stability to U.S. financial assets.

• Watch for signs that the *successor government in Brazil* that will take office after the 2010 elections is committed to continuing the fiscally conservative consensus policies of the conservative Cardoso and populist Lula. President Lula was elected for a second term in 2006 and cannot run for reelection.

• *Look for other countries that may be joining the stability group.* One to watch is South Africa. An improvement in relative stability there would accelerate the interest among international investors in using the country as a platform for expanding exposure to other African economies.

STOCK PICKS THAT PUT THE WIND FROM THOSE TRENDS AT YOUR BACK

BHP Billiton (NYSE ADR: BHP). I've recommended this Australian mining company with a finger in everything from copper to uranium twice before in this book, once as a natural resources pick and once as an inflation hedge. Now I'm recommending it as a way to gain exposure to the stable Australian economy and the Australian dollar, which is likely to be one of the stronger currencies in the world over the next decade thanks to the country's resource-based economy. Australian interest rates were at a high in early 2008 as the central bank tried to slow the economy. As the economy slowed and the bank decided it needed to repeatedly cut interest rates, that weakened the Australian dollar versus other currencies. A weaker Australian dollar will eventually produce a rally in Australian stocks, so I think you've got a good hedge against both weaker U.S. and Australian dollars with this stock.

Cisco Systems (NASDAQ: CSCO). Cisco Systems isn't the fast-growing technology company that rode the dot-com boom to revenue growth of 44 percent in 1999 and 56 percent in 2000 before the bottom fell out. And that's a good thing. The company owns more than 50 percent of the market for Internet routers and switches and 80 percent of the corporate market for routers. Cisco has used that market share as a springboard to build strong revenue streams in Internet security and storage, wireless networking, and Internet telephony and video. Those added revenue streams have turned Cisco Systems into a company capable of delivering steady double-digit revenue growth—16.6 percent annually over the last five years. The Wall Street consensus projects annual earnings growth of 14.2 percent over the next five years.

Encana (NYSE: ECA). Let me count the reasons that this Canadian company is a great way to cash in on stability. Encana has spent the last two years divesting itself of overseas oil and natural gas operations and using the cash to build a leading position in unconventional oil and gas reserves in North America, so no more worries about who's going to seize foreign oil company assets next. The company's properties now include the Barnett Shale formation in Texas, Colorado's Piceance Basin, and oil sands and coal-bed methane in Alberta. Natural gas reserves total 12.4 billion cubic feet. Natural gas is priced in dollars and the global price has a history of rising when the dollar falls. The company also books foreign exchange gains whenever the Canadian dollar climbs against its U.S. counterpart. In the first quarter of 2007, for example, Encana booked an $11 million gain for foreign exchange transactions. The company put off a proposed split into two publicly traded companies in late 2008.

PepsiCo (NYSE: PEP) delivers like clockwork. Take operating margins, for example: 18 percent in 2004, 18.2 percent in 2005, 18.5 percent in 2006, and 18.2 percent in 2007 even as the cost of such raw materials as corn and corn syrup soared. Part of the reason is that PepsiCo is the U.S.-based company that has done the best job at becoming truly global. Today steady North American sales get a powerful boost from a fast-growing international business. In 2008, international sales, which make up about 40 percent of total revenue, are expected to climb by 15 percent. Beverage sales in North America will climb a projected 6 percent to 7 percent and North American sales at Frito-Lay will grow by 4 percent to 5 percent. Earnings, which grew by 12 percent a year on average in the last five years, are projected to grow by an average of 10.8 percent a year in the next five years.

Vale (NYSE ADR: RIO). I've recommended this company (formerly known as Companhia Vale do Rio Doce) in other chapters in this book as a natural resource and inflation pick. Now I'm adding it as a way to profit from the stability premium going to Brazil and Canada. Brazil you can figure out immediately, since this is a Brazilian company selling iron and other ores it mines in Brazil. But the company bought Canadian nickel producer Inco just in time to catch higher nickel prices in 2007, and that gives it big exposure to the Canadian economy and currency. The rising value of the Brazilian real and the Canadian dollar would be a concern in some parts of the global economic cycle, but not in this one. Commodity prices are still on the march upward, and Vale is able to pass along the appreciation of its currencies to buyers scrambling for supplies of iron ore and nickel.

Stocks for Building an Overweight Position in This Sector

- **Canadian Natural Resources** (NYSE: CNQ) for its Alberta oil sands. Recovery of even 10 percent of the oil trapped in these sands would give Canada proven reserves second only to those of Saudi Arabia.
- **Enbridge** (NYSE: ENB) owns or is building pipelines to take

oil and natural gas from Canada and the Rockies to energy-hungry U.S. consumers. The Canadian company paid a 3.1 percent dividend as of May 2008.

- **Fortescue Metals Group** (OTC: FSUMF) is an upstart Australian iron ore producer that delivered its first ore to market in May 2008.
- **Imperial Oil** (AMEX: IMO), Canada's largest refiner, owns 4 refineries, 2,000 gasoline stations, 13 pipelines, and 80 production projects, including a 70 percent stake in the Karl oil sands project and the Mackenzie Delta natural gas development.
- **Johnson & Johnson** (NYSE: JNJ) is the most diversified of the major drug companies. In 2007 41 percent of revenue came from pharmaceuticals, 35 percent from medical devices, and 24 percent from consumer products. That gives the company's earnings growth extraordinary stability.
- **Potash Corp. of Saskatchewan** (NYSE: POT) owns 22 percent of the world's potash capacity. Not a bad thing to own, since prices of potash fertilizer could hit a record $1,000 a metric ton in 2008 and the Canadian company is expecting record production on record exports in 2008.
- **Suncor Energy** (NYSE: SU) holds leases with a likely 15 billion barrels of refinery-ready oil in Canada's oil sands region.

Mutual Funds and ETFs (Exchange-Traded Funds)

There's an exchange-traded fund for each of the non-U.S. markets I've recommended in this chapter.

- iShares MSCI Canada Index Fund (EWC) owns big positions in Canadian Natural Resources, Encana, Potash, and Suncor Energy.
- iShares MSCI Australia Index Fund (EWA) owns a big position in BHP Billiton.
- iShares MSCI Brazil Index Fund (EWZ) owns shares of Petrobras and Vale.

PART III

Becoming a
Compleat Investor

$$\boxed{13}$$

The Importance of

Playing Defense

No team in any sport can just play offense, and investors can't either. Otherwise, no matter how good you are at picking stocks and sectors and how much profit you rack up in the good times, you'll simply give back too much in losses in the bad times when the stock market takes a nosedive. I know this from painful and very expensive personal experience. So listen up. Get the value of my education without paying the tuition. Read this chapter even if you think you're a dyed-in-the-wool buy-and-hold investor who never sells no matter what the market does. It will be worth it to you. I promise.

In 1999, as the great bull market rally went into overdrive, the technology-heavy NASDAQ Composite Index soared to the sky. Powered by stocks such as Yahoo, Amazon, and Cisco Systems, the index gained 86 percent that year—not too shabby considering that the index had climbed 39 percent in 1998.

But Jubak's Picks did even better. I loaded up on the stocks in the technology sector in general and the communications and Internet groups in particular, and in 1999 my online portfolio climbed 102 percent.

So what did I do in 2000? I kept chasing the same trends that had made me so much money in 1999 and I completely forgot about playing defense. In 2000 my portfolio lost 17.2 percent, and that's even worse than it sounds. Since I'd doubled my money in 1999, my loss was magnified. Coming after that 102 percent gain, it was equivalent to a 34 percent drop in the value of my portfolio. I had given back about a third of my gains.

The cost going forward added to the pain. All that money I lost in 2000 wasn't around in my portfolio to start compounding when the market turned back up in October 2002. In 2003 Jubak's Picks returned 45.1 percent. But that gain was on a much smaller base than it would have been if I had played some defense.

PLAY HALFWAY DECENT DEFENSE

And that's all I want you to do. Not time the market and sell everything at the bottom and then move everything back into stocks when your perfect trading system issues a buy opinion. Not go short when the timers yell to sell. Not buy options to leverage your returns on the upside and the downside.

All I want you to do is not give back any more of your gains than you have to when the stock market turns against you. Keep this math in mind: if you gain 100 percent in a year and then lose 50 percent of your total portfolio in a bear market, you're exactly back where you started. To get back to where you were before the bear chewed your portfolio, you need another 100 percent gain. I don't know about you, but I find 100 percent gains scarcer than hen's teeth. Not playing defense just makes investing too hard.

Let's be clear on this: the long-standing and endless debate between traders and buy-and-hold investors about whether some hypothetical market-timing trader can beat the return of some hypothetical buy-and-hold investor is irrelevant. Oh, it's a great way to pass the time around a 2005 Côte de Beaune, but the argument doesn't have much to do with how most of us invest in the real world. You and I aren't likely to go from 100 percent invested to all cash just because some trader's system has suddenly flashed a sell signal. And we aren't likely to put all our cash to work in one bout of buying just because that system flashed a buy signal. Nor are we likely to just sit without doing any selling when the stock market is crashing all around us or avoid some follow-the-leader buying when stocks are climbing. Almost none of us are so stoic that we're able to completely abjure selling when the stock market as a whole panics or avoid getting swept up in the irrational exuberance of a rally that's adding a percent or two to everybody's portfolio four days out of five.

In real life, investing is just a whole lot messier than it is in any academic debate.

In practice, most of us fall somewhere between the extremes of reacting to every sell or buy signal from the overall market and never reacting to the moves of the general market at all, and that's okay. In fact, I'd say that's as it should be for most people who invest to reach a goal rather than as a profession. I just want to show you how to minimize how much of your profit you give back when the stock market turns against you, as it does from time to time.

The system I use in my online Jubak's Picks results in an automatic cascade of selling that will help you play defense in most markets. The cascade starts with individual stocks. I use two triggers that tell me when I need to look more carefully at a stock to see if I should sell.

First, when I buy a stock I set a target price that I'm hoping this stock will reach. When a stock climbs in price and hits that target, it's a signal to make a decision about holding or selling. (You'll find more on how to set a target price in Chapter 14.) You should be familiar enough with the stock by this point so that this decision won't take as much work as the initial buy decision required. But you do, at this point, want to check to make sure that

- The reasons that you wanted to own the stock are still intact
- The stock's chart doesn't show signs that the upward trend is faltering or that the upward trend looks like a rocket that will tumble back to earth after its fuel is exhausted

• The fundamentals justify putting a new, higher price target on the stock

If not, it's time to think about selling.

If you want to try to capture the very last bit of profit from a stock, you can set a sell target about 15 percent higher than the target price you calculate from the fundamentals. Investors know from experience that every trend, good or bad, runs to excess as buyers and sellers get carried away by emotion. Whatever we like to pretend, stock prices are never completely rational, so you might as well try to make a buck or two from the emotional overreaction in the market. A stock that has climbed to $120, for example, will often keep on climbing for the simple reason that investors buy stocks that are going up. They want to jump on the bandwagon. On the other side, investors will often sell a stock that is cheap on its fundamentals simply because everyone around them is selling. If you decide to try to profit from this emotion, make sure you put in a stop-loss limit on the stock. This can be either an actual stop-loss order with your broker to sell when a stock falls to a specific price or a promise to yourself to sell when a stock falls to a specific price. You want to set the stop-loss figure close enough to the stock's current price so that you won't give back too much of your profit and far enough from the current price so that it won't trigger a sell on random ups and downs in the overall market. Depending on the volatility of the market at that moment and the volatility of the individual stock, a stop somewhere around 7 percent to 14 percent below the current price is right. (Do remember to raise the stop limit as the stock continues to climb in price, please.)

Second, I set a percentage position for each stock in my portfolio. Say I have a $200,000 portfolio. I set a full position for my core stocks as $20,000 and a half position for my riskier edge holdings at $10,000. In this hypothetical case, that gives me eight full positions and four half positions. As the portfolio rises in value (we hope), the individual positions rise in value too. But what I look for are stocks that are rising so fast that they outrun the share of the portfolio. If a position gets 25 percent bigger than the average position limit in my portfolio, it triggers a rebalancing review. At the end of the review I might sell just enough shares to get the position back in line with the rest of the portfolio.

Let's say, for example, that your portfolio has had a good 5 percent run in the first four months of 2008 and has climbed from $200,000 to a total value of $210,000 by the end of April. Now a full position in your portfolio is $21,000 instead of $20,000.

But those four months have been spectacular for Potash Corporation of Saskatchewan, as fertilizer prices have rocketed from $700 to near $1,000 a metric ton. By the end of April, the value of your initial $20,000 position in Potash has climbed by almost 24 percent to $24,794. That's $3,794, or about 18 percent more than your full position target value.

That excess above the full position target doesn't trigger a sell, but it does set off an automatic review of the stock. Looking at the strength in the individual trend for the stock and in the macro trend for the sector, you decide whether to let all your chips ride or if it's time to take a few off the table.

I do this kind of review of all the positions in my portfolio at the end of every quarter. Any stock that's more than 25 percent above my position target gets a full review in which I look at the strength of the stock and sector trends. If I'm fully confident of the continued strength of the trends, I let this winner run. If I see signs that the stock or the trend may be leveling off, though, I sell. Not the whole position, but just enough shares to rebalance the portfolio. If Potash had continued to climb so that the position was now $30,000 and the target position was $22,000, I would sell enough shares to reduce the Potash position to the $22,000 level and distribute the $8,000 across the portfolio.

There's another question I ask when a stock exceeds the position target by more than 25 percent. If I sold to rebalance the position, would I be putting the cash to use in stocks with better prospects? If you think Potash stock is looking at 20 percent growth for the next quarter, there's no use selling shares of it in order to put the money into a stock with just 5 percent potential.

You do the same kind of review on the downside. If a position that you still believe in (and see Chapter 13 for how to tell when a stock no longer merits your faith) falls enough in price so that the position is 25 percent less than your target for a position, you buy more shares to top it up. For example, Maxwell Technologies went through tough times in the last quarter of 2007 as orders for its energy storage devices lagged investor expectations. The stock fell to $8.27 at the end of December from $11.63 at the end of September. The value of my original $20,000 position fell to $14,222. That almost 29 percent decline triggered an end-of-quarter position review. I still believed in the company. In fact, a new CEO had come on board with a promise of more focus on profitability. And I certainly still believed in the environmental trend I have outlined in this book. So I bought more shares of Maxwell at $8.27—$5,778 worth—to restore my position to that $20,000. As of May 19, 2008, that had worked out pretty well. Each Maxwell share purchased at $8.27 had climbed in price to $12.82.

If your selling generates cash but there's no position in need of topping up, as there sometimes isn't in the final stages of a bull market rally, then you can just sit on your cash waiting for the inevitable correction before you put it to work. If you want to use this mechanism aggressively, you would hold on to cash whenever you think the market is getting toppy (again, see Chapter 15, on technical analysis) and wait for the correction before putting any cash back to work.

Notice what this rebalancing does: it automatically sells high and buys low without forcing you to sell winners completely or to time the market. In essence, I've borrowed the old tried-and-true method of dollar cost averaging and then added a selling component. In traditional dollar cost averaging you put the same dollar amount into a position each month. So in months when shares are expensive you buy fewer of them and in months when they're cheap you buy more. My method adds a selling tactic that results in selling shares when they're relatively expensive and buying them when they're relatively cheap.

By the way, there's nothing magic about the 25 percent number I used in this example. At 25 percent you'll be employing this method very conservatively and giving winners lots of room to run. If you set the limit at 10 percent, on the other hand, you'll be on the aggressive end of the spectrum and you'll have a better chance of capturing smaller changes in market direction. For what it's worth, in my own portfolio I use a 20 percent trigger.

This mechanism will take you in and out of individual stocks, and when an entire sector rallies more strongly than the overall market, it will lead you to take profits in a sector. So, for example, in 2006 when the S&P 500 climbed 13.6 percent and the oil services sector (represented by the bundle of stocks that trades as an ETF called Oil Services HOLDRs) climbed just 9.09 percent, this system wouldn't have done much at all. Since the sector was climbing but roughly tracking the market, an investor following it would have let any money in oil service stocks ride.

In 2007, however, the story would have been totally different. In that year the S&P 500 index climbed just 3.53 percent but the oil service sector zoomed ahead 44.27 percent. As the year wore on, that relative outperformance would have led you to take profits in the sector—which would have protected some of your profits from the 14 percent drop in the sector in the first month of 2008.

But playing defense shouldn't stop at the level of individual stocks.

ACTIVE DEFENSE AT THE SECTOR LEVEL

At least once a quarter, you should review the charts for the sectors represented in your portfolio. If you detect something in that quarterly review that makes you nervous, you should up the frequency to once a month. You can do this using one of the sector exchange-traded funds that I recommend at the end of each of my ten macro trend chapters. The ETFs that include the acronym SPDR in their names and that track the major sectors in the S&P 500 are a good choice for this purpose.

I'd start with a review of the sector chart. For example, looking at the chart for the Financial Select Sector SPDR in a regular quarterly review at the end of the June 2007 period would have raised if not a red flag at least an eyebrow. You would have noticed that the financial sector ETF had fallen below its 50-day moving average on June 12 and below its 200-day moving average and the bottom of its Bollinger price channel, all really bad signs for the sector. (If you're not familiar with this kind of "chart talk," see Chapter 15 for what all these indicators mean.) By the end of July the 50-day moving average had crossed below the 200-day moving average, and by the middle of October the chart was showing a failed rally—one that didn't take the stocks to a new high before faltering. Depending on how aggressively you play defense, you would have sold out of the sector by selling the stocks in your portfolio that belonged to this sector in whole or part at the end of June, by the end of July, or by October 12. The savings from playing defense in those ways as of January 25, 2008, were 24 percent, 16 percent, and 23 percent, respectively. As you can see, even a conservative defensive player would have saved a considerable hunk of capital by selling out of the sector.

You shouldn't depend solely on technical analysis for your sector defense, though. One reason that I've laid out the positive story for each of the ten trends in this book in so much detail is that with that background you should be able to pick up a temporary downturn in the trend from your own intelligent consumption of business news. It would have been hard to read the news in even a cursory fashion and not pick up on the troubles in the financial sector by August 2007. You would have collected good evidence that the subprime mortgage mess was going to cost banks billions in write-offs over the next few quarters. And on that news, with or without confirmation from the charts, you would have begun to reduce your exposure to the sector in the early fall of 2007.

BEAR MARKETS

The styles of defense I outline in the preceding sections—at the stock and sector levels—are enough to handle most markets. To sum up:

- Sell individual stocks when they climb too far too fast.
- Trim positions when they get too far above the target position value you've set for your portfolio.
- Sell out of sectors that look like they're breaking down in the charts of the appropriate ETF.
- Buy shares in stocks that you still believe in when they fall below your target for a portfolio position.
- Redistribute cash from overly large positions across your portfolio.

If you do all this, then you'll be playing enough defense to handle run-of-the mill dips in the market. What's a run-of-the-mill dip? The measures that I've outlined here are enough to take you through a typical 10 percent correction in the stock prices.

Bear markets, on the other hand, are much less frequent and much more severe. By definition it's not a bear market unless stocks have tumbled 20 percent or more from a recent high. Bear in mind that 20 percent is a minimum. The bear market of March 2000 to October 2002 took the S&P 500 index down 48 percent. The bear market that started on October 9, 2007, had cost the S&P 500 43 percent by October 10, 2008.

Bear markets require their own, more aggressive style of defense. Why? Because a bear market is different from a correction. For example, while corrections often leave the strongest-performing stocks and the strongest-performing sectors of the prior bull market standing—or even push them up in price as investors seek safety from falling prices elsewhere—bear markets take down everything. At some points in a bear market, the stocks that did best in the previous bull market or that even now have the best fundamental stories fall the hardest as investors desperate to raise cash to cover their losses and margin calls decide to sell their best stocks rather than those where they're facing 40 percent losses. To take another example, bear markets are long enough to contain their own rallies. Stocks can climb significantly in a bear market rally and still leave the bear market's downward trend intact.

Bear markets are notorious for repeated failed rallies that crush the last drop of optimism out of investors before stock prices hit a final bottom. The 2000–2 bear market that took the S&P 500 down 48 percent and the NASDAQ Composite Index down 78 percent before it was over produced major rallies in July and August 2000 and in January, May, and December 2001. Investors who used those rallies as selling opportunities did well. Investors who bought into the rallies in the hope that the bear market was over piled losses on top of losses. The NASDAQ Composite Index fell 60 percent from the top of the January 2001 rally to the eventual bear market bottom in October 2002.

It's the unusual investor who can watch rally after rally fail without finally throwing in the towel. And when investors finally decide they can't take it anymore, they're likely to wind up selling at the bottom.

Because they've been burned so many times by failed rallies, having finally sold, they now perversely develop a need to believe that the market will continue to fall. A further decline would justify that belated sell. So investors who have been through the wringer of a bear market and its failed rallies often won't put money back into the market until a rally has been in progress for several quarters. And so the bear inflicts one final bit of punishment by getting these investors first to sell low and now to buy high.

In January 2008 I thought the market had made the transition from a correction to an impending bear market. We wouldn't be in an official bear market until stocks dropped 20 percent or more from their October 2007 highs, I wrote in my column on January 22, 2008. That would mean a decline to the 11,250 level for the Dow Jones Industrial Average, to 1,275 for the Standard & Poor's 500 Index, and to 2,250 or so for the NASDAQ Composite Index.

Frankly, I wasn't willing to wait for the market to earn its official bear market stripes before doing anything to play defense. Waiting for a 20 percent drop means that I don't start doing anything to protect my portfolio until I'm already down 20 percent. Could I be wrong? Of course. That's always a danger. And I'm no more willing to bet the value of my entire portfolio on being able to predict a break to the downside than I am on being able to predict a break to the upside. But the downside is so significant that I am willing to take steps to protect my portfolio even if they mean leaving some profits on the table if I'm wrong. That's especially true when the evidence of an impending bear market in stocks is so convincing to me, as it was in January 2008.

WHAT TO LOOK FOR IN ANY POTENTIAL BEAR MARKET

• **A pattern of lower lows.** The charts showed a breakdown in the stock market and the formation of a strong downward trend. The Dow Jones Industrial Average, for example, showed a dangerous pattern of setting lower lows. The Dow Industrials closed at 12,743 at its November 26, 2007, low, breaking the closing low of 12,861 of August 15, 2007. On January 8, 2008, it closed below that level, at 12,589. And the Dow wasn't the worst-looking index either. The S&P 500 broke through its March 5, 2007, low of 1,374 on January 16, 2008, and the NASDAQ Composite closed within points of its March 5, 2007, low of 2,341 on January 18, 2008.

• **Rising fear among investors.** The S&P 500 Volatility Index (VIX), which uses the volatility of options on the S&P 500 Stock Index to track the rise and fall of stock market volatility, is a good measure of the amount of fear in the market. A higher VIX indicates more volatility and more fear; a lower VIX, the opposite. In July 2007 the VIX surged above resistance at 18 and finally climbed above 30. After sinking back to 18 in October, the VIX went on an upward march again, climbing to near 30 by the end of January 2008. And that's not good for stocks. There are fewer buyers when fear is high.

• **Falling earnings estimates.** The U.S. economy was slowing, but Wall Street analysts had ended 2007 still calling for 16.2 percent earnings growth in 2008 for the companies in the Standard & Poor's 500 Stock Index. Estimates were coming down, though. The estimate for S&P 500 earnings stood at $101 at the end of 2007. By January 14, it had inched down to $100.32. As earnings estimates and earnings growth estimates fall, it makes stocks seem more expensive—and that's not much of an inducement to already fearful buyers. When even well-run segment leaders such as Johnson Controls and Schlumberger report disappointing earnings and guidance, as they both did on January 18, those fears seemed well founded.

• **Bad economic news was getting worse.** For example, new home construction fell again in December by 14 percent and new permits fell by 8 percent. In the banking sector bad debt problems continued to ripple out from mortgages to credit cards and from auto loans to corporate bonds.

For all these reasons, I thought it was worth playing defense at a bear market level.

WHAT GOES INTO A BEAR MARKET DEFENSE?

Here's what I recommended in late 2008:

• **Sell early.** If this is a bear, there's no point in hanging around. Sell now rather than later. Why? You want to avoid as much of the bear market loss as possible. You want to avoid being one of those courageous investors who hangs on through a 19 percent decline but then can't stand it and sells at 20 percent down. Buying high is one way to lose money in a market. The other is selling at the low. And that's what you'd like to avoid. Selling early also helps clear your head. Instead of fighting the last battle, you're ready to look forward to making money with the cash you've got in hand when the market turns in your favor again. By January 22, 2008, I'd moved my online portfolio to 32 percent cash, and I continued to build my cash position in bear market rallies.

• **Get over yourself.** No investor wants to admit that he or she made a mistake, and so we hang on and hang on to stocks down 20 percent or 30 percent hoping that they'll move up to break even in the next bear market rally, and then we'll sell. This sets us up for more losses as the bear runs its course, and it means that we're likely to be selling at exactly the time when we should be buying—when the rally that marks the end of the bear finally comes. But, hey, investing isn't about being perfect, and making a bad investment isn't a judgment on your moral character or intelligence. All investors make mistakes and pick losers. All we really hope for is to pick more winners than losers.

- **Don't count on past winners for safety.** In a bear almost everything gets sold. Worries about the U.S. and global economies have already taken a big bite out of energy and industrial commodity stocks (copper miners, for example). That's not unusual. Those commodity sectors sold off in past bear markets too. Looking back to previous bear markets, about the only sector able to buck the trend has been gold. Gold stocks went their own little correction in early 2008 thanks to a drop in sales of gold into the Indian jewelry market, the biggest market for physical gold in the world. But I think this is just a correction in gold and that gold will be one of the few safe havens in any 2008 bear market.

- **Cash isn't trash.** Rethink your definition of a "good return." A 4 percent to 5 percent return might look kind of puny when stocks are moving up 15 percent, but it's a darn sight more attractive when stocks are plunging. That cash on the sideline can earn you 5 percent in a certificate of deposit (keep the maturity short—six months—so you can put this money to work when the bear is over). Stick to safe U.S. Treasuries and to relatively short maturities such as the two-year so you avoid losses from resurgent fears of inflation.

- **Hedge by going short the market—using an inverse ETF—if you're an aggressive trader and have some familiarity with the basics of shorting.** In the past I wouldn't have recommended anything like this. For investors unfamiliar with options and shorting, a bear market certainly is no place to take a crash course. But the with advent of ETFs I think that's changed. You can now buy an ETF that goes up when the NASDAQ or S&P 500 or Russell 2000 goes down. And you can even buy an ETF that goes up twice as fast as the index that it tracks goes down. ETFs to check out include:

1. The Short QQQ ProShares (PSQ), which bets against the NASDAQ 100

2. The UltraShort S&P500 ProShares (SDS), which tries to go up twice as fast as the S&P 500 goes down
3. The Ryder Inverse 2X Russell 2000 ETF (RRZ), which applies the same two-times strategy to the Russell 2000 small company index
4. The Short S&P500 ProShares (SH), which bets against the S&P 500
5. The Rydex Inverse 2X S&P 500 EFT (RSW), which tries to go up twice as fasts as the S&P goes down

Be careful in chasing returns on the short end—the indexes that have already gone down the most are not necessarily the best picks for defending against future drops. The best time to buy one of these is in a bear market rally. But that means you need to be reasonably confident that you can tell a bear market rally from the real thing and predict when the rally will top out with some confidence. For most of us, I think cash is the better option.

When I made this call in January 2008, I wasn't absolutely certain that we had entered a bear market. My call wasn't, in fact, confirmed until July 2, when the Dow fell to 11,216 and the S&P 500 to 1,262. That made this officially a bear market. It was quite possible that I was making a mistake back in January when I made that call. I'm okay with that. The odds were that protecting my portfolio in this way by moving to cash wouldn't cost me a whole lot. And I knew that if I was correct, I would give my portfolio some valuable protection by making these moves. Nothing in investing is guaranteed, remember. All you can hope to do is to put the odds in your favor as much and as often as you can.

14

Everything You Need to Know

About Fundamentals

All that choice. Investors have a choice of more than 7,000 stocks on the U.S. markets alone. Add in overseas exchanges and the options run in the tens of thousands. You can't possibly own more than a very small fraction of them. In many ways, then, the biggest challenge facing any investor is figuring out what's the best stock to buy out of all those possibilities.

In this book I've given you ten trends to invest in. Pick a stock that benefits from one of those trends and you've gone a long way toward finding the best stock to buy. But you're certainly not all the way home yet. At any one moment, some of the fifty stocks that I've picked in these chapters will be better investments than others on the list. How do you decide which stock is the best stock to buy *now*?

Fundamental analysis—the study of a company's fundamentals, such as growth rates and management efficiency, to forecast future stock prices—can give you an answer to that question. And fortunately, you can learn most of what you need to know by studying just two fundamental measures: the price-to-earnings (PE) ratio and the return on invested capital (ROIC).

In this chapter I'll tell you what you need to know to use these measures to decide what stock is the best one to buy now. And I'll also tell you about other additional fundamental tools that offer context for the PE ratio and ROIC and how to use those tools to make sense of what the PE ratio and ROIC are telling you.

THE PE RATIO

At its simplest, a price-to-earnings ratio divides a stock's price per share by its earnings per share. For example, on March 7, 2008, the price of a share of Apple stock was $112.25 and earnings for the last twelve months were $4.55. The stock's price-to-earnings ratio was $112.25 divided by $4.55, or 24.67.

Most investors I know get this far. What stumps them is whether that PE ratio is good or bad.

Unfortunately, there's no simple answer to this question. PE ratios come in all sizes. On March 7:

- Apple's was 24.67.
- Google showed a PE ratio of 32.60.
- ExxonMobil's was 11.30.
- Devon Energy's was 14.4.
- Monsanto had a PE ratio of 54.80.
- Citigroup's was 33.90.
- PepsiCo's was 20.4.

Which is these is good and which bad? Which is the best? And to put the question in the terms an investor cares about most, which stock does the PE ratio say is a buy?

All other things being equal, you want to buy the stock with the lowest price-to-earnings ratio. That way, an investor is paying the least number of dollars for the largest amount of earnings. Again, all other things being equal, that's a good thing.

Unfortunately, all other things are never equal.

• *High and low PE ratios reflect not just current earnings but fu-ture earnings growth.* Monsanto has such a high PE ratio now, 54.8, because Wall Street analysts expect Monsanto to grow earnings by 40 percent in the fiscal year that ends in August 2008 and 24 percent in the fiscal year that ends in August 2009. PepsiCo, on the other hand, is projected to grow earnings by just 10.5 percent in the fiscal year that ends in December 2008, so the stock deserves a PE ratio lower than Monsanto's.

• *High and low PE ratios reflect the volatility of a stock's earnings from year to year.* All other things being equal, you'll pay more—that is the stock will have a higher PE ratio—for more consistent earnings growth. PepsiCo's earnings go up every year by a steady 10 percent to 12 percent. Over the last five years, the company has averaged an an-nual 12 percent earnings growth. Over the next five years, the com-pany is projected to average 10.8 percent annually. ExxonMobil, on the other hand, is part of the historically volatile oil industry. Earnings were essentially static in 1999, falling to $1.12 a share from $1.15 a share in 1998, and dropped significantly to $1.62 a share in 2002 from $2.16 in 2001. Right now Wall Street expects that after growing earnings by an average annual 26.8 percent in the last five years, ExxonMobil will grow earnings by just 4.8 percent on average for the next five years. Consistent PepsiCo gets a PE ratio of 20.4. Inconsis-tent ExxonMobil gets a PE ratio of 11.3.

• *High and low PE ratios reflect Wall Street's assumptions about the volatility of earnings in a company's industry based on the history of earnings in that industry.* Oil companies have relatively low PE ra-tios because historically oil industry earnings are less dependable and more subject to huge swings up and down. The PE ratio for the Standard & Poor's 500 stocks—commonly used as a measure for the average PE for the stock market—was 18.9 on March 7 when Exxon-Mobil's PE ratio was 11.3. On the other hand, food industry PE ratios are market average or better because historically earnings at compa-nies in this industry have been more predictable and their earnings growth more dependable. Kellogg had a price-to-earnings ratio of 17.9 on March 7. PepsiCo's was 20.4.

- *High and low PEs reflect stock market fads and fashions.* Monsanto, an agricultural chemical and seed company, trades at a PE ratio of 54.8 because a boom in farm commodity prices has sent investors scrambling to find stocks that will let them participate in the boom. Monsanto, widely seen as the leader in the seed segment, is one of small group of stocks that fits this bill. Like Potash of Saskatchewan, a fertilizer stock trading at a PE ratio of 47.5, Monsanto is in fashion.

WHAT'S A GOOD PE RATIO?

So how do you decide what's a good PE ratio (buy) and what's a bad one (sell)? Let me count the ways.

1. *Base the PE ratio not on earnings per share over the last twelve months but on projected earnings for the next year.* After all, you are paying not for past earnings—they're already reflected in the stock price—but for future earnings. This is the difference between what's known as trailing PE and forward PE ratios. So Monsanto's huge 54.8 PE ratio of March 7, 2008, based on trailing earnings for the past twelve months, becomes a still high but not as outrageous forward PE ratio of 37.9 based on projected earnings for 2008. For Potash, a trailing PE ratio of 47.5 becomes a forward PE ratio of 21.5. For a rapidly growing natural gas producer such as Ultra Petroleum, a trailing PE ratio of 66.5 turns into a forward ratio of 31.2. All else being equal, Potash is the best buy of these three because you get more future (projected) earnings for fewer current dollars.

2. *Correct the trailing or forward PE to take account of a company's growth rate.* This results in a fundamental tool known as the PEG (PE-to-growth) ratio. This tool is just common sense. The faster future earnings are growing, the more you should be willing to pay for a dollar of current earnings (the higher the PE ratio). Some investors like to build a PEG ratio based on the current PE ratio and current earnings growth; others like to construct the ratio on forward PE ratio and forward earnings growth. I belong to the second camp: if you're paying for future earnings, it makes sense to me to look at a forward

PEG ratio. To compute a PEG ratio for Ultra Petroleum on March 7, 2008, for example, take the forward PE ratio of 31.20 and divide by the projected earnings growth rate of 22.5 for a PEG ratio of 1.4. (To get a trailing PEG ratio, use the trailing PE ratio and the trailing twelve-month earnings growth rate.) Compare the forward PEG ratio for Ultra Petroleum to that of ExxonMobil. Before computing a PEG ratio, ExxonMobil looks much, much cheaper, with a forward PE ratio of 10.5 to Ultra Petroleum's 31.2. But since ExxonMobil's projected earnings growth rate is just 4.8 percent, the stock has a PEG ratio of 2.2 to Ultra Petroleum's PEG ratio of 1.4. Once you're corrected for the difference in future growth rates, Ultra Petroleum is much cheaper. The same is true with a food stock such as Kellogg. Here the forward PE ratio of 16.5 and the projected earnings growth rate of 9 percent yields a PEG ratio of 1.8—cheaper than ExxonMobil but way more expensive than Ultra Petroleum.

3. *Correct for industry cycles.* When it comes to investing in cyclical stocks—that is, stocks such as those of automakers or mining equipment manufacturers, which show huge swings in earnings from a high when the economy is growing strongly to a low when the economy is struggling—PE ratios work in reverse. The PE of a cyclical stock is highest at the bottom of a cycle. That's not because the P, the price, is so high (it's likely to be in the dumps) but because the E, the earnings, is so low. So, oddly enough to those investors accustomed to growth stocks, the time to buy a cyclical is when the PE is highest. And the time to sell is when the PE is lowest, since that marks the top of the earnings cycle and from there earnings will start to fall, driving up the PE even as the price comes down. Take a look at a cyclical mining equipment stock such as Joy Global. The company showed a loss from 1999 through 2002 (so no meaningful PE ratio in those years, since you can't divide by zero and get a meaningful result) and then swung to a slight profit of 16 cents a share in 2003. At the end of November 2003, the stock showed a price-to-earnings ratio of 36.3 and a price of $9.33. This was the time to buy. Over the next few years earnings per share climbed to 46 cents in 2004, $1.19 in 2005, and $3.37 in 2006. The price-to-earnings ratio fell to 26.9 in November 2004,

19.9 in 2005, and 13.9 in November 2006. By the end of November 2006, Joy Global's share price had climbed to $44.22. That's a 374 percent gain even as the PE ratio was climbing.

4. *Correct for Wall Street error.* PE ratios, and especially forward PE ratios, are only as accurate an indicator of when to buy as the Wall Street projections that they're based on. If the Wall Street consensus is wrong, then the projected PE ratio can't possibly give you a good indication of whether or not it's time to buy or sell. Take a look at what happened to Joy Global after 2006. In that year, you'll remember from the last paragraph, the price-to-earnings ratio for the stock had fallen to 13.9 as earnings had climbed to $3.37 a share. That kind of drop in PE ratio in a year—from 19.9 in November 2005 to 13.9 in November 2006—indicates that Wall Street was expecting that 2006 would mark the earnings peak for the stock. Investors looking at this PE ratio as an indicator of when to buy and sell would have been selling. Earnings for 2007, which dipped to $2.51, would seem to support the Wall Street consensus—Joy Global was a cyclical stock that had seen its earnings peak and was now headed into the downward half of the cycle. But Wall Street was wrong. The fall in earnings in 2007 turned out to be a one-time blip caused not by a fall-off in revenue or operating earnings in 2007 but by a huge gain from a change in tax accounting in 2006. In the third quarter of 2006, the company showed an increase in earnings of 88 cents from the same quarter in 2005, roughly a 131 percent gain in earnings for that quarter in 2006 from the same quarter in 2005. Most of that was a result of a gain from a change in tax accounting. Without that shift, the earnings pattern for Joy Global doesn't show a huge blowout in 2006 with earnings per share jumping to $3.37 from $1.19, and it doesn't show earnings dropping off a cliff to $2.51 in 2007 from $3.37 in 2006. And instead of seeing a cyclical stock that has hit its peak and should be sold, what we see is a cyclical that still has years and years of earnings gains ahead of it. How could you have known that the Wall Street numbers and the signal sent by the PE ratio were misleading? Listening to the company would have been a good first step: Joy Global has said repeatedly that its goal is 20 percent compounded annual growth in earnings through 2012. That's not a sign of

a cyclical company that's hit its peak. You certainly should never just take a company's word on future growth, so you would also listen to the company's market. Joy Global is counting on growth in coal mining in China for a big part of its future growth. Projections that show orders of coal mining equipment from Chinese mining companies climbing at a better than 25 percent annual rate would seem to confirm the company's confidence. Wall Street is now projecting that earnings at Joy Global will climb by 27 percent in the 2008 fiscal year that ends in October 2008 and 23 percent in fiscal 2009. On March 7, 2008, the stock was trading at $66.50 and showed a forward PE ratio of 19.7 and a PEG ratio of 0.74. Despite all the appreciation in the shares, this is still a cheap stock as measured by PE and PEG ratios.

In this last example, you'll notice that I've wandered a far piece away from fundamental analysis based on just earnings and price per share. In digging into the source of Joy Global's earnings to see why they've jumped and fallen and to judge how sustainable they are, I've started to take apart the company's financial reports: its income statement (which reports the company's sales and profits from quarter to quarter or year to year) and its balance sheet (which reports the size and status of the company's assets such as cash in the bank and the debt it owes).

If PE ratios and all the contexts and permutations of them that I've sketched in above are your best fundamental guide to figuring when to buy and sell, then the analysis of the company's balance sheet and income statements is the best fundamental tool available to an investor who wants to figure out the future of a stock.

I know from experience—I remember how daunting my accounting homework could be—and from the e-mail I receive from readers of my column that this part of fundamental analysis is more talked about than performed. Many investors who know that digging into these details is important find the actual work too difficult or too time-consuming. Equally daunting is confusion about where to start if you're going to attempt this part of fundamental analysis. Do you look at receivables or accounts payable? Long-term or short-term debt?

SG&A (selling, general, and administrative) expenses or R&D (research and development)?

So let me propose, if not a shortcut, at least a way to focus your time and energy on a single number. This number isn't by any means the only number that counts, but it does tell the long-term investor the single most important thing about the company.

Is the company compounding its current growth, and if so, at what rate?

You've been told over and over again since you were tall enough to push your passbook across the counter at the local bank that compounding counts. Well, for once the adults weren't fibbing. It's annual compounding that turns $100,000 into almost $200,000 ($196,715 to be exact) in ten years at 7 percent. Without compounding, you'd be stuck with just $107,000 if all you collected was a straight 7 percent on your money regardless of the time involved, or $170,000 if each year you just got 7 percent on your original $100,000. The longer the time period, of course, the bigger the difference.

The same thing that's true for a savings account is true for a stock. A company that earns profits of 7 percent in a year and then has the opportunity to reinvest those profits at 7 percent a year is a better long-term investment than a company earning the same in profits but without the opportunity to reinvest it at the same or higher rates.

The longer your holding period, the more important is a company's ability to compound its earnings. Beyond ten years, I'd argue, there isn't anything more important for an investor.

ROIC

The best single number to look at to judge a company's compounding power is called return on invested capital (ROIC or ROI). To compute ROIC you divide the company's total earnings (that's income before taxes and interest) by its total capital (that's total long-term debt plus total equity), or you can find this information for any stock on the MSN Money site in the section called "Financial Results/Key Ratios."

(Stock reports from Reuters, which are available from many online brokers, also list current and past ROIC.) This ratio tells you how much the company is making on the money shareholders and bond holders have invested. The higher the return, the bigger the effect of future compounding. A company with an ROIC of 11 percent would be able to reinvest its profits in itself next year and the year after and the year after at 11 percent. So it would be compounding its earnings by 11 percent a year. That makes the stock a much better long-term bet—all else being equal, which, of course, it never is—for the investor than a company with a ROIC of, say, 6 percent, which is only compounding earnings by 6 percent a year into the future.

Five years ago, for example, Burlington Northern Santa Fe, in common with most railroads, was truly terrible at compounding earnings. In 2003 the return on invested capital was just 3.2 percent. That was a miserable present return, because in 2003 inflation was running at 2.1 percent, so Burlington Northern's return on invested capital was barely keeping ahead of inflation. It also meant that any income the company did earn—$1.2 billion a year before taxes in 2003—that was reinvested in the company would earn similarly dismal rates for investors in the future.

That year and the next were the end of a horrible span of time for all the country's railroads. With trucks siphoning off freight traffic, the railroads had been trapped in a vicious downward spiral. They were growing, but only slowly—Burlington Northern's revenue climbed by just 5.3 percent between 1998 and 2003. That's not 5.3 percent annually. That's the company's cumulative revenue growth for those six years. Factor in the 2.2 percent annual inflation rate during those years and the company's revenues were lower in real dollars in 2003 than they had been in 1998 by about $440 million, or roughly 5 percent.

Because growth was so slow, the railroads didn't have much money to put back into their business—and little incentive to do so. Why sink earnings into a business growing more slowly than inflation? The railroads weren't exactly begging investors to put new money to work either. Why would they when they would have had to pay more in interest to sell debt than the capital would have earned in the business?

But things started to change for the railroads in 2005. After bottoming at 3.1 percent in 2004, return on invested capital climbed to 5.8 percent in 2005 and then to 6.8 percent in 2006 before taking a dip to 6.2 percent in 2007. Even with that retreat, Burlington Northern's return on invested capital had doubled from 2004 to 2007.

What was going on? Thanks to globalization, demand for the bulky stuff that railroads carry best—coal, wheat, timber—had started to climb and then kept on climbing. Shippers that previously had been indifferent to railroads started to bid up freight rates. And as volumes climbed, railroads discovered they would get paid for delivering better service—and dinged by customers if they didn't. So it became worthwhile to invest in railcars and engines, improved signaling, and new logistics systems not just capable of tracking shipments but also able to prioritize cargoes that needed special treatment. Railroads that had spent the last decade tearing up track started to lay track again.

Not all the railroads are out of the woods yet, but right now it looks like Burlington Northern will soon show a return on invested capital that's higher than its adjusted cost of capital (what it has to pay to raise money from investors). In Burlington Northern, investors are looking at a company that has made the transition from disinvesting in its future to one that is compounding future growth for investors. No wonder that after returning just 2.5 percent in 2001 and losing 7.2 percent in 2002 for investors, the stock has ripped off an extraordinary run of annual returns of 26.7 percent in 2003, 48.4 percent in 2004, 51.6 percent in 2005, 5.5 percent in 2006, and 14.4 percent in 2007.

And you'd have to say that investors believe that this run isn't over. Despite a slowing U.S. economy and despite a stock market that dropped into an extended decline in August 2007, Burlington Northern shares were up 10 percent in the six months from September 10, 2007, through March 10, 2008.

You'd like to invest in companies with high returns on invested capital. So you'd rather invest in ExxonMobil, for example, than in BP because ExxonMobil's return on invested capital is 23.5 percent and BP's is 14.1 percent. That goes a long way toward explaining why

ExxonMobil has returned 24.3 percent a year over the last five years while BP returned just 15.9 percent.

As I keep repeating, though, all other things are never equal. For example, you can't compare returns on invested capital across industries because companies in different industries need to invest different amounts of capital to produce their returns. Oil companies and steel companies both operate in capital-intensive industries—they have to invest a lot of cash in equipment, land, transportation infrastructure, and the like to produce and then sell their products—so it's not too surprising that an oil industry leader such as ExxonMobil and a steel industry leader such as Nucor both show roughly similar returns on invested capital, 23.5 percent and 20.8 percent, respectively. By comparison, software companies are capital-light. A leading software company such as Microsoft has a return on invested capital of 37.9 percent. Despite that, Microsoft shares have returned just 9.9 percent a year over the last five years, trailing both ExxonMobil's 24.3 percent average annual return and Nucor's 42.6 percent.

Just as with PE ratios, you care more about future returns on invested capital than on current returns. Will a company be able to invest today's earnings tomorrow at today's ROIC, a higher one, or a lower one?

BP's lower current return on invested capital, for example, is a reflection of current woes. The company is having an extremely difficult time increasing reserves of oil. According to U.S. Securities & Exchange Commission accounting standards, BP's net crude reserves dropped from 6.36 billion barrels in 2005 to 5.89 billion barrels in 2006. But I'm just as concerned with what I regard as shaky prospects for future exploration. The company has been raising cash by selling declining assets such as its older properties in the Gulf of Mexico, but I have to say I don't see how the company's exploration pipeline is going to deploy cash from earnings and cash from asset sales at even the 14.1 percent return on capital of 2007.

On the other hand, although Chevron's current return on invested capital at 17.1 percent is substantially lower than ExxonMobil's 23.5

percent, Chevron has one of the best lineups of potential production among the industry majors. So I'd expect Chevron's current ROIC to go up as these projects move from potential to production. The company has plenty of places to put its cash to work at rates of return at least equal to today's ROIC. Today Chevron is a pretty decent long-term compounder for investors, and I think it's on the road to doing an even better job in the future.

This isn't exactly a tiny issue for investors in the big multinational oil companies. With something like 80 percent of new reserves and potential reserves in the hands of national oil companies, the international majors are struggling to find places to put their cash to work at anything like historically high returns. ExxonMobil is addressing the problem by investing in the necessary infrastructure to get natural gas from wells to the plants that will turn it into a liquid and by building the terminals that will load the liquefied natural gas into tankers that will take the gas to markets in the United States, Japan, South America, and Europe. This strategy emphasizes one opportunity where its cash and engineering expertise are in global demand.

Chevron, on the other hand, has solved the problem by fighting through incredible political and engineering difficulties to secure new oil and gas supplies in Central Asia and the deep water of the Gulf of Mexico. The prospect that the company will be able to compound future cash at a higher rate is one reason that the stock has outperformed ExxonMobil in average annual return, 27.2 percent to 24.3 percent, over the last five years.

Fundamental indicators are a guide to future stock performance, but the numbers aren't destiny for a stock—at least not without substantial tweaking.

WHAT TO LOOK FOR IN A STOCK'S FUNDAMENTALS

Here are, by the numbers, what I would look for in a stock's fundamentals—but don't forget that tweaking.

- You want a high earnings growth rate.
- Look for a low forward PEG ratio. (The traditional rule of thumb is that low is anything near or below 1.)
- Be willing to pay for a higher PEG ratio in order to buy consistent growth.
- If the stock is a cyclical, you want to buy when growth (and the PE ratio) are high because that marks the bottom of the earnings cycle. (This is the exact opposite of a growth stock.)
- You want that high-growth but low-PEG-ratio stock to have a high ROIC so that the company will be able to compound its earnings at a high rate by reinvesting in its business.

If you find a stock that fits those guidelines exactly, buy it. But remember that this is an imperfect world; there are very few perfect stocks, and those that are perfect are usually priced accordingly and don't stay perfect for very long. In buying stocks, unlike apples, a blemish or two is often a good thing. It gives the stock room for improvement.

15

EVERYTHING YOU NEED TO KNOW

ABOUT TECHNICAL ANALYSIS

THERE ARE TWO OTHER QUESTIONS THAT YOU NEED TO ANSWER as an investor:

1. Should I buy at today's price?
2. When do I sell?

Technical analysis can help you answer those two questions. Technical analysis relies on stock charts, trading volume, and the patterns that price movements sketch out over time to reveal the psychology of the mass of investors.

Let me tell you about a situation where I found technical analysis invaluable.

It was the fall of 2007. The Dow Jones Industrial Average had rallied after plunging almost 9 percent from a high of 13,972 on July 17 to a low of 12,846 on August 16 on fears that the meltdown in the market for debt built on troubled subprime mortgages would spread to stocks and then the economy as a whole. By October 9 the index was at a new high for the year of 14,165. That's a gain of better than 10 percent in roughly a month and a half.

I can still feel the rally mania that set in that October. With stocks rushing higher, the natural reaction was to jump on board. No one wanted to miss a party. As the saying goes, stocks are the only thing that people want to buy more of as the price goes up.

But when I started researching possible buys in this market at the end of October, I got an amber warning instead of a green go-ahead. Many of the stocks that I was looking at had recently gone parabolic. Forget about slow and steady appreciation. These looked like rockets headed for the heavens. Buying at that point meant I had a good chance of buying a rocket just before it ran out of fuel.

For example, here's a simple chart of that period, built using the MSN Money chart tool, of the daily closing price of First Solar, a stock that I'd had my eye on for much of 2007. You can see why from the chart. From a price of $28.34 on November 27, 2006, the shares had climbed to $137.22 by October 9, 2007. That's a gain of 384 percent in less than a year. I missed the dip in August, to my chagrin, when the stock fell back to $81.87. But by October 9, the stock had made up all the ground it had lost and 50 percent more. It was off to the races again.

1–Year FSLR Price History Chart

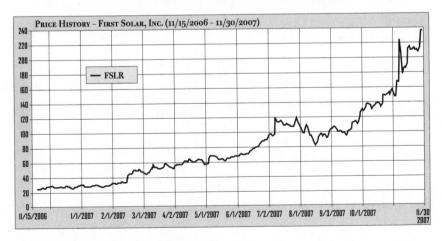

So hit that mouse and buy, no?

Well, no, the chart said. The stock had continued to climb at a gratifying rate from October 9 through the end of October. Shares had climbed from $137.22 on October 9 to $147 on November 2. No way I'd turn up my nose at a 7 percent gain in three weeks.

But then the rate of gain—the speed with which the stock went up in price—accelerated. From a climber of mountains, the stock had turned into a rocket. From November 2 to November 8, it went from $147 to $225 a share, a gain of 53 percent in a week.

First Solar had gone parabolic. A parabolic move—when a stock's rate of gain becomes almost vertical—isn't necessarily a bad thing. Such a move can indicate a breakout after a long period of consolidation at a relatively steady price. But coming after a stock had already racked up big gains, a parabolic move can indicate a blowout top, the last big move up before a stock sinks back, having exhausted the pool of investors (and money) looking to buy.

So how do you tell the difference? Books have been written on how to use price and volume indicators to identify tops and blowouts. But I think the long-term investor can get by—that is, make more money without spending all the hours needed to become expert at technical analysis—with just a few tools. Four, to be exact.

1. **Chart your stock in different time periods to bring out changes in its movement.** If you've been looking at a price chart for a year, as I have in this example, switch to look at a price chart for a week or month. And to give you an even closer look at the stock's action, I've switched from showing just the daily closing prices to using vertical bars that show the high price, the low price, and the closing price for the day. (A small horizontal bar indicates the day's closing price.)

Here's the same stock, First Solar, charted on a monthly basis using high-low-close bars. On this chart I'm looking for what are called gaps, big jumps in price between one day and another that aren't filled by any buys and sells. You'll see just such a gap from November 7 to November 8, exactly the period when First Solar shares went parabolic. By analyzing hundreds of thousands of stocks and charts, experts in technical analysis have discovered that a gap like this one is often a sign of an unsustainable price move. The stock, they say,

1–Month FSLR High-Low-Close Chart

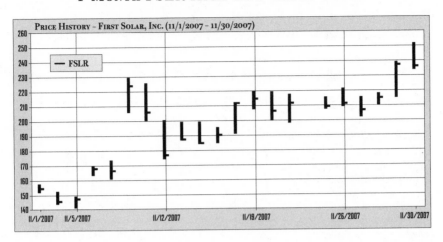

has to come back in price to fill the gap. It's not a good sign either that in the days after the gap, the stock has closed trading near or at the low for the day. Investors haven't stepped in to buy earlier in the day at the highs but instead have stepped aside, deterred, apparently, by the stock's rise in price.

2. **Draw in 50-day and 200-day moving averages on your chart to study the direction and momentum of the trend.** To do this, go back to the original yearlong historical price chart. In the MSN Money charting tool, under "Analysis" you'll see "Moving Averages" in the pull-down menu. Click on both "50-day" and "200-day" to add those to the chart.

Charting a moving average requires a complex calculation (it's hard for me to believe that technicians used to do this by hand in the days before the PC and the Internet) that aims to capture investor psychology. To calculate a 50-day moving average on First Solar in the not-so-good old days, for example, you started on day 1 by calculating the average price for the past fifty trading days. Plot that point on your graph. On day 2, you calculated the average price for the past fifty trading days again—only this time those fifty days include the most recent forty-nine days from the moving average you calculated on day

1 plus the price of First Solar on day 2. On day 3, the moving average used prices from the most recent forty-eight days from the moving average you calculated on day 1 plus the price of First Solar on day 2 and the price on day 3. And so on.

Why go to all this trouble? Because by smoothing out the daily peaks and valleys, a moving average gives you a better idea of the trend in a stock's price and in investor sentiment.

1–Year FSLR Chart with Moving Averages

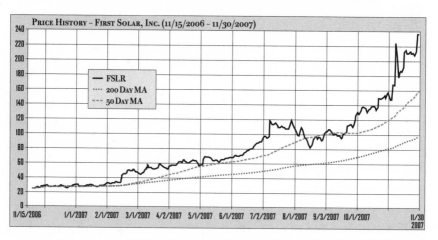

Price History – First Solar, Inc. (11/15/2006 – 11/30/2007)

Looking at a price history chart for First Solar with 50-day and 200-day moving averages, you notice how uniform the pace of the gains in the stock was until October. It's only since the beginning of October that the rate of price increase has really accelerated. You can also see that the August market slowdown, from this longer-term perspective, didn't put a meaningful dent in the long-term trend. If you had been following this chart for a year, you would have been less likely to sell the stock on emotion in August (since the chart reassuringly showed that the trend was intact) and you'd also have been alerted to study the acceleration in price gains. Study rather than act, though, since in contrast to the daily and 50-day moving average charts, the longest-term chart, the 200-day moving average, isn't yet showing a parabolic move.

3. **Look for support (a price level that can stop a decline) or resistance (a price level that can end a rally).** A technician will tell

you that a period of lateral movement around a price or narrow range of prices often creates a temporary floor, or level of support, under a stock. That's because a period when the moving average stays stuck at a price level indicates that a lot of investors have bought or sold near that price. Knowing what we know about investor psychology, you can expect that some of those folks will be feeling seller's regret at the appreciation they missed after they sold and would look to buy to get back into the game at something like their selling price. Buyers at that level, studies of investor psychology say, are likely to hold on even if the price falls through that level because they want to get even before they sell.

The same mass psychology is at work when a stock is on its way up. A price that was support for the stock on the way down becomes a ceiling, what's called resistance, on the way up. That's because investors who bought on the way up and have then wound up underwater as the stock has tumbled are just waiting for the shares to get back to even. They'll sell en masse if the stock should rally to something near their purchase price. Any rally that takes the stock back to the price where a lot of investors bought is likely to fail at that price under a cascade of selling.

In the case of First Solar, the August retreat built some support for the stock at $100 a share. It's reassuring that there is a support level at all—although it's one of rather short duration and therefore relatively weak—but it's also a bit scary that the first real support for the stock is roughly $120 a share below the November price of $220.

This is a stock that looks quite capable of going down as fast as it went up. That's another sign that buying on the parabolic move upward is a risky bet. If you like these shares, and First Solar is one of the stocks I picked to profit from the environmental trend, you'd lower your risk and increase your chance of a profit by waiting for a pullback that tempered that parabolic move.

Of course, First Solar's stock doesn't have a whole lot of history in general. The company only went public in November 2006, so the shares haven't been around long enough to build a lot of support at a range of prices. The stock's climb has been too quick for that.

If you're looking at a stock with more history, however, expanding the time period again can give you useful information about where a stock might find support on the way down or resistance on the way up.

For example, look at a one-year chart for HSBC Holdings, Europe's largest bank, as of November 30, 2007. Like many bank stocks in the fall and winter of 2007, this one was in free fall. The stock plummeted from $99.52 on October 30, 2007, to $88.52 a share on November 26, 2007. That's a drop of better than 17 percent in less than a month.

1-Year HSBC Price History Chart

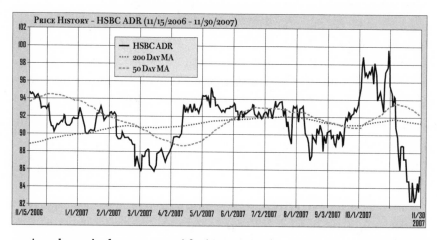

Any bargain hunter considering a purchase, however, is likely to think twice before spending any cash, because while the stock is way down from its highs, the shares don't show any sign of being near a bottom. The price sliced through the 50-day moving average at $93 and the 200-day moving average at $92 like a hot knife through butter. Other potential support levels at $90 and $86—where the stock spent some time in a trading range—didn't stop the fall either. And once the stock broke below $86, there's nothing on the chart that looks like support. There's nothing in this view of the chart to give you any confidence about where to buy.

Switch to a three-year chart, however, and the investor looking for bargains does get exactly that buying guidance.

3-YEAR HSBC PRICE HISTORY CHART

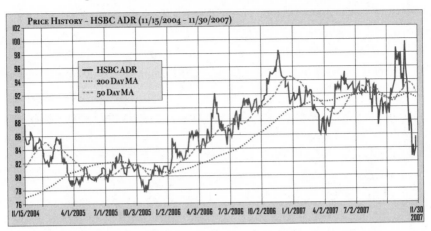

Until HSBC began to peak in October 2006, the shares followed a very steady path upward, with the 50-day and 200-day averages climbing with hardly a bump up or down. That climb was based, the chart shows, on the foundation built at $80 a share from March through December 2005. That's a relatively long nine months at a single price level, and it says that there are a lot of potential new HSBC investors who might jump in at that level as well as a lot of current HSBC investors who would be reluctant to sell below what is, for them, the break-even price of $80.

Looking at this chart, I'd say that any bargain hunter should be willing to consider a buy on the stock near $80. There's no guarantee that the stock won't go lower, of course—it did trade at $52 in March 2002—but your odds of taking a loss at $80 are a whole lot less than if you bought at $90.

And remember, that's what profitable investing is all about. Not about certainty. We never—well, hardly ever—get that about a stock or a stock market. But about improving the odds.

4. **Look for crossovers that indicate a change in the stock's direction.** There's one last way that 50-day and 200-day moving averages can help you make better buy and sell decisions. That's by

looking for crossovers, when the 50-day moving average crosses either above or below the 200-day moving average.

You can see two crossovers very clearly on the 3-year HSBC chart. At the very beginning of May 2005, the 50-day moving average crossed below the 200-day moving average. That's an indication that the stock's upward price trend has been broken and is, according to technical analysts, a strong signal to sell. Following that, the stock stayed stuck in a rut until the end of 2005. Another crossover at that point, with the 50-day moving average crossing above the 200-day moving average, sent a buy signal. Following this indicator, you would have held on to the stock from a buy at $80 in January 2006 until another crossover sent a sell sign at $90 in February 2007. The gain for that buy-to-sell cycle was about 13 percent in twelve months.

5. **Use Bollinger Bands to separate the unimportant price moves from the important ones.** Bollinger Bands can reduce the chance that you'll jump ship on a minor decline or buy at a peak or get whipsawed into buying, selling, and buying again by relatively unimportant gyrations in a stock.

If you look at the chart for HSBC in 2007, you'll see one of the drawbacks in using 50-day and 200-day moving indicators in isolation. Using crossovers as indicators, you would have sold in February at $91, when the 50-day moving average crossed below the 200-day moving average; you would have bought in May at $91 on a crossover in the opposite direction; you would have sold again in September at $91; and then you would have bought one final time at $91 in October. That's the kind of trading that makes your broker rich but does nothing for your portfolio.

Add Bollinger Bands, named after their inventor, John Bollinger, to your chart, though, and a lot of these buys and sells become clearly irrelevant. To do that on MSN Money, go to the Analysis menu, click on "Price Indicators" in the drop-down menu, and then click on "Bollinger Bands." Set the parameters for a period of fifty days and two standard deviations.

3-Year HSBC Chart with Bollinger Bands

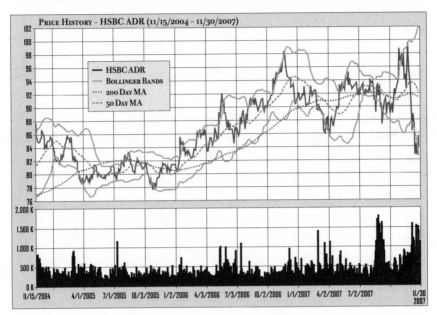

Price History – HSBC ADR (11/15/2004 - 11/30/2007)

— HSBC ADR
Bollinger Bands
···· 200 Day MA
--- 50 Day MA

What Bollinger Bands do is create a kind of price channel based on, in this case, the 50-day moving average. The channel is bounded at the top by the stock's highs and at the bottom by its lows. Bollinger Bands uses standard deviations, a measure of a stock's volatility, above a specific moving average (say the 50-day, although more investors use the 20-day) to create the top and bottom bounds of the price channel. This tool not only filters out the noise to show the price trend in the stock but also shows the trend in the stock's volatility. And that's especially useful for investors trying to limit losses and judge the probability of a top- or bottom-side breakout.

The top of the channel is drawn by looking at the volatility of that average and drawing a line two standard deviations above the moving average. The bottom of the channel is drawn by sketching in a line two standard deviations below the moving average.

Standard deviation is a measure of how much a series of numbers deviates from the mean. The two series 0, 6, 8, 14 and 6, 6, 8, 8 both have the same mean (or average, to most of us) of 7. But the second series has a much lower standard deviation. The standard deviation is a measure of how far from the mean the data points in a series are. If the data fall in a normal distribution, about 68 percent of the points will fall within one standard deviation of the mean and 95 percent will fall within two standard deviations of the mean. So the top and bottom Bollinger Bands follow the moving average and show the stock's deviation from the moving average.

The result—even if you don't understand the math—is a channel that defines a high and a low price for the stock at that point in time. So, looking at HSBC, the chart shows that the stock was not only moving up in 2006 but gradually moving closer and closer to the top of the Bollinger price channel that defines expensive. In November 2006 the stock actually peaked above the top of the price channel, signaling that it had become expensive in relation to its own history. If in November 2006 you had been tempted to buy HSBC because it had been racking up such impressive gains, a look at the Bollinger Bands would have urged you to wait.

The chart with Bollinger Bands also would have saved you from being whipsawed into buying, selling, buying, selling, and buying again in 2007. The moves starting in March 2007 remained within the stock's channel. Not much reason here, according to this indicator, to do anything at all. At the end of September and in early October, however, the Bollinger Bands told a much different story, as the stock's peak clearly took it above expensive. Looking at the chart, you certainly wouldn't have been buying at that point, and if you owned the stock, you might have been selling.

Sixth, use a volume chart to see if buying is expanding or drying up as a stock moves up or down in price.

With a click of your mouse (well, two clicks, actually—one on "Analysis" and one on "Volume"), you can get another view of how investors are reacting to a rise or fall in a stock's price. By adding a volume chart in the pane below the price history chart, you can see how volume—the number of shares being bought or sold—changes with a rise or fall in stock price.

1-YEAR HSBC CHART WITH VOLUME

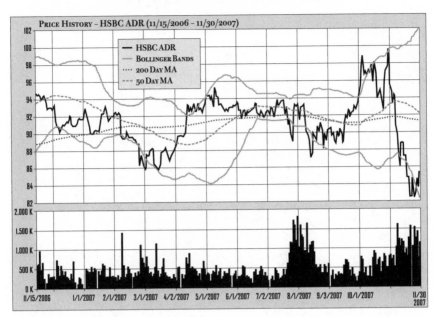

PRICE HISTORY – HSBC ADR (11/15/2006 – 11/30/2007)

— HSBC ADR
— BOLLINGER BANDS
···· 200 DAY MA
--- 50 DAY MA

What can this tell you? For HSBC Holdings, for example, the chart tells you that when the price falls, there's a huge upswing in volume that you can see in the taller columns of the volume chart. Since the stock doesn't climb in price on this volume, as it would if this volume indicated buying, you'd be justified in concluding that when the stock tumbles, panicked owners of the stock sell. This happened in August when the stock fell and everyone rushed to sell, and it happened in November when the stock fell again and everyone rushed to sell. This isn't what you'd like to see if you're thinking about buying the stock. What you'd like to see as a prospective buyer is a very small uptick in volume on a price decline. That's an indication that the selling by what are called "weak hands" has exhausted itself and that those who still hold the shares are what's called "strong hands," who aren't deterred by short-term weakness. This exhaustion is a sign that a stock has bottomed.

You'd like to see exactly the reverse when a stock is climbing in price.

1–Year FSLR Chart with Volume

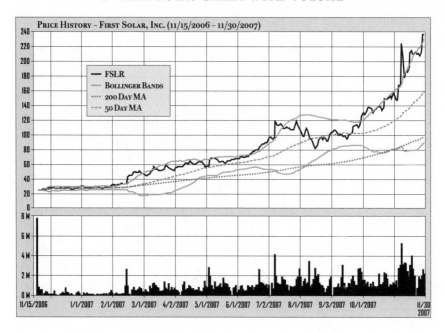

Price History – First Solar, Inc. (11/15/2006 – 11/30/2007)

If you study the First Solar chart, for example, you'll see that volume spikes higher when the stock moves higher in price. A higher share price is bringing more buyers off the sidelines and into the market. Rather than deterring new buying, the higher price is enticing new buyers into the market who are anxious to share in the stock's climb. So far, at least, there's plenty of new buying as the stock moves up in price.

Many long-term investors ignore technical analysis, figuring that it's good for traders picking out short-term trends but doesn't have much to offer long-term buy-and-hold types. And if you've stuck with me to this point, maybe you're saying, "The fifty stocks in this book are all picks for the long term. I don't need technical analysis."

Wrong.

Remember way back in Chapter 2 when I said the hardest thing to do in investing is to get out of your own way? Technical analysis can help you do that. Technical analysis can help the long-term investor avoid selling after a stock takes a short-term nosedive just after purchase. By showing when a stock has started to go up so fast that its rocket-like takeoff isn't sustainable, technical analysis can help you avoid buying high and selling low. By making it easy to tell the difference between a stock that's still falling in price and one that has found a base, technical analysis can help you avoid buying a "bargain" only to discover that it is on a path to becoming an even bigger bargain as the weeks go by. By smoothing out short-term volatility, technical analysis can help a long-term investor stay on board a stock having temporary yips. And by demonstrating that the long-term trend is intact, technical analysis can help a long-term investor control the fears that lead to premature sells.

How does this work in practice? Well, let's go back to HSBC. After studying the charts and concluding that buying the shares in any retreat to $80 made sense, you watched and waited until the end of 2007, when the stock dropped to $80 and you pounced. Unfortunately, the stock kept right on falling through that support. And you, the proud owner, watched, your $80-a-share stock head toward $70. But you didn't panic. You knew there had been strong support at $80, and you thought there was a good chance that after sellers overreacted, the stock would move back to that level. And that's exactly what happened.

After a couple of nerve-wracking months, the shares made their way back to $80 in March 2008, and then kept on going. The stock hit $85 a share in mid-May, and it looked like there was a good chance that the 50-day moving average was about to cross back above the 200-day moving average. That would generate a new buy signal for the stock and bring in new investors who would push the shares even higher.

See what technical analysis has done in this instance for the long-term investor? It has

- Flagged a good buying price
- Kept the long-term investor on board through short-term turbulence
- Helped the long-term investor from selling in relief when the stock climbed back to the original purchase price
- Indicated the likely profitability of continuing to hold

In short, technical analysis helped the long-term investor to deal with the short-term emotions that can get in the way of successful investing.

There are plenty of books and Web sites you can go to if you want to learn more about technical analysis. In print, John Bollinger has written a whole book on Bollinger Bands, called *Bollinger on Bollinger Bands.* Or try Gerald Appel's *Technical Analysis: Power Tools for Active Investors* or Alexander Elder's *Trading for a Living.* On the Web side, you could start with the multimedia tour of technical analysis we've created on MSN Money or subscribe to a site such as the Worden Brothers' Telechart, which offers a combination of technical tools and commentary. John Murphy's Market Message on StockCharts.com sends out a stream of technical views of the market on a daily or more frequent basis to subscribers.

But I think the tools I've described in this brief chapter are enough to help most investors who buy stocks based on macroeconomic trends, sector trends, or fundamentals make better buy and sell decisions. Even if you intend to buy and hold forever, there's no reason not to take a look at a chart to figure out the difference between good and bad times to buy. Charts can help you avoid panicking over an insignificant move in price or rushing to buy just because everyone else is.

If the tools of technical analysis offer insight into the behavior of the market and investor psychology, it seems silly not to take advantage of the information.

PART IV

The List

16

The 50 Best Stocks in the World

I F YOU'VE WADED THROUGH THE PREVIOUS FIFTEEN CHAPTERS, here's the list of all fifty picks that you've been waiting for. If you jumped ahead to this list without reading any of my deathless prose, well, that's okay too. You'll find a reference back to the appropriate trend chapter(s) after each stock pick.

All printed lists like this begin to go out of date as soon as the writer's nimble fingers type that last period. This, however, is a long-term list with picks that I think will be good investments for years—a decade or more in some cases—so it won't go out of date as quickly as a list of thirty-day wonders. But out of date it will get.

Which is where the wonders of the Internet come in. You see, I've created a version of this list as a page attached to every one of my "Jubak's Journal" columns on MSN Money (Money.MSN.com). On that page you'll find:

- This list of fifty stocks with the day's price for each and a cumulative change (up or down) for each pick (and for the portfolio as a whole) since this book was published.
- A short blurb, based on the blurb in this chapter, for each stock,

or in the cases where there's been important news, an updated account that highlights the changes you should note. (The news will quickly replace all the blurbs on this page, I expect.)

• Links to columns about these fifty stocks, charts, and news.

I will also devote a column once a quarter to this portfolio itself, and a link on the page will take you to the most recent column and an archive of old columns.

Finally, there will be a link to a message board where you can share ideas or comments on these stocks. I'll try to visit that as frequently as I can, although I suspect that it won't be every day.

Okay, now on to the list.

1. **Accor** (OTC: ACRFF). Asia is traveling. In China, 44 percent of families plan to travel outside their home province, according to a 2007 report by Calyon Securities. A third of Malaysians have traveled out of the country (a majority to other Asian countries) in the last year. Almost 70 percent of Thais now travel for pleasure. All those folks have got to stay somewhere, and that somewhere is quite likely a mid-price or budget hotel run by Accor. The French company has been redeploying capital from the developed markets of Europe and the United States to its midprice and budget hotel and service businesses in Asia and the rest of the developing world. The company's operating profit from its budget hotels outside the United States climbed 20 percent in 2007 and is projected to climb 12 percent in 2008. *For more on this stock and the trend behind it, see Chapter 3.*

2. **Apache** (NYSE: APA). It's Apache's ability to get more oil out of old fields that makes this an oil stock that I want to own during the supply crunch of the next five years (or longer). For example, Apache bought the North Sea's Forties Field from BP in 2003 for $688 million. Production at the field had declined from a peak of 500,000 barrels a day to fewer than 50,000 barrels a day. Apache invested $911 million in new cranes, pumps, and other equipment and cut operating costs in half. By the end of 2005, the company had increased production to 81,000 barrels a day and raised cash margins per barrel to

$24 from $6. Not that Apache doesn't explore for new oil too. The Houston-headquartered company's recent discoveries include oil and natural gas in Egypt and Australia. The combination clearly works: from 2005 to 2007 Apache expanded oil and natural gas production by 42 percent, and despite producing so much more oil and natural gas, the company raised proven reserves by 16 percent in the same period. *For more on this stock and the trend behind it, see Chapter 7.*

3. **BHP Billiton** (NYSE ADR: BHP) is an Australian mining company with a finger in everything from copper to uranium. With this one pick, you can give your portfolio exposure to most industrial commodities and to a natural-resource-based economy that's likely to make the Australian dollar one of the world's best currencies over the next decade or more. In fiscal 2007 BHP got about 27 percent of its revenue from copper, silver, zinc, gold, and lead mining. Aluminum made up 12 percent of revenue. Iron ore and metals used in stainless steel (nickel, for instance) made up 26.3 percent of revenue. Metallurgical coal accounted for 8 percent of revenues. Energy coal and oil and natural gas accounted for another 22.1 percent. Even with $40 billion in 2007 revenue, the Melbourne-headquartered company is determined to get bigger. In 2007 it launched a takeover bid for Rio Tinto, the third-largest iron ore mining company in the world. As of mid-2008 Rio Tinto had rebuffed that offer. But don't worry about growth at BHP Billiton even if it doesn't gobble up Rio Tinto. The company has $18 billion in new production projects in the pipeline, with the largest growth likely to come in oil and iron ore production. *For more on this stock and the trends behind it, see Chapters 6, 8, and 12.*

4. **Bunge** (NYSE: BG). Bunge is the world's leading oilseed (including soybeans) processing company and one of the top global sellers of vegetable oil. Not a bad place to be, since soybean consumption, up 5 percent a year over the last fifteen years, shows no signs of slowing and since increasing global demand for vegetable oils will lead prices to climb another 50 percent from 2008 to 2015, according to the Organisation for Economic Cooperation and Development. But what I really like about the stock is the company's position as the largest producer and supplier of fertilizer to South American farmers,

with about 25 percent to 30 percent market share. The company controls four of the five major phosphate mines in Brazil. South America,
as one of the few regions where it's possible to bring new land into
production, is increasingly important as a source of wheat, soybeans
(Brazil is the world's second-largest producer), vegetable oils, and
sugar-cane-based ethanol. *For more on this stock and the trend behind
it, see Chapter 9.*

5. **Burlington Northern Santa Fe** (NYSE: BNI). Unbelievable.
Not just a profitable railroad but one earning a return on invested capital higher than its cost of capital. That means that it's actually profitable for Burlington Northern to reinvest in its own business. What a
change from the days when railroads were ripping out track rather
than spending money to maintain it. Give credit where credit is due.
Railroads are making money because of the boom in global commodities such as coal and grain. Nobody in the United States is likely to
ever build another transcontinental railroad. That gives the existing
four transcontinental railroads control of the exceedingly lucrative and
fast-growing business of shipping bulk freight from the U.S. heartland
to ports on the West Coast that serve the growing markets of China
and the rest of Asia. How good is business for Burlington Northern, in
my estimation the best-managed of the transcontinental railroads?
Operating margins are on track to hit 24 percent in 2008, Standard &
Poor's projects. That's up from a recent low of 15.4 percent in 2004.
Revenue, S&P projects, will climb at an annual compounded 8 percent rate from 2008 through 2012. *For more on this stock and the trend
behind it, see Chapter 9.*

6. **Cemex** (NYSE ADR: CX). This Mexican company initially
used free cash flow from its protected and highly profitable home market to build itself into the third-largest player in the global cement industry. In 2005 Cemex bought London-headquartered RMC Group
to continue its attack on the European cement market. In 2007 the acquisition of the Rinker Group gave the company a bigger footprint in
Australia and a substantial premixed concrete business in Tianjin and
Qingdao, China. Now the Monterrey–headquartered company is
using its efficiencies of scale and its skills at balancing sales and pro-

duction around the globe to grow profits and sales faster than its competitors. The company's net profit margin of 13.4 percent over the last five years is almost 4 percentage points higher than the industry average, and sales have grown by about 4.5 percentage points a year more than the industry average over the same period. *For more on this stock and the trends behind it, see Chapter 4.*

7. **Central European Distribution** (NASDAQ: CEDC). Russia—along with China, India, and Brazil, the four big economies of the developing world—is the big prize for the Philadelphia-headquartered company. Central European Distribution is the largest producer and distributor of vodka in Poland as well as one of the leading importers of alcoholic beverages into the country. With Poland's entry into the European Union, Central European Distribution can use its solid base in the country to build exports to the rest of Eastern Europe. And recently Central European acquired the Parliament brand, the third- or fourth-fastest-growing vodka in the subpremium vodka segment in 2007, as its initial entry into the Russian market. Parliament sales were up 19 percent in the first quarter of 2008 from the first quarter of 2007. Another acquisition, of importer Whitehall, in 2008 moves Central European even further into a Russian market that is just starting to shake out relatively inefficient state producers. Sales at the company grew by 79 percent in 2007 and are forecast to increase by 75 percent in 2008 and 2009. Earnings per share climbed 37 percent in 2007 and are forecast to climb 37 percent in 2008 and 30 percent in 2009. *For more on this stock and the trend behind it, see Chapter 3.*

8. **Cisco Systems** (NASDAQ: CSCO). Cisco Systems isn't the same fast-growing technology company that rode the dot-com boom to revenue growth of 44 percent in 1999 and 56 percent in 2000 before the bottom fell out, and that's a good thing. Now San Jose–headquartered Cisco is a company capable of delivering steady double-digit revenue growth. From 2004 to 2007, revenue grew by 16.6 percent a year. That growth is lower than before but far more predictable and sustainable. The company now owns more than 50 percent of the market for Internet routers and switches and 80 percent of the corporate market for routers. Cisco has used that market share as a springboard

to build strong revenue streams in Internet security and storage, wireless networking, and Internet telephony and video. Wall Street analysts are projecting 13.9 percent annual earnings growth over the next five years. *For more on this stock and the trend behind it, see Chapter 12.*

9. **Coach** (NYSE: COH). First Japan and now China. Coach has successfully learned how to translate "accessible luxury" from the U.S. market to Japan. Beginning in 2000 with just 2 percent of the Japanese market, by 2008 the company had grabbed a 12 percent market share going up against such heavyweights in the luxury business as Louis Vuitton, Prada, and Gucci. (Coach now has a bigger market share in Japan than the last two of that trio.) China is next. In 2008 Coach bought out its Hong Kong joint venture partner and opened a new flagship store in the city, its biggest outside the United States. The company plans to open fifty more stores in China in the next five years to go with the thirty it already operates in the country. The target, says Coach CEO Lew Frankfort, is China's emerging middle class. Right now the handbag market in China is about $1.2 billion in sales. And, as in Japan in 2000, Coach has just a tiny sliver of that, about 3 percent. *For more on this stock and on the trend behind it, see Chapter 3.*

10. **Corning** (NYSE: GLW) is one of the survivors of the technology stock crash and bear market of 2000–3. In that era Corning's most exciting business was its fiber-optics unit. The overcapacity generated by the dot-com boom has killed off much of Corning's competition in this area, and now that demand has finally bounced back, this mature technology is generating revenue growth and profits again. And thanks to the company's new ClearCurve product, which reduces signal loss from a bent optical fiber to almost nothing, that business looks ready to boom. But while Corning was waiting for the fiber-optics market to recover, it leveraged its technology skills to become a leader in the new global market for the glass used in LCD screens, with a 50 percent market share. Corning estimates that unit LCD television sales will grow at an annual rate of 31 percent between 2007 and 2009. This business makes up 45 percent of the Corning,

New York–based, company's revenue and 40 percent of earnings. Corning's increasingly important environmental technologies unit produces filters for autos and diesels. The diesel market, for example, will show sales growth of 17 percent in 2008, Corning projects. New technologies such as green lasers and silicon-on-glass are just now about to make the transition from the lab to the commercial market-place. *For more on this stock and on the trend behind it, see Chapter 11.*

11. **Deere & Company** (NYSE: DE). Earnings as high as an elephant's eye. Yes, I'm being corny, but corn is the big story for Deere. Deere gets about 55 percent of its sales from farm equipment, and the company controls about 50 percent of the North American market for agricultural equipment. So you can see why Moline, Illinois–headquartered Deere is the nearest thing there is to a pure play on farm incomes. (Another 20 percent of revenues come from the company's forestry and construction business and its commercial and residential business.) When farm incomes go up, Deere sells more equipment; it's as simple as that. Deere is probably the best-known name in farm equipment because the brand is backed by a relentless commitment to producing a constant stream of new products while removing costs from the company's manufacturing operation. From a low of 5.6 percent in 2001, Deere increased operating margins to 15.9 percent by the end of 2007. Return on equity, negative in 2001, climbed to 24.9 percent by the end of 2007. *For more on this stock and the trend behind it, see Chapter 9.*

12. **Embraer (Empresa Brasileira de Aero)** (NYSE ADR: ERJ). Brazil's Embraer is a major beneficiary of the boom in in-country travel in developing economies. In these countries, it's often cheaper to link cities by air than to connect them with roads or rail lines. The company is the number two maker of regional jets in the world, with almost a 50 percent market share. In 2008 the company was ramping up production on a new generation of planes, the Embraer 190 and Embraer 195 models, which offer longer ranges, greater fuel efficiencies, and more cabin room. The year 2007 finished with an order backlog of $18.8 billion, or about three years' worth of revenue at

2007 revenue rates. *For more on this stock and the trend behind it, see Chapter 4.*

13. **Enbridge** (NYSE: ENB). In 2003 the worry on Wall Street was that the pipeline industry had built all the pipelines North America would ever need and the industry had no place left to grow. Hah! Five years later Calgary-headquartered Enbridge has an impressive number of North American pipeline projects set to start pumping up revenue between 2009 and 2011. The Alberta Clipper Expansion is projected to deliver up to 800,000 barrels a day of heavy crude from Alberta's oil sands to Wisconsin by mid-2010. The Southern Access Expansion will deliver 400,000 barrels a day of heavy crude to Chicago and southern Illinois from Wisconsin in 2009. The Clarity pipeline will transport natural gas from the Barnett Shale and Anadarko Basin in Texas. *For more on this stock and the trend behind it, see Chapter 10.*

14. **Encana** (NYSE: ECA). Natural gas is the bridge fuel between a present dominated by oil and coal and a future of far less carbon-intensive energy technologies. What will be especially valuable during that period—which is likely to last for a decade or more—is natural gas from politically stable countries. Calgary-headquartered Encana has spent the last two years divesting itself of overseas oil and natural gas operations and using the cash to build a leading position in unconventional oil and gas reserves in North America. The company's properties now include the Barnett Shale formation in Texas, Colorado's Piceance Basin, and the Deep Panuke natural gas project of Nova Scotia. The company had announced a plan to split into two independent publicly traded companies in 2009. One, to keep the Encana name, will own the natural gas resources; the other, to be called IOCo, will own the company's oil refineries and its Canadian oil sands joint venture. That plan had been put on hold as of October 2008. *For more on this stock and the trend behind it, see Chapter 12.*

15. **ExxonMobil** (NYSE: XOM). This is the one Western oil major that has found a way out of the box created by the national oil companies' hammerlock on 80 percent of the world's new oil. Texas-headquartered ExxonMobil has decided put its huge cash flow to work by investing in the big capital-heavy projects necessary to get

natural gas from where it's produced to where it's consumed. That means building huge plants in places like Qatar to cool the gas, turning it into a liquid ready to be pumped onto tankers, and then building the infrastructure at the other end in, say, Bayonne, New Jersey, for converting the liquid back into gas and then sending it on into the pipeline system. Add in investments, through 70-percent-owned affiliate Imperial Oil, in Canada's oil sands, as well as profits from the world's most sophisticated refinery system, and you get a return on invested capital of 23 percent—a huge return for a capital-intensive industry such as oil, and a good 6 percentage points above the oil industry average and a whopping 13 percentage points above the average for the big companies in the Standard & Poor's 500 stock index. *For more on this stock and the trend behind it, see Chapter 7.*

16. **First Solar** (NASDAQ: FSLR). The Holy Grail of cost cutting in the solar industry is finding something cheaper than semiconductor-grade (99.99 percent pure) crystalline silicon that will deliver the same or better energy efficiency. One of the most promising technologies is called thin film, and Phoenix-headquartered First Solar is a leader in thin film technologies. The company used a cadmium and tellurium semiconductor to achieve 10.6 percent efficiencies as of the end of 2007 in modules using just 1 percent of the semiconductor material used in crystalline modules. The efficiency is less than the 15 percent to 16 percent efficiencies achieved with crystalline silicon, but high enough with the lower cost of thin film production so that First Solar has started pilot projects that target utility-scale installations. At its December 2007 Wall Street analyst day, the company repeated its target of selling solar modules at a cost of $1.00 to $1.25 a watt by 2012 and at less than $0.70 a watt by 2012. Thin film technologies are projected to grow from 6 percent of the market in 2005 to 15 percent of a much larger solar market in 2010. *For more on this stock and the trend behind it, see Chapter 10. For more on the high volatility of this stock and when to buy it, see Chapter 15.*

17. **Flowserve** (NYSE: FLS). If you need to move water—and in an increasingly thirsty world, who won't?—Irving, Texas–headquartered, Flowserve can do the job. The company makes pumps, valves,

and seals and sells to customers in the industrial, nuclear, oil and gas, and water supply markets. Capital spending in the water/wastewater sector is projected to grow by 10 percent a year in 2008–10. Nothing to sneeze at. But growth in the sector segments of filtration, desalination, and exports of water equipment to China are projected to grow by 15 percent. Looking out beyond the next few years, I think growth rates are more likely to head up than down as growing populations in developing economies with more income demand more clean water. You can see that in the company's backlog of orders, which climbed 27 percent in the first quarter of 2008. *For more on this stock and the trend behind it, see Chapter 10.*

18. **Fortescue Metals Group** (OTC: FSUMF). What a contrast to BHP Billiton, Vale, and Rio Tinto, the three giants that together control 75 percent of the world's seaborne iron trade. While the big iron ore companies bulk up through acquisitions, this Western Australian upstart is just starting production. But what potential. In December 2007 Fortescue announced that its Solomon holding contained 70 percent more iron ore than previously estimated. The company increased its estimate for the area to 1.7 billion metric tons from 1 billion and said it might upgrade estimates for the eastern part of the Solomon project by an additional 25 percent, or 175 million metric tons, during 2008. The company loaded its first shipload of iron ore for—where else?—China in May 2008. *For more on this stock and the trend behind it, see Chapter 8.*

19. **Freeport McMoRan Copper & Gold** (NYSE: FCX). In a world hungry for new supplies of all commodities, this Phoenix-headquartered company sits on the most valuable of all commodities: new commercial-grade deposits of copper, gold, cobalt, and molybdenum. The company expects to up copper production by 25 percent by 2010 and molybdenum production by 42 percent. The total proven and probable reserves of molybdenum total 1.9 billion pounds, and the metal made up 12 percent of 2006 sales. Copper does remain king—especially after the 2007 acquisition of Phelps Dodge. Proven and probable copper reserves total 75 billion pounds. The company's Tenke Fungurume copper and cobalt project in the

Katanga province of the Democratic Republic of Congo is one of the largest undeveloped copper and cobalt concessions in the world today. Ore there grades at a spectacular 2 percent to 5 percent, in contrast to an average mine's 0.5 percent to 1 percent. The company projects production will start in 2009—if, and it's a big if—Freeport McMoRan can navigate politics and corruption in the troubled country. *For more on this stock and the trend behind it, see Chapter 8.*

20. **General Cable** (NYSE: BGC). After years of underinvestment, it's time to start spending on the electrical grid in the United States. U.S. electric companies are projected to spend $14 billion a year over the next ten years to make up for years of underinvestment. That's actually small change compared to the money that China, Russia, and the rest of the developing world will spend in the next decade to build out their grids. General Cable will be one of the biggest beneficiaries of this surge in investment. The company, which once sold only into the U.S. market, has expanded internationally until in 2007 only 45 percent of sales came from North America. The Kentucky-headquartered company's global footprint grew in October 2007 when it acquired the global wire and cable business of Phelps Dodge International from Freeport McMoRan Copper & Gold. General Cable's acquisition gives it equity stakes in two companies selling to China's energy market, and it's a market leader in South and Central America. *For more on this stock and the trend behind it, see Chapter 10.*

21. **General Electric** (NYSE: GE). The one-stop shop for developing economies in need of infrastructure. Need a locomotive, steam turbines, a power plant, a nuclear reactor, or just something mundane like a hundred jet engines? General Electric can sell it to you. And infrastructure, which makes up about 50 percent of the company's revenue, is the fastest-growing part of GE's business. For example, the Fairfield, Connecticut–headquartered, company currently generates about $1 billion a year in revenue from designing and servicing nuclear power plants around the world. GE CEO Jeffrey Immelt recently projected that figure would hit $5 billion a year within the next five to ten years. By selling off underperforming units in order to concentrate on the company's infrastructure businesses, Immelt has increased

return on invested capital to 16.5 percent in 2007 from 12 percent in 2004. *For more on this stock and the trend behind it, see Chapter 3.*

22. **Goldcorp** (NYSE: GG). Goldcorp has got the two qualities that you're looking for in a gold mining company and its stock. First, it's a low-cost producer; in fact, by my calculations, it's *the* low-cost producer among big gold companies. Cash costs in the Vancouver-headquartered company's gold operations—that's costs net of sales of copper and silver—for the quarter were $240 per ounce. Second, gold production at Goldcorp is climbing. Production is projected to climb by 30 percent in 2008 by Canaccord Adams, and to increase further in 2010 as other new mines go into production or older mines expand. For example, in early 2008 the company announced that its big Penasquito mine in Mexico remained on schedule for the first gold pour from ore in 2008. The company recently upgraded proven and probable reserves for the mine to 13 million ounces of gold and 864 million ounces of silver. *For more on this stock and the trend behind it, see Chapter 6.*

23. **Google** (NASDAQ: GOOG). Google is the Internet's dominant search company, with about 70 percent of the global market for search in 2007 compared to a 17 percent share for second-place Yahoo. But the Mountain View, California, company's big technology lead right now is in software that matches the ads that users see on their search page to their queries. The better the match, the more users will actually click on the ad, and the more conversions—clicks that generate sales or requests for more information, for example—will occur. And since advertisers increasingly pay for conversions, the company with the best matching software will earn the highest ad rates. Investors need to remember that while ad growth at Google, Yahoo, Microsoft, and other competitors has been extremely rapid (ad revenue from Google-owned sites climbed 68 percent in 2007), the Internet advertising market is still in its infancy. Internet ad dollars accounted for only 6 percent of advertising spending in 2007. *For more on this stock and the trend behind it, see Chapter 11.*

24. **HDFC Bank** (NYSE: HDB). Only the third-largest bank in India, but under managing director Aditya Pura, the former CEO of Citibank Malaysia, the best-run. Because HDFC's base of retail deposits—

from a network of 761 branches and 1,977 ATMs in 327 cities serving 11 million customers—provides about 40 percent of the capital it lends out, the bank has been able to maintain an amazing 2.3 percentage point net interest margin even as the Reserve Bank of India raised interest rates. A conservative approach to credit quality kept nonperforming loans to just 0.83 percent of all loans in the fiscal year that ended in March 2007. (It doesn't hurt, certainly, that bouncing a check remains a felony in India.) *For more on this stock and the trend behind it, see Chapter 5.*

25. **HSBC Holdings** (NYSE ADR: HBC). The London-head-quartered bank has reacted to its ill-fated entry into the U.S. mortgage market—nothing like making a $17 billion acquisition in the mortgage market just in time to reap $17 billion in losses—by aggressively reaffirming its presence in Asia. It's the largest bank in Hong Kong, the source of about 20 percent of its profits, and owns a 60 percent stake in Hang Seng Bank, the third-largest in the city. In India it is one of the biggest corporate lenders and a pioneer in wealth management for India's growing middle and upper classes. Overall, the bank is the world's biggest collector of deposits, with $1.1 trillion in deposits, and serves more than 125 million retail customers. *For more on this stock and the trends behind it, see Chapter 5.*

26. **Impala Platinum** (OTC ADR: IMPUY). No sector illustrates the difficulties facing the global mining industry—and why those difficulties have pushed commodities prices higher—better than platinum. Early 2008 wasn't an easy period for South African mining companies. Power shortages shut the country's deep mines. Platinum prices on world markets soared even as platinum production in South Africa plunged. News that China had passed South Africa to become the largest gold producer in the world strengthened the impression that the industry's best days were behind it in South Africa. But nothing could be further from the truth in the case of the platinum metal group of platinum, rhodium, and palladium. South Africa was the source of 50 percent of newly mined metal in the group in 2007, and that figure, Deutsche Bank projects, will climb to 55 percent in 2008. Impala Platinum, the second-largest of South Africa's three major

platinum producers, was the only one to increase its output in 2007. *For more on this stock and the trend behind it, see Chapter 8.*

27. **Infosys** (NASDQ: INFY). One of the four horsemen of Indian information technology outsourcing, Infosys combines fast growth with proven management. To thrive in this industry, Infosys has had to win over global clients that now include 113 members of the Fortune 500. These global companies can do business with anyone in the world, and the fact that they're doing business with Infosys should give an investor confidence in the company. In effect, these international clients have vetted the company for you. It doesn't hurt either that Infosys has proven that it can manage its way through challenges. The stronger Indian rupee and rising competition for the best Indian talent in information technology have pushed up costs, but Infosys has been able to raise prices, increase efficiency in India, and move work to markets with lower salaries in Eastern Europe and Latin America. In the fiscal 2008 year that ended in March 2008, the company was able to hold operating margins at 27.6 percent in spite of an 11 percent appreciation in the rupee against the U.S. dollar. *For more on this stock and the trend behind it, see Chapter 4.*

28. **ING Groep** (NYSE ADR: ING). Somebody is going to pick up the pieces of financial business in the world's developing economies dropped by American International Group and Citigroup in the financial crisis of 2007–8. Before the current crisis, I would have identified Citigroup, American International, and HSBC as the leaders in the race to build dominant global financial brands. Stumbles by Citigroup and American International make it likely that this Dutch bank and insurance company will bump one of those two from the global top three. To give you just one glaring example of the way that ING is expanding into markets where challenged competitors are pulling back, in July, Citigroup announced the sale of its German consumer-loan business, with 340 branches and 3.2 million clients. In contrast, just two months earlier ING announced that it would buy German online mortgage broker Interhyp for about $644 million. The company already has 75 million customers around the world, and it's making all the right moves to expand that number. About half

of ING's business is insurance, where ING has been busy shifting capital from mature West European markets to faster-growing markets in Central Europe and Asia. The company is also going after the lucrative and fast-growing market for managing retirement money. On July 1, the company acquired CitiStreet, a retirement plan and benefit service and administration business owned by Citigroup and State Street. The deal makes ING the third-largest defined-contribution pension business in the United States, with $300 billion in assets under management. *For more on this stock and the trend behind it, see Chapter 5.*

29. **Itau Bank Financial Holding** (NYSE ADR: ITU). The second-largest bank in Brazil is the most profitable bank in Brazil—and also one of the fastest-moving. The bank recently bought Bank of America's operations in Chile and Uruguay and is expanding into Argentina. The Brazilian market for auto loans and credit cards is still in its infancy, but Itau Bank already owns 25 percent of both markets to go with its 9 percent share of Brazil's bank deposits. None of these moves has diluted the bank's profitability. Even as higher interest rates and an appreciating currency were cutting into banking sector profits in 2007, Itau Bank still managed a net interest margin of 11.4 percentage points. Neither have they eroded the bank's emphasis on credit quality. Nonperforming loans fell to 4.7 percent in the third quarter of 2007 from 5.2 percent in the third quarter of 2006. Return on equity has averaged 29 percent annually during the last six years. *For more on this stock and the trend behind it, see Chapter 5.*

30. **Jacobs Engineering** (NYSE: JEC). This California engineering services and construction company turns U.S. dollars spent on oil or Chinese manufactured goods into water desalination plants, airports, chemical factories, and other infrastructure projects in the developing economies of the world. The company's largest market is Europe, but its fastest-growing is the Middle East, where dollar-rich oil producers are spending to build up their energy infrastructure and to diversify by investing in refineries and chemical plants. With projects diversified across industries from transportation to petroleum, pharmaceuticals, and defense, Jacobs isn't vulnerable to a downturn in

any one sector. The company's backlog grew by 50 percent in the second quarter of 2007 from the second quarter a year earlier. *For more on this stock and the trend behind it, see Chapter 3.*

31. **Johnson Controls** (NYSE: JCI). In 2005 the company's automotive business, making door and dashboard systems, accounted for 69 percent of sales at Johnson Controls. By the end of 2007 that had dropped to 51 percent. In that short period the Milwaukee-headquartered company has transformed itself from just another auto industry supplier to a technology growth company. In 2007 its building energy efficiency systems made up 37 percent of sales, up from 21 percent in 2005. In this business size counts because customers are increasingly looking for complete, cost-cutting solutions to their heating and cooling problems. Johnson Controls has recently expanded into the energy management side of this business: the company will now undertake to manage a corporate customer's energy use for a fixed fee. Johnson Controls then passes on part of the energy savings it produces to the customer but pockets the rest. The company's most interesting future technology growth potential lies in one of its oldest businesses, automotive batteries. The company has recently signed joint venture agreements to develop the next generation of lithium ion batteries for hybrid and electric cars. *For more on this stock and the trend behind it, see Chapter 11.*

32. **Joy Global** (NASDAQ: JOYG). Milwaukee's Joy Global is one of only three big suppliers of mining equipment to survive the twenty-five-year industry slump—which means that the company doesn't have a whole lot of competition now that mining is enjoying boom times again. Original equipment makes up about 35 percent of sales; the other 65 percent is aftermarket products and services. About 70 percent of Joy Global's equipment goes into the coal-mining industry, with copper and iron mining making up the company's number two and number three markets. Overseas markets make up about half of Joy Global's sales. Of the emerging markets where the company operates, China has shown the fastest growth in recent years, with much of the demand coming from the country's coal industry. *For more on this stock and the trend behind it, see Chapter 3.*

33. **Kinross Gold** (NYSE: KGC). Kinross Gold has merged its way from junior to senior status. The Canadian company has a higher cash cost of production—an estimated $365–$375 an ounce in 2008—than Goldcorp. But Kinross Gold makes up for that with big gains in production in 2008 and 2009. According to Canaccord Adams, those new operations will push gold production at Kinross Gold to 1.92 million ounces in 2008, up from 1.6 million ounces in 2007. That's a 20 percent increase in gold production. In 2009, according to Macquarie Research, the research arm of the Australian investment bank, production will climb by more than 30 percent from 2008 levels as expansion at the company's Brazilian Paracatu mine and new mines in Russia (Kupol) and Chile (Cerro Casale) add to gold output. *For more on this stock and the trends behind it, see Chapter 6.*

34. **LAN Airlines** (NYSE ADR: LFL). A yen to travel isn't arising just in Asia. Everywhere in the developing world where incomes are rising, more people—and goods—are getting on planes, and that includes in Latin America. Based in Chile, LAN Airlines flies passengers in that country, Argentina, Peru, and Ecuador. Freight operations, which include a trucking hub in Miami, account for more than 30 percent of revenue. Earnings-per-share growth for 2007 was 22 percent, but under the impact of higher fuel and other expenses, earnings are projected to decline in 2008 before rebounding to 23 percent growth in 2009. Revenue, however, is projected to grow at a blistering pace even through the earnings drought. According to Deutsche Bank, revenue will grow by 18 percent in 2008, up from 13 percent growth in 2007. Investors used to money-losing U.S. airlines, take note: this isn't your average airline. The Chilean airline's return on equity, a measure of profitability, was almost 50 percent in 2006, compared with the airline group average of 40 percent, and only dropped to 37.5 percent under the impact of higher oil prices in 2007. *For more on this stock and the trends behind it, see Chapter 4.*

35. **Luxottica** (NYSE ADR: LUX). Today the story is North America. Tomorrow the story is China and the rest of Asia. Milan-headquartered Luxottica manufactures and sells glasses and sunglasses

under its own brands (such as Ray-Ban and Oakley) or licensed brands (such as Versace, Chanel, and Prada) through a network of 4,611 branded stores such as LensCrafters, Pearle Vision, and Sunglass Hut. In the last two years the company has acquired Modern Sight (28 stores) in Shanghai, Ming Long (113 stores) in Guangdong, and Xueliang (79 stores in Beijing) to bring its total in China to 270 stores. In September 2007 the company opened a flagship LensCrafters store in Beijing, the first of a planned 90 stores in China. In May 2008 the company licensed its first Sunglass Hut stores in Thailand to go with an existing 220 Sunglass Hut stores in Australia, New Zealand, Hong Kong, and Singapore. *For more on this stock and the trends behind it, see Chapter 3.*

36. **Monsanto** (NYSE: MON). Growing more food for the world in coming decades will depend on developing higher-yielding crops; it wouldn't hurt if they needed less water and were more resistant to pests either. Monsanto created the global seed market and now dominates it—for better (if you've been a shareholder) or worse (if you're a subsistence farmer in Africa who can't afford to buy Monsanto seeds every year). The key here is a research and development budget that spends 10 percent of sales as it turns out a steady stream of new products: modified seeds, disease-resistant seeds, and herbicide-resistant seeds. St. Louis–headquartered Monsanto has gradually strengthened its hold on the market by buying up the best of smaller seed companies. Its DeKalb brand now controls 23 percent of the North American corn seed market, for example, up from 10 percent in 2001. By acquiring Agroeste Sementes in 2007, Monsanto expanded its share of the Brazilian corn seed market to 40 percent from 30 percent. The 2007 acquisition of Delta and Pine Land gave Monsanto a bigger share of the market for cotton seed, and the 2008 acquisition of De Ruiter Seeds upped Monsanto's share of the global vegetable seed market. *For more on this stock and the trend behind it, see Chapter 9.*

37. **Nokia** (NYSE ADR: NOK) owns huge market shares in the markets that are the future of wireless phone technology, with about two-thirds of the handset market in India and a 40 percent share in China. That's turned the Finnish company into an annuity on phone

sales in the world's developing markets, since users tend to upgrade with brands they already own as incomes rise. But Nokia's technology edge comes from the way the company has married this huge base of users of its handsets to software that will enable local wireless operators to turn phones into Internet portals, branchless banks, e-mail desktops, music players, and mapping servers. The bulk of potential wireless customers in the developing world are likely to skip right past the PC-as-Internet-access-device history of the developed world and go straight to a wireless phone delivery model, and Nokia intends to be there. *For more on this stock and the trend behind it, see Chapter 11.*

38. **PepsiCo** (NYSE: PEP). PepsiCo's stock performance screams blue chip. This company delivers like clockwork. Take operating margins: 18 percent in 2004, 18.2 percent in 2005, 18.5 percent in 2006, and 18.2 percent in 2007—even as the cost of such raw materials as corn and corn syrup soared. Part of the reason is that PepsiCo is the U.S.-based company that has done the best job at becoming truly global. Today steady North American sales get a powerful boost from a fast-growing international business. In 2008, international sales, which make up about 40 percent of total revenue, are expected to climb by 15 percent. Beverage sales in North America will climb a projected 6 percent to 7 percent, and North American sales at Frito-Lay will grow by 4 percent to 5 percent. Earnings, which grew by 12 percent a year on average in the last five years, are projected to grow by an average of 10.8 percent a year in the next five years. *For more on this stock and the trend behind it, see Chapter 12.*

39. **Petroleo Brasileiro S.A.** (NYSE ADR: PBR), aka Petrobras. Petrobras isn't just discovering a lot of oil and natural gas. It's discovering them in tough geologies and then drilling for them in really challenging environments. That combination shows the company's emergence as an oil company with cutting-edge technology, which makes the Brazilian oil giant a very attractive partner for national oil companies that don't want any of the Western oil majors as partners. Two 2007 discoveries, the Jupiter and Tupi oil and gas fields, exemplify the company's new stature. Either of these fields alone would be the biggest find since the 2000 discovery of the giant Kashagan oil

field in Kazakhstan. But that oil lies under 4.5 miles of ocean water and then under as much as another 17,000 feet of sand, rock, and salt. Tupi alone could cost between $50 billion and $100 billion to develop. At the end of that process, though, Brazil's proven reserves could equal those of oil powers Nigeria or Venezuela, and Petrobras will be an acknowledged leader in oil field technology. *For more on this stock and the trends behind it, see Chapters 4 and 12.*

40. **Potash Corporation of Saskatchewan** (NYSE: POT). Nothing—next to water—is in more demand by the world's farmers than potash. Any near-term hope of meeting increased demand from a world that needs more food and more plant-based fuel at the same time relies on it. The company is the world's largest producer of potash, a key ingredient in agricultural fertilizers. The company has managed to line up the majority of the world's excess capacity of potash, which makes Potash both the low-cost producer in this market and the swing producer in the industry. When demand is high and supply tight, Potash can bring new supply to market in a fraction of the five years—and $2 billion—it takes to develop a potash mine de novo. The developed world applies about twice as much potash fertilizer to its fields as do Brazil, China, and India. Outside of its potash business, the Saskatoon-headquartered company also has a major cost advantage over many other nitrogen fertilizer makers thanks to its low-cost nitrogen production from natural gas fields in Trinidad. *For more on this stock and the trend behind it, see Chapter 9.*

41. **Q-Cells** (OTC: QCLSF). This German company is the largest producer of solar cells in the world. Q-Cells will be one of the major beneficiaries of the end of the silicon supply bottleneck in 2008, as new supply lowers price for silicon wafers and removes the uncertainties that have hobbled production. The company's cost of silicon wafers will fall 10 percent by 2010, Jefferies International estimates. That will drive its EBIT (earnings before interest and taxes) profit margin to 18 percent from 16.6 percent and the profit growth rate in the company's solar cell business to 43 percent from 39 percent in 2007. Q-Cells also has a promising thin film business. *For more on this stock and the trend behind it, see Chapter 10.*

42. **Rayonier** (NYSE: RYN) owns, controls, or leases about 2.7 million acres of timberland in the United States and New Zealand. About 400,000 acres in the United States are what's known as higher-and-better-use land, more valuable for development than it is as timberland. Rayonier owns about 200,000 acres of higher-and-better-use land in the Georgia-Florida coastal corridor. Recently—even in the middle of the home-building crash—the Florida-headquartered company sold 3,100 acres of that for about $15,000 an acre. But you can pick it up for way less by buying shares of Rayonier. At a December 30, 2007, price of $47 a share, my estimate of 400,000 higher-and better-use acres means that by buying Rayonier shares, you can buy an acre of Rayonier's land holdings for $9,300. See the potential for some real-estate appreciation here? And for some solid protection against rising inflation? The deal is actually even better than that since my calculation didn't give any value to the rest of the company's operations—the production of lumber, pulp, and fibers. And it's the company's other businesses that are generating the cash to pay investors a 4.25 percent dividend (as of the end of 2007). *For more on this stock and the trend behind it, see Chapter 6.*

43. **Schlumberger** (NYSE: SLB). If Schlumberger did its work in clean rooms in Silicon Valley, everyone would understand that this is a world-class technology company and price the shares accordingly. Fortunately for us, most investors still don't get it, so you can buy the shares at a discount to more traditional technology stocks. Schlumberger increased spending on research and engineering by 18 percent in 2007. Why is that important for a company that provides services to the oil and gas industry? Because the oil and gas industry has developed an insatiable appetite for new technology, such as 3-D seismic imaging, and innovative services, such as real-time data management from drills thousands of feet under the surface. Companies exploring or drilling for oil in increasingly difficult geologies need to find ways to increase the odds that increasingly expensive test wells will produce significant volumes of oil and gas. And that's where Houston-headquartered Schlumberger steps in. For example, in 2007 Schlumberger introduced a family of services that fractures underground rock formations to free trapped oil

and natural gas so that it will flow to a well and eventually to the surface. As oil companies run out of easy-to-produce oil and natural gas, they have to do more and more fracturing. Schlumberger's new technology increases the amount of oil and natural gas production after fracturing and—here's the big kicker—lowers the cost of fracturing. Win/win. No wonder revenue grew by 21 percent in 2007. *For more on this stock and the trends behind it, see Chapters 7 and 11.*

44. **State Street** (NYSE: STT). Somebody's got to manage all that money, and increasingly it's State Street. Stability and innovation aren't a bad combination in any company in any sector, but they're especially valuable in the financial sector, where innovation is so hard to come by and all the more valuable for that scarcity. First, stability. State Street is one of the largest global custodians and asset managers in the world. Clients such as mutual funds or insurance companies use State Street for their back-office bookkeeping in exchange for a fee. And since clients don't want to muck up their bookkeeping and alienate their customers, custodial clients don't tend to move from one institution to another with great frequency. Second, innovation. On the asset side, where State Street directly manages $2 trillion in assets, the company is now one of the biggest players in the fast-growing market for ETFs (exchange-traded funds), the most serious threat to traditional mutual funds since the rise of the modern mutual fund in the 1960s. *For more on this stock and the trend behind it, see Chapter 5.*

45. **Suntech Power Holdings** (NYSE: STP). You can actually follow the technology path that produces higher yields and increased profits at this Chinese solar cell maker. That's critical to investors because the solar industry is—or soon will be—all about increasing efficiency (in manufacturing and in electrical production from the cells) as increasing global production capacity drives down the price of solar cells. Suntech introduced a new technology—called Pluto by the company—in 2008 that will increase manufacturing efficiency by 6 percent to 12 percent. At the same time, the company's increasing scale (Suntech is already the number four producer of solar cells in the world) will drive down the costs of silicon wafers. *For more on this stock and the trend behind it, see Chapter 3.*

46. **Tejon Ranch** (NYSE: TRC). Raw land, despite the 2007 meltdown in the housing market, is a great way to profit from inflation. As they say, God isn't making any more land, so the world has a limited supply and increasing demand. And you know what that does to the price of a commodity over time. But that saying is even more true if we're talking about land within commuting distance of Los Angeles. Tejon Ranch, based in Lebec, California, owns about 270,000 acres sixty miles north of Los Angeles and within spitting distance of Interstate 5. The company raises cattle, grapes, almonds, and pistachios on the land but has plans to turn some of it into commercial development and three residential communities. On May 8, 2008, Tejon Ranch and a coalition of environmental groups announced an agreement that would conserve 240,000 acres of the company's 270,000 acres but permit development to go ahead on the remaining 30,000 acres. That will let the company move ahead with its plans to build three residential centers with a total of 26,000 houses plus hotels, condominiums, and golf courses at the southern and western edges of the ranch. At the stock's closing price on May 8, investors are getting an acre of developable land for about $23,800 when they buy shares in the company. *For more on this stock and the trend behind it, see Chapter 6.*

47. **Tenaris** (NYSE ADR: TS). Selling things like pipes and pumps to the oil exploration and production industry has grown into a very nice $10 billion (in sales) business at Tenaris. And the company would do quite well on volume alone since it dominates some segments of the market. (The company has about a 50 percent market share in Saudi Arabia, for example.) But the company's big drive now is to increase the profit margins in that business. The company knows that as companies drill in ever more challenging geologies, they'll pay extra for pipe that can withstand extremely high temperatures and pressures, flex to accommodate new trends in horizontal and guided drilling, and won't surrender to extremely corrosive conditions. That's increasingly what Tenaris delivers—sales of its new Tenaris Blue high-performance connection technology, for example, continue to push margins higher. Gross margins climbed to 45.8 percent in 2007 from a five-year average of 41.5 percent. Sales of higher-end,

high-technology products such as Tenaris Blue are projected to climb to 50 percent of sales by the end of 2008, up from 40 percent in 2007, according to Deutsche Bank. *For more on this stock and the trends behind it, see Chapter 7.*

48. **Thompson Creek Metals** (NYSE: TC). Thompson Creek, the second-largest publicly traded producer of molybdenum (copper, gold, and molybdenum producer Freeport McMoRan is number one), projects that production will climb to 16.5 million to 17 million pounds in 2008, up from a projected 15.9 million pounds in 2007, and then undergo a big ramp-up to 34 million pounds in 2009 as the company starts to work richer grades of ore in its mines. In 2006 it cost the company about $6 to produce a pound of molybdenum. That was down from more than $7 in 2005. Molybdenum prices should average somewhere between $30 and $35 in 2008 and remain well above $20 a pound through 2010. You do the math. *For more on this stock and the trends behind it, see Chapter 8.*

49. **Ultra Petroleum** (NYSE: UPL). What energy supply could be more secure than natural gas from Wyoming and Utah in the good ol' U.S. of A.? And Ultra Petroleum owns a lot of it. I mean *a lot.* The company's proven reserves total 2.4 trillion cubic feet of gas. But the real prize here is Ultra Petroleum's 4,800 undrilled locations that are projected to yield 5 billion cubic feet of gas each and the 150,000 acres Ultra Petroleum owns in the heart of the Green River Basin. Only about 15,000 of those acres have been developed, so this company has years and years of expanding production ahead of it. Standard & Poor's projects an increase in production of 17 percent in 2008 and 18 percent in 2009. That expanding production should be very profitable too, since according to Morningstar, Ultra Petroleum shows the lowest cost per unit of natural gas produced of all North American producers over the last five years. *For more on this stock and the trends behind it, see Chapter 7.*

50. **Vale** (RIO). Formerly known as Companhia Vale do Rio Doce, this Brazilian company is the largest producer of iron ore in the world and has 23 percent of the Chinese market for iron ore. (It certainly

doesn't hurt that iron ore prices at Vale climbed 60 percent to 70 percent in 2008.) The company's iron ore mines are the lowest-cost producers in the world. The company bought Canadian nickel producer Inco just in time to catch higher nickel prices in 2007. Production of nickel climbed 14 percent in 2007. The company's biggest new mines, in Brazil and New Caledonia, are projected to begin production in 2008 and 2009, respectively. *For more on this stock and the trend behind it, see Chapter 12.*

Appendix 1

WHY MY STRATEGY WORKS:
EVIDENCE FROM THE ACADEMIC DEBATE

THERE'S A VERY HEATED AND LONG-STANDING DEBATE AMONG academics about whether or not it is possible over the long term for an investor to beat the stock market. What's come to be called the "random-walk school" after the very convincing book *A Random Walk Down Wall Street* by Burton Malkiel contends that it's not. The best any investor can hope for is to match the market return, minus transaction costs. Any investors who beat that market return are just the temporary beneficiaries of the random movement of stock prices.

The other side in this debate, exemplified by academics such as Andrew Lo—with Craig MacKinlay the author of *A Non-Random Walk Down Wall Street*—disagrees. Research from this camp has found evidence of market inefficiencies that savvy investors can exploit. The stock market predictably overreacts to news and rumors, for example. Trends and momentum persist in predictable ways. Seasonal patterns in stock prices do exist to a degree that makes following them profitable.

Having written a book on how you can beat the stock market, it should be obvious which side of the debate I agree with. The argument is a long way from settled, certainly. I'd say we need another hundred years of good stock market data—carefully controlled to eliminate all changes in the structure of the financial markets, of course—before we've got a chance at a solid conclusion. In the meantime, though, I think the debate does suggest some theoretical reasons why the system I set out in this book can beat the market. I'll try to summarize those reasons here.

Want to Beat the Market?
Pick the Right Asset Class

Exactly how much of an investor's return comes from picking the right asset class is a matter of academic debate. Back in 1986 in the article that started all the debate, Gary Brinson and his coauthors showed in a study of ninety-one pension funds from 1973 to 1985 that replacing the active stock, bond, and other picks that these pension managers had made in their portfolios with corresponding index funds resulted in equal or better performance. The mix of asset classes—stocks, bonds, and cash in this study—accounted for about 94 percent of the volatility of the pension portfolios.

That finding wound up getting distorted into a belief that the choice of asset classes accounted for 94 percent of a portfolio's returns. And even though that isn't what the Brinson study said—there's a huge difference between saying that asset classes show a 94 percent correlation with a portfolio's degree of volatility (its tendency to move up and down) and saying that 94 percent of performance (the net of those ups and downs) is produced by the choice of asset classes—the distortion was enough to produce repeated attacks on this research.

A 2000 paper by Meir Statman took on both the original research and the studies that questioned it head-on by looking at both volatility and performance. Statman's research into volatility produced numbers strikingly similar to those in the Brinson study—89 percent (instead of the earlier study's 94 percent) of the portfolio's volatility was a product of asset classes. On the basis of the Brinson and Statman work, I think it's fair to say that something like 90 percent of a portfolio's tendency to go up and down is explained by the asset classes of the investments in the portfolio.

But Statman also took an explicit look at performance—the net gain or loss after all the up-and-down volatility is over and done with. And Statman found that picking the right asset classes did make a huge difference. A hypothetical portfolio manager who was able to perfectly zig in a portfolio when asset classes did—moving in and out of asset classes with perfect foresight—would have outperformed the actual pension fund managers by 8.1 percentage points a year.

That may not seem like much until you remember that the average annual return (before inflation) delivered by the stock market is just 10 percent a year. For long-term government bonds it's just 5.3 percent, and for short-term U.S. Treasury bills it's just 3.8 percent, according to Ibbotson Associates. The 8-percentage-point gain represents a potential near doubling—or more—of an investor's returns over the long haul.

What did that perfect manager do? Not pick shares of Merck instead of Pfizer, to be sure. No, instead that perfect manager shifted the odds in favor of his portfolio by looking at the big top-down moves in the markets. Instead of trying to find the drug stock that would outperform other drug stocks, that manager moved into bonds when that asset class was in market favor and moving up in price, and into stocks when the market was moving in favor of that asset class. And that manager moved out of those assets and into cash when the market turned sour on them.

Statman and Brinson were both talking about a relatively conservative definition of asset classes—stocks, bonds, and cash. But I became intrigued by a 2000 follow-up to Brinson's research by Roger Ibbotson and Paul Kaplan that used five asset classes—big-company U.S. stocks, small-company U.S. stocks, non-U.S. stocks, U.S. bonds, and cash. Ibbotson and Kaplan found that this kind of more detailed strategic asset allocation also beat the market over time.

Ibbotson and Kaplan's study raises what is for me an interesting question: what would happen if you both narrowed the range of asset classes to include only stocks, but then sliced and diced the world of stocks into more pieces than just the big-company, small-company, and international categories that Ibbotson and Kaplan used? So instead of stocks being a single asset class, natural resources stocks, real estate stocks, retail stocks, technology stocks, and so on would each be an asset class. That would work, I conjectured, as long as the stock groups were sufficiently independent. That is, as long as gold stocks, for example, moved up when financial stocks moved down or retail stocks moved up when oil stocks went down. That would enable me to put big tidal moves from one stock group or another behind my portfolio and improve the odds that my stock picks would work.

If you can figure out which stock groups are moving together and which aren't, and then move between them in time to catch some of the ups and avoid some of the downs in those groups, then you should be able to beat the returns you'd get from either investing in a stock market index or from trying to pick the best stock.

WHY THIS STRATEGY CAN BEAT THE MARKET

Academic research from the "non-random-walk" camp suggests why this strategy can beat the market.

- By moving into strong stock groups, you pick up on the momentum effect. Common sense and your experience as an investor say that stocks that have been going up tend to keep going up. Academic research says this effect lasts for anywhere from six to eighteen months and gradually gets weaker. Common sense says that a company delivering good news will continue to deliver good news for a while. A company with a product that clicks will see sales rise for more than just the quarter when the product was introduced. A company that discovers new efficiencies and reduces costs will reap the benefit quarter after quarter. Academic research supports this: a company that reports surprisingly strong earnings results in one quarter stands a good chance of reporting better-than-expected earnings for the next two quarters.

- By moving into strong stock groups, you pick up on the expectations lag effect. Common sense and experience tells us that we don't change our minds easily. Reality often has to hit us over the head repeatedly before we revise our opinions. Investors and Wall Street analysts aren't any different. In the great bull market for oil stocks, for example, analysts had to see month after month of oil prices at $40 a barrel before they decided to use $25-a-barrel oil in their calculations. Wall Street analysts aren't unusual. It takes most investors months or quarters to catch on to a trend. The good news here is that you and I don't have to buy into a trend on day 1 to make money. We can be reasonably late and still make reasonable profits.

- By moving out of stock groups as trends start to fade, you avoid being the last buyer. We've all been there and done this: we buy into a stock that's been a rocket just at the point where the rocket starts to run out of gas and fall back to earth. By constantly staying alert on the news on each trend—focusing on the potential turning points I've identified in the "Ripped from the Headlines" section at the end of each chapter—you've got a good chance of not buying in when a trend and a stock are about to fade and of getting out when a trend and a stock have exhausted their momentum.

- And since you're constantly on the lookout for new trends and groups of stocks that will make you money, I think you're less likely to buy into overpriced manias for "must-own" stocks. One great way to avoid feeling that you must own this stock or that one, no matter what the price, is to have lots of other great alternative investments always in front of your eyes. If you've got three or four stocks competing for your limited pool of investment cash (hey, every investor, even Warren Buffett, has some limit), you've got to be more critical of each of them in order to decide among them. That lets you take the kind of deep breath investors often need in order to avoid doing something stupid.

None of this is conclusive, of course. To me the best proof that this strategy works is that it has worked for me and the readers of my Internet column on MSN Money for more than ten years. That will have to do as "proof" while we wait for the next hundred years of market data.

Appendix 2

A SPECIAL NOTE ON COMMISSIONS

INVESTORS WHO HAVE BOUGHT AND SOLD STOCKS ONLY IN THE discount and deep-discount age of Internet brokerage services don't pay much attention to commission cost anymore. They're used to $5 or $8 or $12 trades, so why pay much attention?

Which is why you might be in for a shock when you try to buy and sell several of the overseas stocks in my list of fifty. By and large, I've tried to use U.S.-traded stocks or the U.S.-traded ADRs (American depositary receipts) of overseas companies in my list. Buying and selling those will result in the low commissions that most of us now take for granted.

But every once in a while you'll come across a stock that only sells on an overseas exchange. The symbol for these shares ends in an "F." You can still buy them through the international desk at your brokerage, but quite possibly you can't buy them online—you might have to pick up the phone—and the commissions can be substantially higher. How high? Fidelity, which has a very good international desk, charges $50 for a buy or a sell on a foreign stock such as Fortescue Metals Group or Q-Cells. I've run across discount brokerages that charge $75 each way.

I think the few stocks like this that I've put on my list are worth the extra commission, but I certainly wouldn't want to trade these stocks frequently at this price.

And besides, the lag between an order and its execution can be horrendously long.

If paying that kind of commission is too much for your purse or frugal nature, there are lots of other stocks here that trade at the normal low everyday commission price.

Acknowledgments

THIS BOOK WOULDN'T HAVE BEEN POSSIBLE WITHOUT THE MIL-
lions of investors who have read my "Jubak's Journal" Internet column
over the last eleven years. Their comments in e-mails and in person at
conferences have all helped me shape first the column and now this book.
I've tried to include all that I've learned from those interchanges in this
book. To all who have read and written over the years, "Thank you."

I've been fortunate to work with three wonderful editors at Microsoft
during the ten-plus years that my column, "Jubak's Journal," built up
the track record behind this book: Dan Fisher, who let me have my head
as I worked to figure out what an Internet stock-picking column was;
Mark Pawlosky, who kept hammering away at me to connect the column
more directly to people's lives and what they experienced in the everyday economy; and Richard Jenkins, my current editor, who let me have
the rope to write this book and has never once held our initial, very
strange job interview against me. (Well, at least not in public.) At MSN
Money I've also had a chance to bounce ideas off Jon Markman, Chris
Oster, Des Toups, Charley Blaine, and Ron Prichard. Allan Townsend,
Jeff Quiggle, Wendy White, and Chris Donohue have all been valued
partners in crime. Aaron Whallon was a latecomer to the "Jubak's Journal" scene, but after two years of four videos a week he knows the foibles
of this enterprise inside out.

Outside my MSN Money coconspirators, I'd also like to thank John
Koten, a cranky insomniac of an editor who taught me, more frequently
than I like to recall, that it's never too late for a rewrite—if it makes an

article better. My thanks also to the editor on this book, John Mahaney at Crown, whose structural suggestions made this book so much better, and to Susan Ginsburg, my agent, who's been down the long road with me on this and other projects.

And finally, I'd like to thank my family: Luna and Finn, who put up with weekends without Dad and always asked, "How's it goin', Dad?" and Marie, who held down the fort, put up with foul moods, and allowed me to vent and rant when the writing wasn't going as well or as fast as I wanted. Without you three, this book wouldn't have been possible.

Index